Marcos Engelken-Jorge · Pedro Ibarra Güell
Carmelo Moreno del Río (Eds.)

Politics and Emotions

Marcos Engelken-Jorge
Pedro Ibarra Güell
Carmelo Moreno del Río (Eds.)

Politics and Emotions

The Obama Phenomenon

Bibliographic information published by the Deutsche Nationalbibliothek
The Deutsche Nationalbibliothek lists this publication in the Deutsche Nationalbibliografie;
detailed bibliographic data are available in the Internet at http://dnb.d-nb.de.

1st Edition 2011

All rights reserved
© VS Verlag für Sozialwissenschaften | Springer Fachmedien Wiesbaden GmbH 2011

Editorial Office: Dorothee Koch | Priska Schorlemmer

VS Verlag für Sozialwissenschaften is a brand of Springer Fachmedien.
Springer Fachmedien is part of Springer Science+Business Media.
www.vs-verlag.de

No part of this publication may be reproduced, stored in a retrieval system or transmitted, in any form or by any means, electronic, mechanical, photocopying, recording, or otherwise, without the prior written permission of the copyright holder.

Registered and/or industrial names, trade names, trade descriptions etc. cited in this publication are part of the law for trade-mark protection and may not be used free in any form or by any means even if this is not specifically marked.

Cover design: KünkelLopka Medienentwicklung, Heidelberg
Printed on acid-free paper
Printed in Germany

ISBN 978-3-531-18120-2

Contents

Introduction

Marcos Engelken-Jorge
Politics & Emotions: An Overview 7

Emotions & Contemporary Political Theory

Ramón Maiz
The Political Mind and Its Other: Rethinking the Non-Place of Passions
in Modern Political Theory 29

Methodological Issues

Brad Verhulst & Mary-Kate Lizotte
The Influence of Affective States on the Depth of Information Processing ... 73

Andrew J.W. Civettini
Barack Obama and the Political Science of Hope 95

Perspectives on Politics & Emotions: The Obama Phenomenon

Oliver Escobar
Suspending Disbelief: Obama and the Role of Emotions
in Political Communication 109

Alan Sandry
Persuading the Intractable: Charisma and Emotional Engagement
within the Dialogue of Politics 129

Åsa Wettergren
"I'm Still Standing for Hope and Glory!" Reflections on the Obama
Phenomenon and the Politics of Resentment vs. the Politics
of Cosmopolitanism 141

Deborah Gould
Desiring Politics: Wanting More in the Age of Obama 155

About the Authors 189

Politics & Emotions: An Overview

Marcos Engelken-Jorge

This book is a joint effort aimed at advancing our understanding on the role of emotions in politics. Traditionally, politics in democratic societies has been conceived of as a matter of power and competing interests. Emotion, for its part, has been largely disregarded or conceived as a threat to a rational and well-ordered society. In the last decades, however, this dominant hyperrationalist liberal viewpoint has been challenged. A number of scholars have started to consider the role of emotions in political behaviour, political mobilization, political judgement and decision-making, political communication, et cetera. Even some normative political theorists have included emotions in their research agenda and challenged, also from within the field of normative political theory, the dominant hyperrationalist liberal perspective. In this regard, this book is not path-breaking. It attempts simply to contribute to advance our understanding of the complex and multidimensional role played by emotions in politics. Nowadays, emotions are not simply ignored, as they used to be, by political scientists and political sociologists. However, after years of research, many of the conundrums revolving around the topic of politics and emotions remain unsolved. In addition, research has contributed to raising new questions. This book aims at clarifying some of them and posing new ones which should lead future research.

The book is divided into three sections. The first approaches the issue of politics and emotions from a theoretical perspective, while the second focuses on a series of methodological questions. The selection of essays composing these two sections and that following is far from exhaustive – this would be an impossible task. The essays have been selected to provide the reader with a sense of the plurality of approaches available to politics and emotions, the cutting-edge debates in this area of research and the possibilities, and also limitations, associated to each theoretical and methodological approach. Due to their nature, the essays that compose the first two sections of this volume do not rely heavily, or do not rely at all, on the case-study selected for this book; namely, the Obama phenomenon. In contrast, the essays that compose the third, and longest, section discus this case-study more thoroughly. By focusing on a single case, they do not only contribute to clarify the Obama phenomenon, which merits attention in its own right, but they illustrate empirically how emotions, approached from different angles, can enrich political analysis. This combination of a single empirical case and different theoretical and methodological approaches has an additional virtue on which we should insist. The varied perspectives adopted by the authors of this book overlap to a certain extent, but they also diverge, even conflict, in many aspects. Some authors prefer a more individualistic methodology, while others opt for a contextual analysis of emotions. Some scholars adopt a quantitative approach to politics and emotions, while others favour a qualitative one or resort to ad hoc proxy indicators. The work of some contributors shows the salutary effects of certain emotions on politics, while other essays reveal the ambiguous and complex effects emotions can have. These divergences, and to some extent also contradictions, not only highlight the difficulties faced by political scientists and political sociologists as they consider emotions, but they also illustrate – as mentioned before – the benefits and limits of the different approaches adopted in this book.

In the introductory chapter, we first consider the somewhat exaggerated, though absolutely not false claim that emotions have been marginalized in Western intellectual tradition. This sets the context for our joint effort to the study of politics and emotions. We then deliver some notes on the main controversies that surround the concept of emotion, focusing in particular on those more relevant to political scientists and sociologists. The third section gives a brief review of the main areas of research in which the consideration of emotions has been particularly productive. Succinct methodological notes are provided on how to approach the study of emotions. Finally, the fifth section gives a summaring review of the main contents and structure of this book.

Have emotions been marginalized in Western Tradition?

Most accounts about the traditional marginalization of emotions or the naïveté of the West about emotions are, at best, exaggerations. This is the thesis of Michael Neblo (2003), which he maintains convincingly. Not only does he argue that some authors (for instance, Damasio 1994; Marcus *et al.* 2000) have unhelpfully overstated the alleged marginalization of emotions in our Western philosophical tradition, but contends, moreover, that the new research on emotions is merely articulating insights already advanced by Western tradition. In other words, modern political philosophers for example, used to start their accounts with what they purported to be the human nature and, thus, with the consideration of passion and emotion. This is the case of major scholars such as Machiavelli, Hobbes, Spinoza or Tocqueville (cf. Arteta 2003: 50-51; Patapan & Sikkenga 2008), whose works do not display this categorically and consistently negative vision of emotions that some claim is typical of the West. However, this does not imply that the relation of our intellectual tradition to emotions has been unproblematic.

Liberalism, for instance, has marginalized emotion in two ways, as contended by Cheryl Hall (2002: 732-726). In one way, classic liberalism has given a place to emotions, though in order to argue for them being banned from the political realm. Classic liberalism did not conceive human beings as rational subjects oriented by self-interest, but rather as irrational beings moved by irrational desires. Hence, public institutions – so goes the argument of classic liberalism – were supposed to hinder the arousal of passions, transforming them into interests, which were thought of, in turn, as including the positive aspects of both passion and reason.

In a second way, emotion has been marginalized by contemporary liberalism by simply disregarding passion. Its conception of human beings as seeking their own self-interest and reduction of reason to instrumentality, tend to exclude practical questions, i.e. moral ones, from the horizon of consideration. Thus, emotions have been simply relegated to the private realm. As Nancy Rosenblum (cited in Hall 2002: 735) asserts: "Liberalism has difficulty assigning a place to the family, for example, or patriotism, or the politics of personal leadership – except to warn against it." In other words, passion has been chiefly conceived of by contemporary liberalism as a threat that promotes instability, violence and injustice (Hall 2002: 736-738).

A similar vision is also maintained by David Ost (2004: 230-233), for instance, though he draws the marginalization of emotion in the Western tradition back to the reason/emotion dualism propagated during the Enlightenment and to the association of emotion with superstition. This dualism, according to Ost, also triggered the association of reason with the realm of power, in particular with the institutionalized exercise of power, and emotion "with the underlings" (Ost 2004: 231). Incidentally, this explains why emotions were considered until the 1960s "a key – for some, *the* key – to understanding virtually all political action that occurred outside familiar political institutions." (Goodwin *et al.* 2001: 2) In fact, mass psychology thought of social movements and masses as irrational phenomena triggered by exacerbated and irrational passions (for instance, Le Bon 1895; Blumer 1939).

In the second half of the 20th century, behaviourism contributed to the exclusion of emotions from the allegedly legitimate field of inquiry of the social sciences. Emotions were conceived of as insufficiently tangible and not subjectable to quantification (Ost 2004: 233; Calhoun 2001: 46). In this regard, the lack of methodological rigour with which some authors, especially within the field of cultural studies, initially approached the analysis of emotion also contributed to this widespread perception (Calhoun *op. cit.*).

Notwithstanding what has been called *marginalization* of emotions in Western tradition, social sciences like sociology have considered emotions and their contribution to social and political analysis. Scholars such as Marx, Weber, Durkheim, Simmel, Pareto and Cooley, have all paid attention to emotions. However, as Jonathan Turner puts it, "early sociology was not devoid of a concern for emotions, but perhaps with the exception of Cooley, these concerns were secondary, implicit, and under-theorized." (Turner 2009: 340) Nevertheless, over the last three decades, sociologists have tried to correct this drawback, and nowadays dramaturgical and cultural theories of emotions, ritual theories, symbolic interactionist theories, structural theories, exchange theories, et cetera, are trying to make sense of emotions and their imbrications with social reality (cf. Turner & Stets 2005: 23 ff.; Turner 2009).

Another interesting discipline to be considered is philosophical psychology (Calhoun & Solomon 1984). Sensation theories, like the one developed by Hume, have been interested in highlighting how people experience their emotions. Psychological theories (e.g. William James) have focused on the psychological basis of emotional experience. Behavioural theories (Darwin, but also Dewey or psychological behaviourists like Watson, Skinner or Ryle) have concentrated on observable emotional behaviour – arguing interestingly that if a person can make mistakes about his/her emotions or be unaware of them, but an external observer can identify them, then the behaviour must be the primary thing of an emotion. Evaluative theories (Brentano, Scheler, Sartre or Solomon), in turn, have maintained straightforwardly that emotions are chiefly evaluations, that is, that they are epistemologically important mental phenomena and, although they can sometimes lead us astray, they do not do so on principle. Finally, cognitive theories (e.g. Bedford) have been interested in how people name and speak of emotions and the logical restrictions governing the use of terms referring to them.

As we will see, all these theories highlight different aspects which we should consider in the next section. For the moment, however, suffice it to conclude from this very broad and oversimplified account that the importance attributed to emotions in the Western tradition, as well as the conceptions that the major scholars have advanced of them, are less clear than what is commonly assumed. Furthermore, the status attributed to emotions varies depending on the discipline and the period of time considered. On the whole, it is true that emotions have been somewhat disregarded, in particular in the field of political science. This provides one good reason for bringing together this book. However, it also gives a grounding for the initial chapter, written by Ramón Maiz (this volume), which offers a nuanced and, as we see it, also very necessary account of the roles played by emotions in the fields of political science and political theory, as well as adjacent disciplines (especially sociology and epistemology).

Controversies Revolving around the Concept of Emotion

We should turn now to the concept of emotion. More precisely, what exactly is an emotion? How can we define it? We have already seen from the above broad review of philosophical-psychological theories of emotion that behaviours, feelings, evaluations or, more broadly speaking, cognitive components, as well as linguistic rules and social conventions, may contribute to the definition of emotions. Similarly, Turner and Stets (2005: 9-10) cite the following elements as constitutive of emotions: "the biological activation of key body systems," "cultural definitions and constraints on what emotions should be experienced and expressed," "the application of linguistic labels (...) to internal sensations," "the overt expression of emotions through facial, voice, and paralinguistic moves," and "perceptions and appraisals of situational objects or events." All these elements, as both authors acknowledge, interact in complex ways, and none of them can be said to have a privileged role in the definition of emotions. Usually the definitions of emotions vary depending on which aspects a researcher finds more relevant (Turner 2009: 341).

We think this is a legitimate way of approaching the definition of emotions. As political scientists and sociologists, it is not emotions *per se* that we need to define. Rather, what we are interested in is in reaching a definition of emotion that is useful *for political analysis*. This means that we may be interested in more parsimonious concepts, which should be, however, complex enough for rigorous analytical work, though not more complex than strictly necessary. This is not to prejudge the potential interest of any of the aforementioned aspects claimed to be constitutive of emotions. Rather, we are suggesting that, in this context, we should only consider those elements of emotions relevant to political analysis.

For Aurelio Arteta (2003: 49), for example, it is sufficient to consider just three aspects of emotions: their valence, that is to say, whether they are positive or negative emotions; their cognitive components, and their motivational force. Martha Nussbaum, in turn, advances a far more complex concept of emotion than Arteta, but argues contrary to conventional wisdom that bodily processes need not be considered in the definition of emotions, mainly because they do not make any difference.

> "We should certainly grant that all human experiences are embodied, and thus realized in some kind of material process. In that sense human emotions are all bodily

processes. But the question is, are there any bodily states or processes that are constantly correlated with our experiences of emotion, in such a way that we will want to put that particular bodily state into the definition of a given emotion-type?" (Nussbaum 2001: 58)

Considering the plasticity of the human organism, Nussbaum answers this question in a negative way (Nussbaum 2001: 58-59).

In line with the argument so far, this section will be devoted to the discussion of several aspects of emotion that are relevant to political analysis. Since they are also controversial and this is just an introduction chapter, we will refrain from advancing a fully-fledged definition of emotion. Instead, we will simply introduce the main issues and arguments that structure the debate on emotion and political analysis.

The first question to be considered is whether emotions can be differentiated from other adjacent phenomena, such as moods or feelings. In this regard, Chesire Calhoun and Robert Solomon (1984: 23) warn against considering emotions as "a set of homogeneous phenomena." There are, for instance, calm and violent emotions, as well as episodic and more dispositional ones. However, for many scholars it has been useful to distinguish emotions, albeit heterogeneous, from other similar phenomena with which they tend to be (mistakenly?) conflated. For instance, emotions have been distinguished from moods. Both are supposed to constitute "amorphous states," but the former are directed to specific objects, while the latter are claimed to lack any specific referent (McDermott 2004: 692). Appetite is another close notion. Appetite has been said to refer to "'blind' cravings or desires that operate largely at the most fundamental bodily level" (Hall 2002: 729). Feelings, in turn, allude to "emotional states about which a person is consciously aware" (Turner & Stets 2005: 286). Since there are unconscious emotions, and they can be useful for political analysis, emotions need to be differentiated from feelings.

However, as Nussbaum (2001: 129 ff.) acknowledges after distinguishing between "bodily appetites," "emotions," and "moods," it can be very difficult to differentiate between these phenomena, especially between certain emotions and moods. "One may feel generally fearful, and that will be an emotion with a vague object, if its content is that some (vague) danger is viewed as impending. It will be a mood to the extent that even that type of highly general or vague object is absent." Nevertheless, she contends that this should not be seen as a problem, "for what would be a problem in an account of emotion would be an excessive rigidity or definitional dogmatism." (Nussbaum 2001: 133)

Surely, such an argument can be regarded as a mere excuse for a deficiency in Nussbaum's account of emotions. However, her claim is not without merit. The usefulness of such a theoretical account that refrains from making "boundaries seem unrealistically sharp or rigid" (*Ibid.*) can be seen, for example, in Connolly's analysis of the "evangelical-capitalist resonance machine" (Connolly 2005). His main argument is that the alliance in the United States between "cowboy capitalism" and "evangelical Christianity" rests upon shared spiritual dispositions that create a common ethos, which is in turn amplified by the media politics of resonance. "Ethos" and "spiritual dispositions" are some of his key analytical concepts, into which emotions, moods, desires, judgements and so on are conflated. In one passage of his essay, for instance, he argues that the ethos of the evangelical-capitalist political movement in the US is energized by a sort of "existential resentment" (Connolly 2005: 878). This is a resentment that can whirl "in a larger complex, producing a hurricane out of heretofore loosely associated elements" (*Ibid.*), which comprise emotions, desires, drives, beliefs, feelings, patterns of perception, et cetera. This is just but one example of the usefulness of keeping the conceptual boundaries between emotions and other close phenomena porous and fluid. Similarly, Verhulst and Lizotte (this volume) advise us not to overemphasize the differences between moods and emotions, since both emotions and moods may have the same implications for certain politically-relevant phenomena.

Some scholars go beyond this point. The "Lacanian-left", for example, is a label that refers to authors such as Slavoj Žižek (1989), Jason Glynos (2001), Glyn Daly (1999; 2009) or Yannis Stavrakakis (1999; 2005). They do not speak of "emotion" but of "enjoyment", defined as a sort of "existential electricity" (Daly 1999: 227). Similarly, Patricia Clough (2008) prefers not to speak of "emotion" but "affect." Both the Lacanians and Clough are referring to a kind of pre-symbolic emotional or affective energy, focusing not so much on stable, more or less discernible, emotional states but on concealed, malleable and shifting aspects of subjectivity. By violating the conceptual boundaries between emotions, moods, feelings and so on, and focusing on aspects that purportedly underlie them (thus highlighting implicitly their common origin and somehow their porosity), these authors have managed to explain compellingly the motivational components of political change and the resistance that it usually encounters (e.g. Glynos & Howarth 2007) – though not without analytical drawbacks (cf. Engelken-Jorge 2011).

In short, what conceptual framework should be privileged over the rest in the analysis of politics is not a settled question. While some authors prefer to keep (allegedly) different emotional phenomena apart and to draw clear-cut distinctions between them, others favour alternative and less rigid conceptual frameworks. Both conceptual strategies can be said to have advantages but also deficiencies. The perils are, on the one hand, excessive conceptual rigidity and, on the other, lack of analytical rigour.

A second controversy which merits consideration refers to how to classify emotions. It is not clear at all how many emotions can be identified or which of them are relevant to political analysis. One common way of tackling this issue is to classify emotions according to a typology, which offers a door for introducing emotions into discourse in a parsimonious fashion. The most common of these typologies, which can be traced back to classic authors, for example Hobbes (cf. chapter 6 of the *Leviathan*) or Spinoza (cf. 2009: 134-5), is the grouping of emotions into positive and negative valences, on the assumption that these "positive" and "negative" emotions are related to a fundamental approach-avoidance behavioural system in the human being (Turner & Stets 2005: 11).

Recently, however, it has been argued that political analysis has to move beyond this conceptualization (cf. Huddy *et al.* 2007). In this regard, political psychologists have shown that two different negative emotions can trigger dissimilar effects. Anger tends to promote action and to underestimate the risks associated to a particular situation, while anxiety fails to trigger action and tends to promote the overestimation of risks (cf. Huddy *et al.* 2007). Consequently, scholars have argued for other theories to substitute the prevalent valence-based approach; for instance, appraisal theories or what Huddy *et al.* call the "functional neuroscience perspective" that either posits a model of emotion-specific influences or a more differentiated set of emotional and behavioural responses than the valence-based approach (Huddy *et al.* 2007; Lerner & Keltner 2000; Lazarus 2001). Nevertheless, research focusing on discrete emotions is not without problems either, as argued by Verhulst and Lizotte (this volume).

Another way of dealing with the complexity of emotions and the plurality of effects that emotions can trigger is to identify and focus on *political* emotions, i.e. typically political emotions. For some authors, anger is the central political emotion, in line with Schmitt's (1932) definition of the political. Ost (2004), for example, makes a case for this thesis. Though implicitly, this argument can also be found in the work of other authors such as Laclau & Mouffe (1985; see also Laclau 2005; Mouffe 2005 and the critique of Laclau & Mouffe's position in Barnett 2004). Other scholars, in contrast, extend the list of emotions or passions that can be considered typically political and include, among others, the following: *libido dominandi*, fear, greed, envy, resentment, compassion and indignation (cf. Arteta 2003: 53-62).

In short, it is still controversial what is the best strategy for integrating emotions into political analysis. Traditionally, emotions have been grouped into positive and negative valences, though the deficiencies of such a typology have been shown recently. Other scholars, however, prefer to adopt a more fine-grained approach, and either focus on specific emotions or on more differentiated sets of emotions. Still others concentrate solely on one or a few emotions that can be said to be typically political.

There is a third aspect that we should consider; namely, to what extent are emotions and their political effects related to personality traits and/or to a specific situation. To begin with, it seems obvious that the identification of any emotion requires the consideration of its context. This is an old and, to a great extent, uncontroversial idea (cf., for instance, Spinoza 2009). If we move beyond this idea, namely that the context is relevant for the identification of an emotion, it seems obvious that some personality traits can make people more or less prone to experience certain emotions. This is the case, for instance, advanced by Civettini (this volume). He speaks of "high and low hope individuals" and claims that hope is both a "dispositional trait" and an "emotional state." Indeed he does not disregard certain contextual factors, but argues that focusing on the individuals might help understand why *some* individuals are politically more active than others. Yet for other scholars it is "unhelpful to associate emotions primarily with the individual rather than with the social and cultural." (Goodwin et al. 2001: 11) Gould (this volume) makes a case for this thesis. In her chapter, devoted also to the analysis of the political effects of hope, she shows how important the context and the discourse triggering this emotion can be. The *same* emotion, namely hope, has had very different consequences with Bill Clinton and with Barack Obama, and she traces back these differences to both the context of hope and the political discourse that promoted the feeling.

In summary, it remains controversial to what extent individual traits or contextual aspects are relevant to an understanding of the political effects of emotions, i.e. whether we should pay the same attention to both aspects or, on the contrary, if it would be more fruitful to concentrate more on one aspect than on another. Possibly, the answer to this question will depend on the political phenomenon under research. In any case, research programmes such as the one proposed by Civettini (this volume), or lucid analyses, such as the one by Gould (this volume), should contribute to solving this puzzle.

Finally, a fourth question merits discussion; namely, the cultural variation of emotions. Nussbaum (2001: 152-157), for instance, speaks of "intersocietal differences in the emotional life", which is due to the following factors: the physical conditions (to the extent that they influence certain cultural patterns), the metaphysical, religious and cosmological beliefs held by a social group, certain social practices (of child rearing, for example), language and the way emotions are labelled and distinguished from each other, and certain social norms that determine what is valuable in a society and how people (or just men, or just women) should behave. These factors are said to influence the behavioural manifestations associated to emotions, the objects that are deemed appropriate for a particular emotion, as well as the emotional taxonomies and the judgements about the worth of a particular emotion, which, in turn, affect the experience itself of this emotion (cf. Nussbaum 2001: 157-165).

Calhoun (2001), in contrast, goes a bit further. Acknowledging this inter-societal variation of emotions, but also recognizing that there are always intra-societal variations, i.e. that the way emotions are displayed in a society varies over time and that there are also differences among individuals, he speaks of "emotional habitus." That is to say, the inculcation in individuals of "a sense of how to act, how to play the game ["of relating emotions to each other, and of relating emotions to cognition and perception"], that is never altogether conscious or purely reducible to rules." (Calhoun 2001: 53)

To tackle this issue, namely, the inter- and intra-societal variation of emotions or, in short, their cultural variation, some scholars have distinguished between primary and secondary or higher-order emotions. Happiness, fear, anger or sadness are primary emotions, while secondary or higher-order emotions are usually conceived of as combinations of these primary emotions or as emotions that are less natural and more socially constructed. Yet both the distinction between primary and secondary emotions and the number and categories of emotions that belong to each group are still unsettled questions (cf. Turner & Stets 2005: 10-13; Turner 2009: 342; Goodwin et al. 2001: 13).

Altogether, the challenges faced by political scientists and political sociologists, in order to integrate emotion into political analysis, are nothing short of formidable. There is still no clear definition of what an emotion is; neither do we know what the most useful conceptual framework is to integrate emotion into political analysis – not to mention other conundrums pertaining to the role played by contextual, cultural and individual elements in emotions and their political effects.

Areas of Research

The consideration of emotions has been particularly fruitful for certain areas of research within the disciplines of political science and political sociology. Emotion has advanced our understanding of cognitive processes and the mechanisms that influence political judgement, as well as decision making. It has helped understand certain aspects of political participation and political behaviour. Furthermore, it has provided some insights into the nature of the social bond and of social cohesion. Besides, some scholars have resorted to emotions in order to explain certain dynamics of the public space and to advance some insights into how best to cope with some of the challenges appearing in the public space.

Debates on political socialization have also pointed out the importance of the education of emotions – an issue, on the other hand, closely related to debates on restorative justice. Studies on political communication and rhetoric have also relied on the analysis of emotions. Last but not least, normative political theory has also benefited from the consideration of emotions. Though very briefly, let us consider these areas of research in turn.

Emotion has been studied at different phases of the decision-making process. Research has analysed emotion during and after decision-making, anticipated emotions and memories of past emotions (McDermott 2004 reviews the most relevant literature). However, better known examples of research at the intersection of emotion, cognition and decision making are the work of Marcus *et al.* and research on the influence of emotion on information processing. According to Marcus *et al.* (1993; 2000), both anxiety and enthusiasm greatly determine political judgement. While anxiety triggers political learning and stimulates attention toward new information, enthusiasm fosters political engagement and influences candidate preferences. Besides, emotion might, though not necessarily (Turner 2009: 342), generate self-re-productive cognitive processes (cf. Endert 2006). In this regard, the literature known as "motivated reasoning" documents the variety of ways in which people who are strongly committed to a given view interpret evidence to support their view. People fail to consider evidence that disconfirms their view, or reject its validity, and accept evidence as valid if it confirms their view (cf. Mendelberg 2002: 168). Furthermore, an emotional state or a mood can affect the reasoning style; for instance, by generating recurring ideas and images in a subject's mind or by causing her or him to consider a great number of diverse aspects but to consider them superficially (Damasio 1994: 146 ff.). Moreover, it can influence the evaluation of possible outcomes resulting from a course of action; for example, by overestimating the odds of positive outcomes when in a positive mood or the probabilities of negative results when in a negative mood (McDermott 2004: 696). In summary, it is out of doubt that affective states influence directly and indirectly political judgment, as well as the depth of information processing (Verhulst & Lizotte this volume).

That emotion can motivate and guide social and political behaviour is also a well-known thesis (Arteta 2003: 49; Hall 2002: 739-41; Turner & Stets 2005: 290). However, it would be even more interesting to be able to specify the mechanisms that rule this motivational force. The compilation by Goodwin *et al.* (2000) provides important insights into the effects of emotions on political mobilization and collective political behaviour. As stated above, Marcus *et al.* (1993; 2000) maintain that enthusiasm fosters active campaign involvement. Civettini (this volume) advances an interesting distinction between "prospective emotion" and "current state emotion", arguing that the former holds the key to understanding action-oriented political behaviour. Gould (this volume), for her part, shows that the effects of hope on political behaviour depend on context, as well as on the discourse that triggered hope in the first place.

It has also been claimed that emotion holds the key to understanding the nature of the social bond and for promoting social cohesion (Hall 2002: 739-41; Markell 2000). For Ahmed, for example, collectives materialize "as an effect of intensification of feelings," which are, in turn, influenced by "histories that stick," i.e. by "associations that are already in place" (Ahmed 2004: 39). Markell (2000), relying on Habermas' notion of "constitutional patriotism", clarifies the structural ambivalence of the dynamics of affect that promote social cohesion – in other words, the identification with a common entity. The chapter of Escobar (this volume) provides important insights into a kind of social relationship that is somewhat cognitive in nature, but not reducible to *logos*. His underlying thesis is that emotions propel certain dynamics of their own that help to understand a symbolic, although not strictly linguistic, form of communication (hence, a kind of social bond).

Emotion has also played a role in identifying the dynamics of the public space and in clarifying how best to cope with the challenges appearing in this public space. Both Wettergren and Sandry (this volume) highlight the essential ambivalence of emotion. For a political leader, attracting the support of parts of the population also implies gaining the attention of many detractors. Similarly, Mouffe (2002; 2005) insists on this essential ambivalence of emotional dynamics. For her, the ambivalence of politics, which is due to the "passions" involved in politics, implies from a normative viewpoint an agonistic conception of democracy and, thus, an acknowledgement of the conflictive nature of politics, which cannot be managed by resorting to deliberation or to sheer market procedures. Connolly (2005: 881-884) maintains that the adequate management of public emotions, which appear in his account in the form of "existential dispositions", first require their explicit recognition and then the promotion of alternative "modes of spirituality" – not their exclusion to the private realm. Regarding the former aspect, i.e. the recognition of the emotions that are already in place in the public realm, Markell (2000) advances that the study of public emotions should provide more realistic expectations about how we can, and to what extent, cope with certain challenges appearing in the public place. This is a question, moreover, which has been explicitly addressed by some Lacanian political theorists (Glynos 2001; Glynos & Howarth 2007; Stavrakakis 1999). Escobar and Wettergren (this volume) also tackle this issue. Their analyses clarify certain symbolic strategies that deal with the complexity and ambiguity of some public emotions, which are managed by the "versatility" or – in Laclauian terms

(Laclau 1994; 2005b: 91 ff.) – "emptiness" of certain symbolic signifiers; in particular, Obama himself.

Debates on political socialization have also benefited from the consideration of emotion. Classical authors, such as Plato or Aristotle, already considered the importance of the education of emotions. As Ben-Ze'ev puts it (1995: 198), for Plato, for instance, "a sound education consists in training people to find pleasure and pain in the right objects". Contemporary authors working in the neo-Aristotelian tradition (e.g. Nussbaum), but also other scholars outside this tradition (e.g. Rorty), have considered the literary education of emotions as a fundamental strategy for achieving virtuous citizens (cf. Straßenberger 2006; Rorty 1989). The premise of this argument is usually that emotions carry a cognitive component of their own, usually, though not always, of a special kind (Nussbaum 2001: 67). "Emotions typically have a connection to imagination, and to the concrete picturing of events in imagination, that differentiate them from others, more abstract judgemental states." (Nussbaum 2001: 65) That is to say, emotions manage to generate more vivid and texture-rich judgements.

This idea of educating citizens is also somehow at the heart of debates on restorative justice (see, for instance, the special issue dedicated by the *European Journal of Social Theory* [2008, vol. 11, num. 3] to this topic). The main concern underlying this area of research is how to build or re-establish "a sense of shared humanity, a political community based on equality of respect, and shared civic trust" after a violent conflict – a task that "requires victims, perpetrators and beneficiaries to undergo an emotional catharsis and transformation that cannot be achieved through conventional criminal and civil laws and practices." (Ure 2008: 285) Close to this area of research, Yanay's work (2002) shows that hatred can be turned into a positive mode of attachment once its ambivalence is acknowledged.

The study of political communication has also benefited from considering emotions. Informal logic, for example, distinguishes between an "emotional system [of argumentation]" and "the deliberate, intellectual system", each being preferable depending on the circumstances (Ben-Ze'ev 1995: 198). From a normative viewpoint, both emotional argument and deliberative, intellectual argument are to be conceived of similarly, according to Michael A. Gilbert (2004). In other words, both are governed by certain rules, and it is the adequacy of a statement, be it emotional or logical, to these rules that determines its acceptability – not the emotional or the logical nature of the statement *per se*. As Gilbert (2004: 261) puts it:

> "There certainly are rules for emotional argument. They are similar to the rules for logical argument, and include such factors as veracity, non-exaggeration, justification of evidence, avoidance of bias, consideration of alternatives, and so on. Emo-

tional intimidation, for example, is wrong not because it is emotional, but because intimidation in an argument is often wrong."

The role played by emotions in political communication has usually been studied from a pragmatic perspective, assuming, thus, that "communication is the observable practice of a relationship" (Penman quoted in Escobar this volume; also see Sandry and Wettergren this volume). Among other things, such a perspective widens the usual scope of discourse analysis. Not only sheer linguistic elements should be studied, but the consideration of emotions (and also communication understood as a social relationship) demands including further aspects into analysis; for instance, the significance of the human body and of body language and the meaning conveyed by the personal history of the speaker (cf. Escobar this volume; Wettergren this volume), as well as the contribution of other social actors to the creation, and communication, of a certain discourse (in this regard, see the remarkable analysis of "Obama's hypervisibility" by Escobar this volume), the condensation of emotional and symbolic meaning in a particular symbol or word (e.g. Obama himself – cf. the chapters by Escobar this volume, and Wettergren this volume – or certain words, like the Welsh term *hiraeth*, analysed by Sandry this volume).

Nevertheless, the abovementioned acceptance of emotion as a legitimate form of communication and argument is not without problems. Indeed, Gilbert's words are compelling: "Emotional intimidation, for example, is wrong not because it is emotional, but because intimidation in an argument is often wrong" (Gilbert 2004: 261). However, the chapter by Sandry (this volume) raises a crucial question: How can emotion transfer itself to actual political decision-making? Though emotions carry a cognitive component, it can be very often vague and undefined. As Sandry formulates it, emotions can play a positive role in political rhetoric, and they are surely unavoidable components of rhetoric, but from a normative viewpoint, we shall remain well aware that emotional rhetoric may be intended to just "buy our support"; that is, to manipulate the population so that "it becomes easier to hand over responsibility for political decision making to someone else" (in this regard, also see the chapter by Gould and her analysis of the different effects of hope with Clinton and Obama). Normative political theory has considered this and adjacent questions. As the chapter by Maiz (this volume) points out, "hyperrationalist" normative theories do not only lack motivational strength, but also have a normative deficit. The underlying assumption behind this latter claim is that by reflecting on our strongest responses we may identify our higher goods and moral values. In other words, emotions may convey normative insights that normative theories that disregard emotions fail to consider or fail to explain appropriately (see the chapter by Maiz this volume for a more detailed discussion on this issue). Alternatively, other scholars suggest that research on emotions from an evolutionary perspective may also contribute to clarify certain moral intuitions (Damasio 2003: 155-173). In this regard, normative political theory, akin to the abovementioned areas of research, has also benefited from not ignoring emotions.

Emotions and Research Methods

As we stated earlier, emotions have been conceived of, in particular by behaviourists, as insufficiently tangible and not subjectable to quantification, and thus have been largely disregarded by mainstream social scientists. Moreover, as we concluded from our brief survey of the central controversies revolving around the concept of emotion, political scientists and political sociologists lack any clear and agreed definition of emotion. Controversies abound on how to approach best the study of emotions and how to integrate them into political analysis, as well as on the role played by contextual, cultural and individual aspects in emotion. These deficiencies are by no means unimportant. However, it is safe to claim that the study of emotion is not much more difficult than the identification, measurement and analysis of other political and social phenomena. If we think, for instance, of racism and xenophobia, both are also complex and to a great extent elusive phenomena – possibly because both are also affect-laden phenomena. The crucial point, however, is that both racism and xenophobia have been successfully subjected to empirical enquiry. Indeed, there are many questions which still remain unsettled, but our understanding of racism and xenophobia has advanced greatly thanks to empirical research (cf. Wieviorka 1991). We deem that despite the abovementioned difficulties, the same holds true for the analysis of emotions and politics.

A wealth of research methods are currently available for the analysis of emotion and politics. Qualitative methods include, among others, in-depth interviews (Gould this volume; Engelken-Jorge 2010), focus groups (cf. Escobar this volume; Moreno del Río 2010), discourse and frame analysis, not only restricted to sheer textual analysis, but also considering audiovisual data (Escobar this issue; Moreno del Río 2010), and participant observation (Polletta & Amenta 2001: 313; Gould this volume). Quantitative-oriented researches usually rely on survey data. The most basic alternative is to gather data from self-reported feelings (Huddy *et al.* 2007), though self-reported feelings can be sometimes misleading (Verhulst & Lizotte this volume). Other scholars favour instead the use of scales (Civettini this issue) or, when the emotions to be studied are particularly elusive (e.g. those related to xenophobia), special, subtle items are used (Cea D'Ancona 2009). Other researchers, in contrast, resort to proxy indicators, such as voting statistics or the number of volunteers in a political campaign (Gould this volume). Last but not least, some scholars propose to use more sophisticated research strategies in experimental settings, from experimentally inducing an emotion and observing its effects on later cognitive processing (Verhulst & Lizotte this volume) to using resonance imaging machines to measure brain activity (Turner & Stets 2005: 314-315). As usual, each method has its own limitations but also possibilities. Thus, a triangulation research strategy, such as the one used by Escobar (this volume), or a systematic research agenda, such as the one proposed by Civettini (this volume), are usually preferable to the use of a single method.

The Book

The book has been divided into three sections. The first is a comprehensive literature review by Maiz. The section provides a detailed description showing how emotions have been largely excluded from contemporary political theory and political science. The main argument of Maiz is that the *reason/emotion* dualism is at the heart of this exclusion. A review is provided giving the most important contributions from diverse disciplines (sociology, epistemology, neuroscience...) challenging this dualism. Following is a discussion of the new theoretical approaches within the field of political philosophy that are leading the path toward a new conceptualization of politics not influenced by the aforementioned dualism.

The second section is devoted to methodological questions. In the first chapter of this section, Verhulst examines the cognitive processing styles of individuals during the time when they experience emotions, and links these to how political science research typically measures and assesses emotions in the mass public. The review of several different models of emotions that tackle the cognitive processing styles of individuals leads him to identify the commonalities of these models, as well as the questions that future research needs to address. Civettini's chapter, in turn, focuses on hope, which he shows to be a crucial emotion for understanding political behaviour. The chapter clarifies the notion of hope and advances a systematic research agenda for its study.

The third section tackles the issue of emotions and politics by focusing on a case study; namely, the Obama phenomenon. In the first chapter of this section, Escobar outlines the core elements of the political communication dynamics by which Obama has achieved worldwide stardom. He analyses the use of grassroots mobilization and media technologies, as well as the master narratives of the Obama phenomenon that have managed to transcend the dispassionate politics mindset that had dominated the communication strategies of the Democratic Party for most of the past decades. In the second chapter, Sandry concentrates on several aspects of rhetoric. He draws on evidence taken from the Obama phenomenon, among other empirical material, which help him to advance a very interesting critique of Obama's 'now' agenda and use of rhetoric. In her chapter, Wettergren concentrates on the concepts of resentment and cosmopolitanism in politics from an emotion-sociological perspective. Her discussion draws on the Obama phenomenon as it appears from this perspective. Finally, Gould uses the Obama phenomenon to explore the renewed political desire in the United States. Rather than revolving solely around Obama the man as the bearer of change, Gould argues that the excitement, enthusiasm and hope surrounding his campaign and election derived in large part from Obama's incitement to a renewed relationship to the political. Obama spoke on behalf of political desire, presenting the political realm as a site that should and could be responsive to the citizenry's desires and thus as a site worth engaging. Bracketing the question of Obama's intentions, Gould considers the effects, even if unintended, of repeated injunctions to "believe" not just in his ability to bring about real change, but in the citizens' ability. In this context, the more general question about variations in the sources, contours, and effects of political hope is addressed.

Taken together, the essays contained in this volume reflect the plurality of approaches available to politics and emotions. They introduce, and contribute to, the cutting-edge debates in this area of research, highlight the commonalities of these approaches, but also their contradictions, and reveal the potentialities and limits of each theoretical and methodological perspective.

References

Ahmed, Sara (2004). Collective Feelings. Or, The Impressions Left by Others. *Theory, Culture & Society* 21(2), 25 – 42.
Arteta, Aurelio (2003). Pasiones Políticas. In Aurelio Arteta Aisa (coord.), *Teoría política: poder, moral, democracia*. Madrid: Alianza.
Barnett, Clive (2004). Deconstructing Radical Democracy: Articulation, Representation, and Being-With-Others. *Political Geography* 23(5), 503 – 528.
Ben-Ze'ev, Aaron (1995). Emotions and Argumentation. *Informal Logic* 17(2), 189 – 200.
Blumer, Herbert (1939). Collective Behaviour. In Alfred McClung Lee (ed.), *Principles of Sociology*. New York: Barnes & Noble. 1951.
Calhoun, Cheshire and Robert C. Solomon (1984). Introduction. In Cheshire Calhoun and Robert C. Solomon, *What Is an Emotion? Classic Readings in Philosophical Psychology*. New York & Oxford: Oxford University Press.

Calhoun, Craig (2001). Putting Emotions in Their Place. In Jeff Goodwin, James M. Jasper and Francesca Polletta (eds.), *Passionate Politics: Emotions and Social Movements*. Chicago & London: The University of Chicago Press.
Cea D'Ancona, Mª Ángeles (2009). La compleja detección del racismo y la xenofobia a través de encuesta. Un paso adelante en su medición. *Revista Española de Investigaciones Sociológicas* 125, 13 – 45.
Clough, Patricia T. (2008). The Affective Turn. Political Economy, Biomedia and Bodies. *Theory, Culture & Society* 25(1), 1 – 22.
Connolly William E. (2005). The Evangelical-Capitalist Resonance Machine. *Political Theory* 33(6), 869 – 886.
Daly, Glyn (1999). Politics and the Impossible. Beyond Psychoanalysis and Deconstruction. *Theory, Culture & Society* 16(4), 75-98.
Daly, Glyn (2009). Politics of the political: psychoanalytic theory and the Left(s), *Journal of Political Ideologies* 14(3), 279-300.
Damasio, Antonio (1994). *Descartes' Error. Emotion, Reason, and the Human Brain*. New York: Putman's.
Damasio, Antonio (2003). *En Busca de Spinoza*. Barcelona: Crítica. 2010.
Endert, Elke (2006). *Über die emotionale Dimension sozialer Prozesse. Die Theorie der Affektlogik am Beispiel der Rechtsextremismus- und Nationalsozialismusforschung*. Konstanz: UVK.
Engelken-Jorge, Marcos (2010). The anti-immigrant discourse in Tenerife: assessing the Lacanian theory of ideology. *Journal of Political Ideologies* 15(1), 69 – 88.
Engelken-Jorge, Marcos (2011). La Teoría Lacaniana de la Ideología: Su Potencial Explicativo y Limitaciones. *Política y Sociedad* 48(1), 93 – 108.
Gilbert, Michael A. (2004). Emotion, Argumentation and Informal Logic. *Informal Logic* 24(3), 245 – 264.
Glynos, Jason (2001). The grip of ideology: a Lacanian approach to the theory of ideology. *Journal of Political Ideologies* 6(2), 191 – 214.
Glynos, Jason and David Howarth (2007). *Logics of critical explanation in social and political theory*. London: Routledge.
Goodwin, Jeff, James M. Jasper and Francesca Polletta (2001). Introduction: Why Emotions Matter. In Jeff Goodwin, James M. Jasper and Francesca Polletta (eds.), *Passionate Politics: Emotions and Social Movements*. Chicago & London: The University of Chicago Press.
Hall, Cheryl (2002). 'Passions and Constraint': The Marginalization of Passion in Liberal Political Theory. *Philosophy & Social Criticism* 28(6), 727 – 748.
Huddy, Leonie, Stanley Feldman and Erin Cassese (2007). On the distinct Political Effects of Anxiety and Anger. In Neuman, Russell, George E. Marcus, Ann N. Crigler and Michael Mackuen (eds.), *The Affect Effect: Dynamics of Emotion in Political Thinking and Behaviour*. Chicago: Chicago University Press.
Laclau, Ernesto (1994). Why do empty signifiers matter to politics? In Ernesto Laclau, *Emancipation(s)*. London: Verso. 1996
Laclau, Ernesto (2005). On 'Real' and 'Absolute' Enemies. *The New Centennial Review* 5(1), 1 – 12.
Laclau, Ernesto (2005b). *La razón populista*. Buenos Aires: Fondo de Cultura Económica.
Laclau, Ernesto and Chantal Mouffe (1985). *Hegemonía y estrategia socialista. Hacia una radicalización de la democracia*. Madrid: Siglo XXI. 1987.
Lazarus, Richard S. (2001). Relational Meaning and Discrete Emotions. In Klaus R. Scherer, Angela Schorr and Tom Johnstone (eds.), *Appraisal processes in emotion: Theory, methods, research*. London: Oxford University Press.
Le Bon, Gustave (1895). *The Crowd: A Study of the Popular Mind*. Atlanta: Cherokee. 1982.
Lerner, Jennifer S. and Dacher Keltner (2000). Beyond Valence: Toward a Model of Emotion-Specific Influences on Judgement and Choice. *Cognition and Emotion* 14(4), 473 – 493.

Marcus, George E. and Michael B. Mackuen (1993). Anxiety, Enthusiasm, and the Vote: The Emotional Underpinnings of Learning and Involvement During Presidential Campaigns. *The American Political Science Review* 87(3), 672 – 685.
Marcus, George E., Russell W. Neuman and Michael Mackuen (2000). *Affective Intelligence and Political Judgement*. Chicago: Chicago University Press.
Markell, Patchen (2000). Making Affect Safe for Democracy? On "Constitutional Patriotism". *Political Theory* 28(1), 38 – 63.
McDermott, Rose (2004). The Feeling of Rationality: The Meaning of Neuroscientific Advances for Political Science. *Perspectives in Politics* 2(4), 691 – 706.
Mendelberg, Tai (2002). The Deliberative Citizen: Theory and Evidence. In Michael X. Delli Carpini, Leonie Huddy and Robert Y. Shapiro (eds.), *Political Decision Making, Deliberation and Participation: Research in Micropolitics, Volume 6*. New York: Elsevier Science.
Moreno del Río, Carmelo (2010). El 'Zejas' y la 'niña de Rajoy'. Análisis sobre el papel del humor en las elecciones generales españolas de 2008. *Revista Española de Ciencia Política* 22, 69 – 93.
Mouffe, Chantal (2002). *Politics and Passions. The Stakes of Democracy*. London: Centre for the Study of Democracy.
Mouffe, Chantal (2005). *En torno a lo político*. Buenos Aires: Fondo de Cultura Económica. 2007.
Neblo, Michael A. (2003). Impassioned Democracy: The Role of Emotion in Deliberative Theory. Paper presented at the *Democracy Collaborative Affiliates Conference*, 2003, Washington, US.
Nussbaum, Martha (2001). *Upheavals of Thought. The Intelligence of Emotions*. Cambridge: Cambridge University Press.
Ost, David (2004). Politics as the Mobilization of Anger. Emotions in Movements and in Power. *European Jorunal of Social Theory* 7(2), 229 – 244.
Patapan, Haig and Jeffrey Sikkenga (2008). Love and the Leviathan. Thomas Hobbes's Critique of Platonic Eros. *Political Theory* 36(6), 803 – 826.
Polletta, Francesca and Edwin Amenta (2001). Second that Emotion?: Lessons from Once-Novel Concepts in Social Movement Research. In Jeff Goodwin, James M. Jasper and Francesca Polletta (eds.), *Passionate Politics: Emotions and Social Movements*. Chicago & London: The University of Chicago Press.
Rorty, Richard (1989). *Contingencia, ironía y solidaridad*. Barcelona: Paidós. 1991.
Spinoza, Baruj (2009). *Ética demostrada según el orden geométrico* (edited and translated by Atilano Domínguez). Madrid: Trotta.
Stavrakakis, Yannis (1999). *Lacan & the Political*. London: Routledge.
Stavrakakis, Yannis (2005). Passions of Identification: Discourse, Enjoyment and European Identity. In David Howarth and Jakob Torfing (eds.), *Discourse Theory in European Politics. Identity, Policy and Governance*. Hampshire: Palgrave Macmillan.
Straßenberger, Grit (2006). Die politische Theorie des Neoaristotelismus: Martha Craven Nussbaum. In André Brodocz and Gary S. Schaal (eds.), *Politische Theorien der Gegenwart II*. Opladen & Farmington Hills: Barbara Budrich.
Turner, Jonathan H. (2009). The Sociology of Emotions: Basic Theoretical Arguments. *Emotion Review* 1(4), 340 – 354.
Turner, Jonathan H. and Jan E. Stets (2005). *The Sociology of Emotions*. Cambridge: Cambridge University Press.
Ure, Michael (2008). Post-Traumatic Societies: On Reconciliation, Justice and the Emotions. *European Journal of Social Theory* 11(3), 283 – 297.
Wieviorka, Michel (1991). *El espacio del racismo*. Barcelona: Paidós. 1992.
Yanay, Niza (2002). Hatred as ambivalence. *Theory, Culture & Society* 19(3), 71 – 88.
Žižek, Slavoj (1989). *The Sublime Object of Ideology*. London: Verso.

Emotions & Contemporary
Political Theory

The Political Mind and Its Other

Rethinking the Non-Place of Passions in Modern Political Theory

Ramón Maiz

"There are only two solutions: one is the use of emotion, and ultimately of violence, and the other is the use of reason, of impartiality, of reasonable compromise"
Karl Popper

"Nothing great was ever achieved without enthusiasm"
Ralph Waldo Emerson

There is a hidden tension underlying current debates on issues such as liberalism, communitarianism, multiculturalism or nationalism in the field of political theory.[1] This hidden tension is at least as problematic as the tensions expressed by other, more explicit binary codes, such as community/individual, monism/pluralism or universalism/particularism. In this chapter, I will argue that the *Reason/Emotion* dichotomy, a foundational dichotomy or more precisely a dualism, originating in a partial and radical interpretation of Enlightenment thought, lies as an undisputed assumption behind those other binary codes, hindering the very possibility of arriving at new developments in the theory of democracy and of politics itself. The *Reason/Emotion* dichotomy induces with the "blissful clarity" of myth – using Barthes' expression – an undisputed and omnipresent *hyper-rationality*. In turn, this has very negative de-politicizing effects on a large part of the arguments advanced by political theorists. In this respect it is revealing that egalitarian liberalism is built on the notions of *rational/reasonable* and *public reason/non-public reason*. Furthermore, the creation of community networks is usually presented as a kind of escape from moral subjectivism by appealing to a presumptive objective rationality of tradition. Moreover, it is striking that demands for representation of individuals or social groups are normally defended by resorting to an individual or group *interest*. Also, deliberation is based on the ideas of 'rational consensus' and 'force of the

---

[1] Translated from the Spanish by Marcos Engelken-Jorge en *Livérbula s.l.*, under the supervision of the author. This chapter is part of the project SEJ2007-67482: *The Quality of Public Deliberation in Contemporary Democracies*.

better argument'. Nationalism is regarded as morally justifiable only if it adopts the *reasonable* form of 'civic patriotism' within the alleged cultural neutrality of the State. Last but not least, it is also revealing that some feminist theories are controversially constructed in opposition to the aforementioned aspects by appealing to the notion of 'Eros', with an aim to freeing the repressed political dimension of affect. In my view, all these aspects show clearly the foundational marginalization, if not the theoretical exclusion, of emotion, passion, and feeling. Moreover, one crucial aspect of the problem in this chapter is the modern conceptual displacement of the classical notion of 'passion', which includes both affective and cognitive elements, by that of 'emotion' conceived as the other of Reason (Dixon 2003; Oatley 2004). In the following pages, however, I will be using these terms, i.e. emotion, passion and feeling, as synonyms, to refer to the structurally-banned affective dimension of politics.

In close relation to the aforementioned uncritical and – as I argue here – untenable dualism, *reason* and *emotion* are concepts that have built each other reciprocally, I would say in a sort of bi-univocal correspondence, by means of a long process of overdetermination which has produced a semantic matrix of conceptual associations and oppositions. As a result, both concepts have eventually come to be thought as belonging to two mutually-exclusive and self-evident horizons of meaning – to put it in the words of Kosellek. Only within this antagonistic horizon of interpretation and reception (reason *vs.* emotion) do both notions begin to make sense in theoretical discourse.

The list of classic readings that have helped modern authors define the notion of liberty has been biased favouring a very specific and reductive notion of reason which is clearly opposed to that of emotion. Other possible theoretical resources, from Spinoza to Fergusson and Tocqueville via Hume, have been misinterpreted or simply dismissed. In short, politics has been conceived of theoretically as pertaining to the realm of the rational, i.e. as an achievement of reason. Indeed, the State itself, when thought of as the monopoliser of political power and legitimate violence, is justified by its unbeatable capacity to domesticate passions: "Why has government been instituted at all? Because the passions of men will not conform to the dictates of reason and justice, without constraint." (Hamilton *The Federalist Papers 15*). The idea of reasoning person who is isolated and loosed from any affective bond with fellow citizens; the tenet that emotion distorts, clouds or disturbs reason, and that it should be kept under control so as to achieve a rational reasonability, which constitutes the basis of modern politics; the reduction of rationality to a form of calculus, free from any contaminating affect, metaphor or interpretative frame (*raciocinatio est computatio*) and its reduction to the principle of self-interest maximization; the design of institutions as a combination of various mechanisms of aggregation and intermediation of interests, of checks and balances and other sorts of filters aimed at 'cooling' the passions, or at deactivating them to 'calm passions' which are ultimately reducible to the discourse of interests, so as to exclude emotion from the public sphere, are a few of the diverse arguments variously formulated and combined, and with different scope, by authors as varied as Descartes, Weber, Kant, Stuart Mill, rational choice theorists, Rawls or Habermas.

As pointed out by George Lakoff, from said perspective, coming to dominate politics by the end of the 20th century, you will be inclined to "think that all you need to do is give people the facts and the figures, and they will reach the right conclusion. You will think that all you need to do is point out where their interests lie, and they will act politically to maximize them. (...) You will not have any need to appeal to emotion – indeed, to do so would be wrong! You will not have to speak of values; facts and figures will suffice." (Lakoff 2008: 11)

However, the reason/passion dichotomy, whose subtle and nuanced contestation by Aristotle and the Hellenistic thinking had sank into oblivion, has been subjected for over 20 years to renewed critical scrutiny by authors working within the disciplines of neuroscience, philosophy, psychology, sociology and the epistemology of the social sciences, more radically than ever before, exploring new paths and multiple ranges (Marcus *et al.* 2000; Neuman *et al.* 2007; Castells 2009). However, this untenable and misleading dichotomy still governs the dominant paradigms that inform empirical and normative research in the fields of political science and political theory – precisely, those disciplines that are supposed to deal with the *bios politikos* and the *vita activa*. Moreover, this happens although political scientists and social psychologists are well aware of the presence of emotional appeals in electoral campaigns, as well as of the relevance of emotional factors (e.g. fear or enthusiasm) for understanding electoral behaviour and the outcome of political campaigns (Brader 2006; Westen 2007) – let alone other more extreme phenomena such as religious, ethnic or nationalist violence.

The aim of this chapter is to provide arguments to criticize the above mentioned misleading dualism present in the fields of political theory (and political science). This dualism is responsible for an unacceptable narrowing of *the political*. This is because the reason/passion dichotomy is a key premise of an underlying theoretical logic in which: *1)* The foundational exclusion of emotion leads to an unfeigned hyperrationality that, 2*)* leads to the overvaluation of consensus and the correlative negation of deep conflict as an inescapable dimension of politics. *3)* Processes of collective identity construction and mobilization are neglected, hand in hand with rational individualism, and *4)* a displacement is promoted of politics by morality, law or economy.

Towards said aim, first, I will explain how the reason/emotion dichotomy is semiotically structured, by using a complex semantic chain of significations *(1)*. Then, I will show that this dichotomy has a decisive influence on the chief paradigms of contemporary political theory by overburdening the notion of reason and excluding passion *(2)*. Third, I will introduce some of the most important contributions appearing in diverse disciplines and that are relevant for the questioning of several crucial aspects of the emotion/reason dualism in politics *(3)*. Finally, I will discuss new theoretical approaches within political philosophy that have clearly surpassed the old analytical frame and that are in the origin of a non-dichotomic conceptual horizon that is crucial for the normative thinking of democracy *(4)*. It should be stated from the outset that my argumentation does not intend to support a case for 'more passion' in politics. Rather, it aims at providing the basis for a new way of articulating reason and emotion in the *vita activa*. More precisely, the focus is on a new way rooted in contemporary wisdom that transcends a reduction of *the political* to morality, law and the analysis of public policies and public management.

The Semiotic Structure of the Reason / Passion Dichotomy

The dichotomy between reason and passion has been constructed by the gradual superposition of various sets of binary codes, homologies and semantic antagonisms. These have generated an hegemonic narrative of political discourse that clearly assigns a positive value on reason, while presenting different dimensions of emotion as the negative antithesis of reason. This symbolic structure of associations and oppositions underlies in the form of an ideal type beneath the notion of *political reason* coined by the moderns. However, the notion has been given several meanings depending on case and empirical development. A summary can be found in table 1, of the most common and persistent chains of equivalences and oppositions upon which the reason/emotion dualism has been based (according to the classic division between matter and spirit established by Christian Wolff in *Psychologia Rationalis* 1734 §34). Based on this dualism, emotion, feeling and passion have been excluded from the conceptual-cum-semantic field giving rise to the conception of modern politics as the empire of reason. The argument is very briefly provided below.

The opposition between reason and emotion was formulated by Descartes as a radical division between spirit and matter, mind and body, *res cogitans* and *res extensa*, i.e. between an indivisible and non-measurable thinking 'thing' (*res*) and a mechanical and infinitely divisible non-thinking body. In this way, an undisputed assumption was born that still perdures; namely, "the suggestion that reasoning, and moral judgement, and the suffering that comes from physical pain or emotional upheaval might exist separately from the body." (Damasio 1994: 320) This point of departure is characterized by a normatively-biased division between an upper sphere (that of the mind, the spirit...) and an inferior sphere (related to body, to the sheer biological dimension, to "visceral factors", in the words of William James) – summing up, by a divide between "head" and "heart" (Koziak 2000: 153). From said point of departure, an hyperrationalist notion of *cold reason* has been postulated, in which thought (i.e. *reason*-ing) opposes feeling by separating the cognitive from affective elements, i.e. by separating self-controlled from automatized elements (Spezio and Adolphs 2007: 74).

In this way, the idea that a pure, objective, consensual, non-contradictory and *dispassionate* form of knowledge is possible is substantiated. The idea is conceived of as having the sole ownership of all the cognitive, evaluative and motivational components of the human soul. From this viewpoint, passions are depicted as the completely other of the brightness of reason. Indeed, they are thought of as unpredictable and having an irrational, unconscious, innate (i.e. not learnt), obscure, suspicious, conflictive and contradictory origin. Moreover, their etymology shows that they have been conceived as opposed to the principle of the *vita activa*; namely, as characterized by *passivity*. They are regarded as something that happens to us, which befalls us in an unforeseeable manner, depriving us of self-control and enslaving us (for instance, we are 'overwhelmed' or 'roused' by passion). Within this framework, emotions are thought of as irrational forces that hinder action, i.e. that create *heteronomy*, and are alien to our true selves, that is, to our conscious selves (*cogito ergo sum*). Moral and political actions are conceived of as the conscious and rational prosecution of the goals set by a self-determined person (*sapere aude*). Hence, passion is thought of as something threatening, external to our thinking selves; something disturbing and blinding, clouding judgement and agitating the mind, making it sectarian, partisan and unpredictable, overwhelming and alienating us. Thus, passions are often metaphorically equated to natural disasters: passions are stormy or torrential, eruptive... In short, they disturb the Apollonian and Saturnian harmony of reason, science, wisdom and moral and political righteous judgement (James 1997: 13). From this perspective, emotions are seen as subjective forces that hamper self-control and reasonability, bring us back into the obscure world of prejudice, superstition and dependency. In short, emotions make us return to, in the words of Kant, "self-imposed immaturity" (*selbstverschuldeten Unmündigkeit*). In contrast, reason is equalled to science and objective knowledge by authors of the Enlightenment, and thus, is thought of as speaking a universal language, one associated to *Light* (En*light*enment, *Siglo de las Luces, Iluminismo, Lumières, Aufklärung*), in opposition to the subjective partiality of passions, from the "dark night" of Romanticism (Reddy 2001: 211) – if we were to understand this period of history, probably exaggerating some of its features, as a total and traditionalistic rejection not only of modernity but also of science and reason.

Since the work of Madison, Kant or Sieyès, the consequences of the passion/reason division for the creation of a free political order are clear: passions trigger sectarianism, subjectivity; they hinder the achievement of impersonal and objective agreements, of consensus, as well as the genuine negotiation of the common interest and the common good. Thus, the intrusion of affects, as well as of personal and expressive factors in the public realm is conceived not only as something that perturbs the use of public reason but also as something potentially authoritarian and despotic (Rosenblum 1987: 167). Civilization – or even Culture, if it is imagined in a universalistic fashion, i.e. as heading toward progress and truth – is supposed to dominate, channel and tame passions, for emotion brings us back to our animal condition; in short, to nature. Therefore, modern politics are conceived theoretically as an artificial realm, i.e. as the realm of social contract allowing us to abandon the state of nature, in which hope and fear are the dominant passions (*homo homini lupus*). Moreover, reason facilitates entering the realm of institutional design, i.e. the design of sophisticated mechanisms intended to calm political passions (for instance, the writing of a Constitution, the separation of powers, bicameralism, the creation of a system of checks and balances, et cetera) (Holmes 1995). In this regard, Sieyès, who analysed politics as though they were an "ordinary machine", designed "machines" and "*rouages*", and thus felt the imperious need for abandoning the rhetoric of emotions, the "language of sentiment" and the "language of affect", in order to defend that politics are used in the "abstract" terms of science, judgement and principles (Maiz 2007: 81). In summary, in the context of the aforementioned dualism, emotion is thought of ultimately as the completely other of political reason; that is to say, as a sort of atavism or primitive remainder, as a symbol of everything that has been left behind by civilization and progress, and that has no proper place in the enlightened realm of liberty created by the moderns.

Now, this discourse of rationalist foundation of politics descends a step further in its materialist secularization; is reformulated in instrumental terms, losing in this way most of its normative and moral content, which would have led to the provision of *principles* (Sprangens 1981). This discourse takes shape as a less philosophical and more empirical concept. The concept of *interest* is discrete, can be operationalized and measured, and abandons excessively abstract and inefficient notions related to the metaphysics of morals, moral philosophy, or ethical and political principles. Even the notion of motives understood as *convictions* is brushed away by the new concept (Walzer 2004: 123). This is the key functionality of the concept of *interest*. It provides a common language and a common measuring rod, it facilitates the use of rationality and calculation, and it furnishes us with an idea of the Good facilitating communication in the public sphere of market society. Indeed, interest can be clearly expressed ('interest will not lie'), and is furthermore undeniably individual ('each person is the best judge of his interests'). On the other hand, it allows to bridge the gap to legitimate decision-making; to the generation of majorities by mechanisms of preference aggregation (decision-making rules, parliaments, political parties, and so forth). It should be noted that this process has three distinct components: *1)* the substitution of principles (convictions, moral reasons), which should provide the moral basis of institutions, by the notion of *interest*, which is better attuned to negotiation (Hirschman 1977: 2). *2)* The translation of some types of passions to the language of interest (for instance, the pursuit of profit or other *calm passions,* associated to *le doux commerce*). *3)* The concomitant exclusion of other more indomitable passions from the realm of politics (e.g. indignation or compassion), and their confinement to private life. In short, the notion of *interest* does not only imply the exclusion of passions from the political sphere but also the debilitation of ethical and political principles, and their substitution by a utilitarian feeble notion of the Good that is allegedly shared by everybody and is the rationalist maximization of individual interest.

This reductionistic notion of reason underlies the image of the modern individual as a singular citizen furnished with interests and individual rights, in opposition to collective or group identities and to amorphous *masses* driven by irrational loyalties or the passionate identification – *Einfühlung, Empathy* (Morrell 2010) – of the self not only with another person but with the whole group. Moreover, it is this notion of reason at the heart of modern citizenship that has enabled us to imagine a type of nationalism, or better said *civic patriotism*, that has structured the relations, i.e. rights and duties, between citizens and the State; the only notion providing the foundations of a type of political Constitution that is indeed conceived as a shelter against passion (*precommitment*). This type of patriotism is therefore totally different to 'ethnic nationalism', or even to nationalism *tout court*. In fact, from this perspective 'nationalism' is held to be invariably influenced by an organic link between nature and passion and creates a holistic totality in which individual reason disappears. Thus, it is a patriotism that elevates liberalism above populism, which is related to collective passions and to charismatic (thus, non-rational) leadership.

In this way, politics is imagined as a rationalized realm of order, stability and coherence, but also as the realm of work and legitimate power exercised by the rational machinery of the State (interest aggregation, majority rule); that is, a realm that is thought of as constituting the other side of the domination of scientific reason over nature. Within this reason/passion dualism, passion is always conceived of as the problem, while reason appears as the only possible solution. Because passions are debilitating, generate dependencies, unpredictability, partiality and subjectiveness, they ought to be confined to individual privacy and excluded from citizenship, i.e. from the public sphere.

Table 1: The Reason/ Emotion Dichotomy

Reason	*Emotion*	*Reason*	*Emotion*
Mind	Body	Science	Art
Res cogitans	Res extensa	Civilization	Nature
Thought	Feeling	Universal	Particular
Cognitive	Affective	Modern	Primitive
Head	Heart	Interests	Passions
Objective	Subjective	Calculus	Impulse
Rational	Irrational	Negotiable	Unnegotiable
Calvinism	Pietism	Individual	Mass
Conscious	Unconscious	Civility	Nationalism
Literal	Metaphoric	Liberalism	Populism
Active	Passive	Consensus	Conflict
Control	Automatism	Liberty	Tyranny
Judgement	Prejudice	Order	Disorder
Autonomy	Dependency	Coherence	Incoherence
Lucidity	Obfuscation	Stability	Instability
Sanity	Insanity	Work	Sensuality
Constructive	Destructive	Apollonian	Dionysian
Impartiality	Partisanship	Power	Weakness
Justice	Arbitrariness	Public	Private
Enlightenment	Romanticism		

Last but not least, this privatization of passion is also placed in the feminine realm, that is, the realm of passivity, irrationality, weakness and ultimately, privacy. Reason is a primarily 'masculine' capacity to take action, to make decisions, to master self-control, to exercise dominion and to govern the public sphere achieved through personal and institutional harnessing and exclusion of emotions (Hall 2005: 36). Thus, women have managed to open a space for themselves in the public sphere by entering unambiguously into the signification chain and behaviours fitting this hyperrationalist vision of politics, in other words, by assuming all the features that are supposed to be related to reason – at the price, however, of being under suspicion of acting against 'their nature', in a cold and manly fashion.

Hyperrationality and the Theoretical Exclusion of Emotion in Mainstream Political Theory

In this section, I will tackle succinctly this foundational exclusion of emotion and passion in four influential strands of modern political theory: utilitarianism, Marxism, (post-)Kantian liberalism (Rawls) and communitarianism (MacIntyre). To do so, I will consider four figures that illustrate the ideal-typical arguments advanced by these theories. However, it should be stated from the outset that these ideal-typical arguments necessarily simplify both the complex arguments advanced by each of the authors considered and, in particular, the complexity and inner plurality of each of the aforementioned theories. Nevertheless, they will help to demonstrate that an unthought space underlies those theories, that is to say, a space that appears in the form of an undisputed assumption, i.e. a theoretical non-place that is the non-place of passion and affect.

Let us consider first *utilitarianism* (Figure 1). It advances a consequentialist argument; namely, it provides a criterion for assessing norms and actions that rests upon the evaluation of the consequences derived from these actions and norms, not upon their accordance to ethical and political principles. What matters is whether actions and norms lead to the greatest happiness for the greatest number of people (Goodin 1995). Utilitarianism departs from an allegedly realistic image of the individual, i.e. it does not presume altruism or perfect information in decision-making but a materialist type of 'rationality', that is, one that is based upon the notion of *interest*, as well as on the idea that interests are given and revealed. This secularized perspective assumes, then, a notion of the Good that is not linked to moral, metaphysical or religious principles. In contrast, individual happiness is taken to be the mere *utility maximization* of individual interests. At this point, a crucial problem arises; namely, how are we to cross the gap that separates, on the one hand, the initial scenario of a group of *individuals*, who are separated by their conflicting interests, from the expected scenario of a well-ordered *society*, characterized by legitimate decision-making. The answer provided by utilitarianism is clear: through mechanisms of aggregation that, with minimal processing, allow the grouping and the selection among various sets of compatible and transitive scales of individual preference. The common good is, thus, conceived as the maximization of the sum of individual utilities. On the basis of this conception, principles of justice are inferred, which are to govern the aggregation of individual preferences by public institutions.

By this mechanism, the pursuit of each person's self-interest should lead to collective happiness. At this point, two aspects of this basic utilitarian argument should be highlighted: *1)* A classic notion of reason, characterized by having a substantive ethical and political content (principles and convictions), is displaced by another one that is more instrumental and that rests upon the notion of interest. *2)* The idea of the Good is theoretically purged of any content departing from the principle of utility maximization. What is excluded, in particular, is the consideration of civic virtues and the emotions that reinforce those virtues, being both virtues and emotions necessary motivational and normative components of a well-functioning democracy.

Figure 1: Utilitarianism

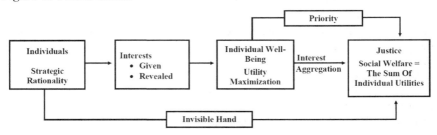

In *Marxism's* classic paradigm (cf. figure 2 – major corrections by Gramsci, Althusser or Marx himself are not included), the point of departure is a theory of history built on a materialist philosophy (historical materialism) focusing on the economic infrastructure of society; namely, on the relationships of production (Cohen 1978). In this context, the *productive forces*, which are taken to be the key explanatory factor, are conceived as related to the *relations of production*. In other words, it is claimed that the relations of production have changed through history – namely, are specific for each *mode of production* (Asiatic, feudal, capitalist) –, managing in this way to increase the human capacity of production. Moreover, they are held to group individuals into *social classes*. The concept of *social class*, in turn, rests upon the notion of *class interest*, which refers to collective shared interests. Finally, according to Marxism's classic argument, legal and ideological superstructures adapt to the relations of production so as to promote the development of the productive forces. Assuming these premises, Marxism argues *1)* that in the capitalist society, the proletariat is the overwhelmingly majoritarian social class, owing to the process of proletarianization of the middle classes, and *2)* that the interests of the proletariat are increasingly universal, i.e. increasingly widespread, objective and transparent. This is due to the growing exploitation and impoverishment of the great majority, which owes to the inherent dynamics of capitalism, as well as to processes of urban and industrial concentration. *3)* This causes *class consciousness*, which is thought of as the awareness of the objective interests shared by the working class, to become more consistent and to prevail over other differences of religion, nation, culture, etcetera. *4)* Since class antagonism rests upon economic determinations, it is held to inevitably lead to a radical change, which is conceived of as a *social* revolution (leading to changes in the mode of production), not as a mere *political* one (which would have an effect solely on the superstructure). *5)* Finally, the aspiration of achieving equality, i.e. of satisfying the interests of the proletariat in a classless, free of injustice and exploitation-free society, prevails over liberty (associated to superstructure rights). Liberty thus becomes dispensable and the State adopts authoritarian forms such as the dictatorship of the proletariat. In this manner, a scientific analysis of reality (historical materialism), which eliminates the need for a merely normative, philosophical, political or moral analysis, uncovers the hidden rationality that lies behind *commodity fetishism*, as well as the tendencies and inner contradictions of capitalism, highlighting the authentic interests of the workers.

Figure 2: Marxism

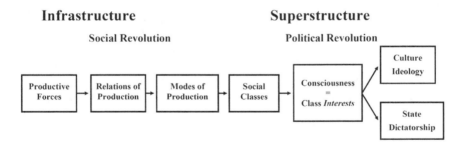

In short, *1)* the censure of the "poverty" of moral and political philosophy, linked to *2)* the need for a social revolution, which pursues equality – not simply political, i.e. formal, change – and *3)* fulfils the objective class interests of the proletariat. Thus, it can be argued that notions like *scientific reason, universalism, economic class interest* and so on, which are essential to Marxism, emerge within an objectivist and hyperrationalist account of social change. This account, moreover, disregards the complex group of mechanisms at work in a process of collective action, in two ways: *1)* it ignores the costs associated to processes of collective decision-making and mobilization, i.e. the resources invested, possible collateral effects, opportunity costs, et cetera, or *2)* the unavoidable *normative* (i.e. convictions, principles: justice, equality, fraternity), as well as *motivational* components (i.e. political virtues and emotions, which are capable of activating convictions: solidarity, compassion, indignation and so on). As the later Cohen believed: "a change in the social ethos, a change in the sentiments and attitudes people sustain toward each other in the thick of daily life, is necessary for producing equality" (Cohen 2000 145).

Let us turn now to the post-Kantian version of Liberalism exemplified in the works of Rawls (cf. figure 3). Here, another, substantially different conception of reason is at play, different from the previous two. *1)* The ethical and political impulse of the classic enlightened notion of reason is taken up again, and *2)* a nuanced splitting of the concept of reason is postulated, into *rationality*, or the faculty of determining one's own interests and conception of the Good, and *reasonability*, i.e. the capacity to arrive at cooperative agreements in order to form the basis of democratic institutions. On the one hand, the exercise of moral autonomy, that is to say, of individual rationality, generates an incommensurable pluralism of comprehensive doctrines and conceptions of the Good. On the other hand, by contrast, a neo-contractarian hypothesis argues that reasonability (i.e. political autonomy) is capable of generating an overlapping consensus shared by different conceptions of the Good that, in turn, found the principles of justice that should govern public institutions. Two arguments advanced by Rawls are decisive at this point: *1)* The thesis that justice should prevail over the Good, in contrast to what utilitarians argue, and *2)* the idea that conceptions of the Good should not belong to the realm of *public reason* but that of *non-public reason*, that is, to the private sphere. From this follows that "devotions and affections" (*sic.*), which are related to the "bonds of loyalty and fidelity" that are characteristic of conceptions of the Good, should be excluded from the principles of justice. In other words, passions and emotions that are associated to conceptions of the Good, even "the convictions and passions of the majority," should remain excluded from the realm of politics (Rawls 1971: 373). The only exception allowed to this foundational exclusion is "moral sensitivity." However, it should be noted that this exception has not been elaborated theoretically, although it contradicts the dominant rationalist paradigm of Rawls' work. By taking into account "moral sensitivity," which affects conceptions of the Good and conceptions of justice, "attitudes" – in fact, they are emotions, e.g. "sympathetic identification," "sense of justice" or "love of mankind" – are allowed to enter into the public sphere, since they are taken to be both rational and reasonable. But what else can be "moral sensitivity" but a passion, an expression of 'enthusiasm' toward justice and cooperation or the desire for a *well ordered society*? However, this hidden normative and motivational dimension of emotion is not adequately tackled within the theoretical territory of public reason expressed as the overlapping consensus on the principles of justice, nor behind *the veil of ignorance* of the *original position*. In short, there is a significant tension between the dominant rationalist (Kantian) paradigm and a subordinated almost Humean perspective in the work of Rawls. Although the latter standpoint is not theoretically articulated, it manages to re-introduce the unavoidable dimension of emotion and to place it at the very heart of the Apollonian political constructivism, at work in the deduction of the principles of justice.

Figure 3: J. Rawls

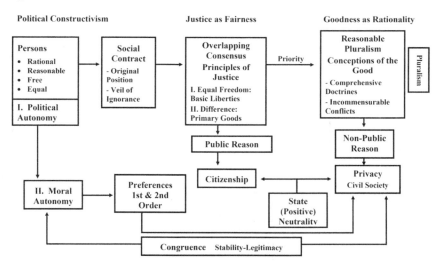

Finally, let us turn to another theory that could be expected to have a larger focus than the previous ones on the rational-cum-affective dimension of politics; namely, communitarianism, in its neo-Aristotelian version (MacIntyre 1981) (cf. figure 4). Mirroring the Aristotelian distinction between potentiality and actuality, communitarianism argues that the transition from a non-educated human nature to its *telos*, i.e. its inherent purpose or end, is mediated by certain *virtues*. According to the argument, they provide humans with the necessary moral dispositions to reach their *telos*. However, the genesis and development of these virtues is not a matter that depends solely on the individual person but also on the *polis*, that is, the political community. Virtues will be unable to prosper in the absence of a favourable context. Thus, virtues will only prosper if there are public institutions promoting a shared conception of the good life, of the idea of Good, giving the coordinates of the shared *telos* of a life worth living. In this regard, it is the political community who provides the necessary moral resources to cultivate these virtues, and it does so through *customs* and *tradition* (articulated group of customs). For this reason, *paideia*, i.e. a system of instructions that should teach pupils the civic obligations of their *polis* and of citizenship, and *phronesis*, i.e. practical wisdom, are held to be the most basic activities for the cultivation of virtues. Therefore, morality, conceived as a rational and intelligible undertaking, is taken to be unable to exist outside a specific political community.

Figure 4: MacIntyre

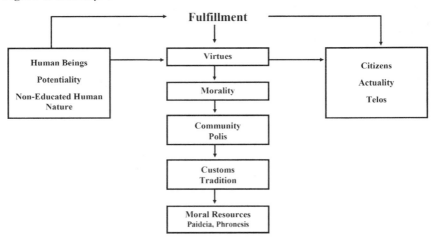

Contrary to the subjectivist and individualistic conception of morality held by the liberals (autonomy), communitarianism advances an objective conception of morality (authenticity) that is based upon the notion of *community* and leads to regain impersonal and rational ethical standards of justification. It should be noted that this departs significantly from Aristotle's, for who good politics depended on the ability to develop emotional dispositions in essential link with rational judgements about the good life. In this regard, what is lost in the rationalist and objectivist analysis of MacIntyre (1990), greatly influenced by neo-Thomism in this respect, is the Aristotelian notion of *thumos*, or the emotive capacity (the Aristotelian equilibrium between indignation, fear, compassion and affect) to acquire and practice the civic virtues in the *polis*, the psyche's capacity for emotion that is then organized by virtues and the institutions. For Aristotle, the justification of the emotional and practical dispositions is based on the notion of *eudaimonia*, or capacity to flourish and cultivate the simultaneous exercise of emotional and rational capacities within an institutional context that promotes both of them. However, this articulation of emotion and reason is omitted from the argumentation of MacIntyre, who does not consider at all the Aristotelian notion of *civic passion*, i.e. the complex amalgam of beliefs, values, moral evaluations, physical sensations and communitarian narratives (Koziak 2000: 164). The omission of this dimension by MacIntyre has been to some extent corrected by other authors such as Sandel (1982) or Walzer (2004), also associated to communitarianism. These two authors have re-introduced the affective dimension into this theory, though in a very unsystematic fashion, in an attempt to correct the normative and motivational deficit of the rationalist idea of the good life advanced by MacIntyre.

The Contemporary Critique of the Reason/Passion Dichotomy: From Neuroscience to Philosophy and the Social Sciences

For over more than 20 years, research in neuroscience, psychology and other fields such as philosophy, epistemology of the social sciences or sociology, has been undermining the very basis of the traditional dichotomies between reason and passion, and mind and body. It has been shown that, first, hyperrationalist approaches, which have been usually uncritically assessed and overrated, are plagued with inconsistencies and other drawbacks (Kahneman and Tversky 1979; 1992), as is the case, for instance, of neoclassical economy. Second, there is evidence that reflection is not free-standing but conditioned by *interpretative frames* (Lakoff 2008). Third, it has also been argued that it is the brain's emotional system what explains why the mind functions by connecting emotion and cognition and by using interpretative frames (Trepel *et al.* 2005; Parrott 2001). Moreover, there is growing evidence that emotion is involved in reasoning. Indeed, it enhances rather than undermines reasoning, as was previously assumed (Evans 2001; Evans and Cruse 2004). Furthermore, emotion is nowadays considered capable of influencing decisively and in predictable ways political judgement, decision-making and information processing (Marcus *et al.* 2000; Cassino and Lodge 2007), as well as judgement and moral evaluation, as has been shown by contemporary neuroethics (Baertschi 2009; Evers 2009). On top of that, it has also been shown that human action is triggered by processes of decision-making in which both emotion/sentiment and reason concur (Damasio 2003: 149).

There are two different emotional circuits, which are ruled by different neurotransmitters: The circuit of dopamine is associated to positive emotions (happiness, satisfaction, enthusiasm), while the circuit of norepinephrine is linked to negative emotions (fear, anxiety, anger). In this chapter, we shall focus on two aspects of this rich, multidisciplinary literature: *1)* Emotion is the brain function that motivates, directs and prioritizes human behaviour. *2)* Emotion and cognition interact in complex ways – the former one can either enhance or undermine the capacity of deliberation (Neuman *et al.* 2007: 15). Moreover, emotion provides subjects with the feeling that their goals and plans are somehow related to the broader context in which they take place. This is a crucial feeling, since in its absence decision-making would be deficient or even impossible. Indeed, "flat emotion and feeling" is related to "decision-making defect," thus suggesting that "[t]he powers of reason and the experience of emotion decline together" (Damasio 1994: 54).

More precisely, emotions perform two functions that are crucial for politics: *1)* They act as relevance detectors, i.e. they trigger the feed-back mechanism that determines the significance that internal and external stimuli have for the achievement of each person's goals (Frijda 1986). Moreover, *2)* emotions function as re-orientation mechanisms that prepare mind and body to respond adequately to new challenges and conditions (Damasio 1994; LeDoux 1996).

In summary, emotions are no longer considered an impediment to the appropriate use of reason. On the contrary, they are regarded as one decisive precondition for its correct use (although, similarly to arguments, emotions can be appropriate or inappropriate). Furthermore, there is a great deal of research in psychology in the widest sense that has demonstrated experimentally the indissoluble connection between emotion and reason, and between sentiment and mood, and rationality (Zajonc 1980; Frank 1988; Mackie and Worth 1989; Cornelius 1996; Parrott 2001; Greco and Stenner 2008; Sluds 2009; Rifkin 2010).

Ronald de Sousa, Robert Solomon, Dylan Evans, Robert Frank, Antonio Damasio and J. LeDoux, and many others, have not only shown that the absence of emotion engenders irrational decisions – contrary to conventional wisdom – but also that it strongly hinders the capacity to take *any* decision at all. According to these authors, decision-making without its affective dimension would be deprived of its crucial 'saving time devices'. It would thus take too long and end up being irrational. It is now finally established, against the inherited stereotype of abstract reason, that reason is "embodied reason, reason shaped by our bodies and brains and by the interaction with the real world, reason incorporating emotion, structured by frames and metaphors and images and symbols, with conscious thought shaped by the vast and invisible realm of neural circuitry not accessible to consciousness." (Lakoff 2008: 14)

In parallel to neuroscience and psychology, philosophy initiated a current of substantive recovery of the theme of emotion both through new reinterpretations of classic works – Aristotle, Spinoza or Hume – or based on contemporary research advances in neuroscience and psychology. In my view, two authors – Solomon and De Sousa – are crucial to this new philosophical approach to passion; because of their significance to the field of political theory.

Robert Solomon, for instance, has advanced a complex argument that similarly to Nietzsche or Sartre has placed passion at the centre of human life; in particular, regarding the following two dimensions: *1) Intentionality*: "All emotions are intentional, ultimately 'about' both ourselves and the world." Emotions are defined by the very objects with which they deal; hence different emotions have different ontologies. This leads us to *2) evaluation*: Value judgements constitute the crucial components of emotions (good or bad, right or wrong, just or unjust, gained or lost). Moreover, to the extent that emotions imply value judgements, they require standardized criteria for judging and attributing responsibilities. This, in turn, brings us to *3) action*: Contrary to the etymology of emotion, which suggests that emotions are passive, i.e. they are something that simply occurs accidentally, overwhelming us, emotions are actions, they imply power, the capacity to do whatever we want and express in this way our emotions. This is why Solomon (1993: 222) contends (maybe in a too categorical and exaggerated manner) that "every emotion is a subjective strategy for the maximization of personal dignity and self-esteem."

Ronald de Sousa, in turn, develops a philosophical analysis of emotional rationality in his well-known book *The Rationality of Emotion*. Briefly, he proposes an ideal of an "adequate emotional response." His notion of *emotional rationality* implies a tragic image of life, which departs from the linear and reductionist hyperrationality of certain enlightened authors. For de Sousa, the complex intentionality of emotions, which combine object-directedness with intentional and informative elements, provides the capacity for them to play a crucial role in rationality. They play this role, at least partly, by supplementing the formal rules that are usually taken to be crucial to the exercise of rationality. The absence of an "adequate emotional response" does not only undermine the rationality of decisions but hinder decision-making itself by deferring decisions. According to de Sousa, emotion contributes to rationality by reducing the amount of information to be considered, as well as by limiting possible interferences and the number of relevant options to be taken into account each time; that is to say, emotion supplements reason by complementing the deficiencies of the latter (de Sousa 1987: 195).

Summarizing some of the most relevant arguments advanced in this varied literature we can contend that:

1. Emotions have a cognitive dimension. Thus, it is not sensible to distinguish between emotion and knowledge, for the former contributes to the solution of problems that demand creativity, judgement and the adoption of decisions that require processing large amounts of information (Damasio 2003; LeDoux 1996).
2. Emotion and reason are both anchored to the body. Hence, it is not sound to maintain the mind/body dichotomy (Damasio 1994 and 2003).
3. Reason relies upon procedural memory and declarative memory and hence upon previous learning. In this regard, to the extent that emotions play a role in learning processes, reason is also emotion-dependent (Marcus 2002).
4. Reason relies on emotion to determine what is crucial and vital for us. In this respect, emotion determines which problems should be solved by reason and supplements it by limiting the number of possible alternatives. In other words, emotion combines an evaluative mental process with a dispositional response to this cognitive-cum-evaluative process (de Sousa 1987; Solomon 1993).
5. Reason depends on the emotional systems to trigger the actions that cannot be carried out by reason itself. Consequently, emotions are necessary to fill the gap between reason and conscious or unconscious action (Frijda 1986; Ben-Ze'ev 2000).
6. In turn, emotions are influenced by judgements (i.e. values and beliefs), since the former emerge once an object or event has been appraised in a particular situation. This constitutes a major difference between human and animal emotions (Nussbaum 2001; Elster 1999a).
7. Emotions have a cognitive dimension that is not only determined by certain genetic factors but is also in part socially constructed. That is to say, emotions are determined by cultural and socio-structural factors. Moreover, emotions are transmitted by processes of emotional socialization (Evans 2001; Turner and Stets 2005 and 2007; Barbalet 2001; Clarke *et al.* 2006).

In summary, emotion has four fundamental dimensions: *cognitive* (i.e. information about certain specific circumstances), *evaluative* (i.e. personal relevance attributed to this information), *motivational* (i.e. the disposition to act once this information has been evaluated) and *sensitive* (i.e. an objectless mood) (Ben-Ze'ev 2000).

Considering everything that has been advanced in this section, it is not surprising that various research programmes, usually influenced by social-psychology and neuroscience, have emerged since late 1970s in the field of sociology. In this regard, several books dealing with the role of emotion in social relations have been published since the 1980s (Flam 1998 and 2002; Turner and Stets 2005 and 2007).

Based on their detailed diagnosis of post-modernity, Michel Maffesoli and his research team at the *Centre d'Étude sur l'Actuel et le Quotidien* at the *Université Paris Sorbonne* have been highlighting for some time the affective dimension of contemporary "emotional communities," as well as the decisive political role of emotional and sensible bonds, of the "emotional quotient," of a "sensitive reason" and of the "ethics of aesthetics," etcetera, arguing against the Cartesian hyperrationalist, contractarian and voluntaristic conception of politics advanced by the moderns. All these issues – i.e. the growing political mobilization of emotional energies and feelings of belonging, the mobilization of the human being "longing for roots," the topic of the affective *pacte societal* and so on – have been ever-present in the work of Maffesoli from *Le Temps des Tribus* (1988) to *Iconologies* (2008) via *La Transfiguration du Politique* (1992) and *Éloge de la Raison Sensible* (1996).

For many sociologists, emotions can be regarded as the 'glue' of social bonds. They generate support for social and cultural structures and furthermore sustain the viability of the social and symbolic systems themselves. However, concurrently there will be occasions when emotion may estrange individuals from their cultures and societies, leading to challenges to their own cultural and social traditions. In this respect, emotions have been considered a vantage point for micro-sociological analysis, since they are considered a crucial link between the micro and the macro dimensions or, better said, between social systems and actual social action. Hence emotion has attracted the attention of many scholars working in different areas; just to mention a few, symbolic interactionism (Goffmann, Burke), the theory of "Interaction Ritual Chains" (Randall Collins), psychoanalytic symbolic interactionism (Turner), social exchange theory (Homans, Blau), macrostructural approaches (Barbalet) or postmodernism (Maffesoli) etc. (Turner and Stets 2005).

Recently, Castells has synthesized superbly the growing connection between neuroscience, psychology and sociology: "Feelings and the constitution of the self emerge in close relation, but only when the self is formed are emotions processed as feelings. By becoming known to the conscious self, feelings are able to manage social behaviour, and ultimately influence decision-making by linking feelings from the past and the present in order to anticipate the future by activating the neural networks that associate feelings and events." (Castells 2009: 197)

Nevertheless, Jon Elster's work is perhaps the most outstanding example of all these attempts to incorporate emotion to social scientific analysis. In recent years, Elster has elaborated a theory of *explanation* in social science, from the starting point of rational choice theory. He advanced an original interpretation of Marx's work, characterized by a methodological individualism at odds with Cohen's functionalist interpretation. His epistemological account has then expanded gradually in scope, finally incorporating the *mechanisms* that mediate between cause and effect, and proposing a theoretical account based on an interactive articulation of the following three dimensions: *(1)* rational choice, *(2)* social norms and *(3)* emotions. In this way, Elster denies both "economic imperialism" and "cultural-studies imperialism," for these accounts try to explain behaviour and decision-making by presenting them as results of rational choice processes, revised and amplified according to models of biological adaptation, or as social constructions that are infinitely malleable. Indeed, Elster has been increasingly critical with the hyperrationalist reductionism of many models of rational choice theory. In particular, he has censured the practice of attributing 'objective interests' to social actors, that is, allegedly 'objective' interests that are defined depending on the context. Such an account is problematic, according to Elster, because it fails to consider the role that other key factors (e.g. social norms or emotions) may play in a specific situation (Elster 2007: 463). Notwithstanding, he does acknowledge the importance of interests and material incentives, as well as the usefulness of expanded rational choice models and game theory, Elster contends that the interaction between emotion and interest is far more complex than admitted by cost/benefit models, given that emotions contribute to determine the preferences and rewards at stake.

Following Solomon in this respect, he suggests that emotions give sense to our lives, and thus they are decisive, i.e. "the stuff of life." In other words, emotions constitute the most powerful bond capable of linking human beings together, we feel them intensely, and they can be highly pleasant or unpleasant. Indeed, many manifestations of human behaviour would be unintelligible, if we were not to take emotion into account (Elster 1999a: 486). In this regard, Elster contends that emotions are capable of influencing action in three different ways: *1)* They constitute sources of happiness and unhappiness, pleasure and displeasure, as well as *2)* impulses to action. *3)* They manage to influence mental states and, in particular, beliefs.

According to this author, emotions have an undeniable cognitive dimension (in the broad sense, i.e. including moral beliefs), which allows *1)* to differentiate human from animal passions, since animals are unable to develop complex beliefs about their own emotions (there is no cognitive link between emotion and action). Furthermore, *2)* emotions vary depending on the cultural and social environment, and in particular, depending on the dominant cognitive and moral principles (Elster 1999b: 21).

Besides, in Elster's view some emotions are essentially *social*, in the sense that they are triggered by beliefs about other human beings, whilst others are just contingently social. The influence of the former ones upon human behaviour depends to a great extent on the social norms internalized by social agents (cf. figure 5). More precisely: "social norms in general operate through the emotions of shame and contempt." (Elster 1999a: 140)

Figure 5: Elster

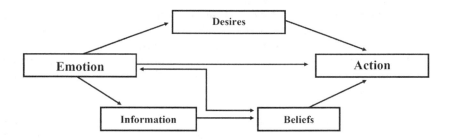

In the following, the main characteristics of emotion pointed out by Elster will be listed – at least those features that are relevant for the purpose of this chapter (Elster 1999a, 1999b and 2007). It should be noted that his thought in this respect has been greatly influenced by Frijda (1986), and that many of the arguments advanced by Elster overlap with those made by Ben-Ze'ev (2000). Plainly:

1) Cognitive antecedents: Emotions depend upon beliefs that we hold about ourselves and others. This is a feature that, in turn, is referred to the cultural context, which is understood as a set of shared values, beliefs and concepts. In this regard, Elster highlights three crucial aspects: *a)* Emotions support social norms by, for instance, inducing shame for not having accomplished a duty or scorning those who are unreliable. Furthermore, he argues *b)* that each culture has its own qualitative and quantitative repertoires of emotions, and finally, *c)* that

emotions that are integrated within the axiological repertoire of a specific culture are subjected to diverse social norms.
2) Observable physiological effects (such as changes in heart rate, body temperature, blood pressure, breathing pattern, or other, visible changes on the skin) and physical expressions (e.g. the posture assumed, the tone of voice, and other visible expressions such a shouting, smiling or crying).
3) Action tendencies: Emotions are actions, "states of readiness to execute a given kind of action" (Frijda 1986: 70), or better said, "modes of relational action readiness, either in the form of tendencies to establish, maintain or disrupt a relationship with the environment or in the form of mode of relational readiness as such" (Frijda 1986: 71). Furthermore, emotions do not only promote action in general, but more precisely, they promote the most immediate action possible.
4) Intentional objects: Emotions, unlike feelings, which are taken to be just an element (among others) of emotions, are always intentional, i.e. they are 'about' something: a person, an object or a situation.
5) The pleasure/pain valence which varies in intensity: Emotions can be pleasurable or painful. Action tends to achieve pleasure and to act on conditions generating displeasure.

Unlike disciplines such as neuroscience, psychology, sociology and epistemology of the social sciences, in which the conception of emotion has been cut loose from the classic reason/passion dichotomy for over 20 years, political analysis remains alien to "emotional rationality" (McDermott 2004: 702) and under the hegemony of hyperrationalist explicative models – notwithstanding that the concept of reason initially deployed by these hyperrationalist models has been revised and broadened (*bounded* rationality, *framed* rationality and so forth). Nevertheless, there is a belief that is gaining increasing acceptance; namely, that there might be certain emotional factors underlying the classic explicative variables (i.e. utility maximization, political opportunity structure, political culture, et cetera). Thus, this belief holds that these emotional factors might play a relevant role in explaining political phenomena, too. If we limit our considerations to the last decades, this belief can be traced back to Raymond Williams (1977), who coined the notion of "structures of feeling" to refer to the deeply rooted dispositions and sensibilities that, located beyond the realm of ideas and principles, are at the very basis of different modes of life. This concept, moreover, was taken up by researchers such as Hetherington (1998: 79) to account for the expressive dimension of political processes of identity construction. More recently, other authors have demonstrated, for instance, that emotional and cognitive elements are intertwined in matters such as the fight against terrorism or the Iraq war. Moreover, going beyond classic hyperrationalist studies, these analyses have proved that passions such as fear, anxiety or patriotic enthusiasm play crucial roles in public opinion's mobilization and manipulation, and, moreover, that these roles vary according to the passions considered. In general terms it is safe to say that the effects of passions are more complex than what is suggested by the simple distinction between positive and negative emotions (Huddy *et al.* 2007; Castells 2009).

The affective dimension of politics can be found in other phenomena such as electoral behaviour, which has normally been explained by resorting to hyperrationalist and mainly spatial analytical models based on the principle of utility maximization (rational voter), disregarding in this way other aspects such as emotion or discursive frames, which underlie the behaviour of the electorate, or are even required by the chain of thought prompted by the explicative hyperrationalist model itself (Nardulli and Kuklinsky 2007; Lupia and Menning 2007; Elster 2007; Lakoff 2008). However, the electorate is confronted in every electoral process with a plurality of alternatives, which are sorted out with the help of mechanisms such as the felt sympathy toward a political leader or a political party (apparently forgotten mechanisms, notwithstanding the work of Campbell 1960), which implies an "affective orientation." More precisely, the electorate is to a large extent an "emotional constituency." In fact, "people vote for the candidate who elicits the right feelings, not the candidate who presents the best arguments" (Westen 2007: 125). Research on affective intelligence has demonstrated that voters are influenced by emotions such as enthusiasm or anxiety. In this regard, it has been shown that *enthusiasm* lessens the amount of reflection and encourages resorting to pre-established heuristic devices, such as political identification, when deciding who to vote for (Marcus 2002; Cassino and Lodge 2007). Other studies have claimed that feelings of impotence or solitude, fostered by the secret ballot, are responsible for political apathy, low levels of political participation and political cynicism (Barbalet 2001), while Marcus (2002: 104) has shown that *anxiety* affects the political judgement of the voters. It has an influence on the quality of this judgement, on the effort to search for new information and on the voters' processing capacity of this new information. In summary, *1)* "the political brain is an emotional brain" (Western 2007); accordingly, *2)* "the rational (…) voter is an emotional voter" (Brader 2006: 195); and as a corollary, *3)* "emotion is both central and legitimate in political persuasion" (Lakoff 2008: 8).

The most relevant emotional systems play a visible role in many citizens' and politicians' activities, thus undermining the traditional image of cold, dispassionate reason, which has been normally thought of as independent, self-sufficient and opposed to emotion. Emotional systems gather information from the environment, process it and produce sensations. This information, in turn, influences procedural as well as declarative memory. It also has effects on habits and learning processes, and precedes and prepares conscious activity. Following McDermott, an optimal – according to standard neuroscientific knowledge – decision making model must consider the multiple roles played by emotion: mobilization to action, calculation, future discounting, information gathering and selection, memory, historical analogies, risk perception etc. (McDermott 2004).

The emotional dimension becomes more evident if we consider one unavoidable feature of politics; namely, the processes of collective mobilization, as well as the conflicts for power among social groups. This implies both the construction of the group itself as a shared, protagonist social identity (an 'us') and the construction of a 'them', which acts as the antagonist. In turn, these two crucial activities of political action imply and articulate in complex manners and in one single movement the following elements: *1)* material elements (interest); *2)* ethical and political elements (principles, convictions, ideals); and *3)* emotional elements (positive and negative affective bonds). Political action, be it cooperative or conflictive, consensus-oriented or dissenting, requires that political actors have the capacity to take heed to the intentions and goals of the actors with whom they interact. Contrary to what a well-known expression suggests – 'it's nothing personal, just politics' – it has to be concluded that, strictly speaking, 'the personal is political', i.e. that politics is a personal experience that is guided by emotional perceptions. This is obvious in some extreme cases such as ethnic conflicts. For instance, Petersen has developed an "emotion based approach" that highlights the role played by passions such as hate, fear or resentment in these conflicts. According to this author, the former two emotions are not as relevant as the latter one, but resentment is shown to be decisive, since it connects structure to information; information to beliefs and emotions; and beliefs and emotions to political action and the repertoires of action (Petersen 2002).

However, not only in processes of political mobilization do (negative) passions play an important role but also in those of de-mobilization. In this regard, Helena Flam has analyzed systematically the crucial effects of *fear* on the protests that took place in the authoritarian regimes of East Germany and Poland before 1989 (Flam 1998). Based on over 100 in-depth interviews, she contended that fear was a crucial factor that brought those protests to a standstill and deteriorated the chances of overcoming the problems associated to collective action. And Cass Sunstein has provided a sophisticated discussion of the ambivalent effects (action or inaction) of fear in risk-evaluation and decision-making processes in his systematic critique of the "precautionary principle" (Sunstein 2005).

It is not necessary though to look at antagonisms that are so emotion-laden. Regarding other more common cases, it can be claimed that it is crucial to connect a problem with an emotional reaction so as to achieve that citizens take deep care of that particular problem and act co-ordinately – since the rational understanding of a problem has been shown to be insufficient and in need of being supplemented by emotion. In other words, without this emotional connection, sheer rational comprehension does not lead to action. In short, emotional processes link together these three aspects: behaviour, memory and learning processes, which are crucial in politics to maintain a habit, defend a regime, change an attitude or an institutional pattern, or to challenge a political order. For example, Gamson has suggested that framing a situation as unjust, during a process of collective mobilization, cannot be seen as a sheer cognitive or intellectual judgement about what is just or unjust, but has to be regarded as an expression of moral indignation – as a "hot cognition," to put it in social-psychological terms (Zajonc). From this follows that the more concrete both the goals of collective action and the problem that this action tries to correct and the more specific the antagonist (i.e. the social group held responsible for the problem under consideration), as well as the more colourful the terms used to describe this problem, the stronger the motivation of the participants and the more vivid the emotions felt by social actors, which reinforce the sense of indignation and thus enhance the probability and intensity of social mobilization (Gamson 1992: 32). In summary, passion plays a vital role in the political construction of collective identities and therefore in the unavoidable agonistic dimension of politics, which cannot be made to fit completely into a consensual and 'rational and reasonable' model of politics without eliminating the very essence of democratic politics (Mouffe 2002).

Actually, strategic and instrumental aspects of politics are intrinsically related to expressive elements, turning interests and principles inseparable from the underlying emotions. This is especially evident if we consider the political logic of collective action. Considering the inner dynamics of political parties, groups and movements, it can be argued that they generate, through their political action, collective identities that are capable of merging individuals into a common project, as well as capable of fostering solidarity bonds and feelings of belonging, which emerge not only from shared goals but also from shared memories and the idea of a common future. The emotional ties of these collective identities are, moreover, strengthened by participating in collective action and by the existence of an us/them opposition, i.e. a political antagonism. In this context, the emotional dimension of revolutions and political protests constitutes a promising research strand, which can be regarded as supplementing traditional structural models and those based on resource mobilization theory, as well as culturalist approaches. This research strand will certainly highlight the role played by emotions (fear, hope, indignation, resentment) in this type of political processes, in which emotions may work as 'mental frames' or 'action tendencies' (Jasper 1997; Goodwin *et al.* 2000; Reed 2004; Flam and King 2005).

All these shared emotions, ideas and projects tend to crystallize forming networks of varying stability, which reproduce, in turn, the initial structures of meanings, emotions, cognitive praxes, memories and symbols. In this regard, it would be safe to use the expression 'emotional scheme' (analogously to Sewell's "cultural schemes") to refer to the set of emotional meanings and memories of shared sensations, as well as the repertoires of common or conflicting actions occurred during the interactions between participants, opponents and audiences.

Every process of identity construction requires a certain emotional transference that, though varying in intensity and duration, manages to promote the feeling that one belongs to a cause, a movement or a party, i.e. to something that transcends the individual, and thus that is charged with a certain amount of collective emotional energy. In this regard, *frame analysis*, for instance, which is still influenced by a limited notion of rationality, is marked by rationalism and cognitivism (Goodwin *et al.* 2000: 6). Surprisingly, emotions play a very limited role, or no role at all, in the constructivist explanation of collective action advanced by frame analysts, who were expected to more open and sensitive to the emotional dimension of politics than authors resorting to structural or rational-choice theory approaches. However, strictly speaking the normative-cum-cognitive framing of 'reality' must be accompanied by its emotional framing (Flam and King 2005: 24). In this respect, cognitive-linguists who analyse interpretative frames (Lakoff) are paying increasing attention to insights developed by researchers on political emotions (Westen), since both fields of research are complementary. Cognitive science and neuroscience have demonstrated that frames, metaphors and narratives are imprinted in the brain's neural circuitry; that is to say, cultural models reside in our brains. It has also been shown that narratives are neurally articulated, i.e. physically wired in our brains – at least concerning their dramatic structure, the distribution of protagonist and antagonist roles, and their emotional structure, i.e. Damasio's "somatic markers," which link the dramatic structure with the double circuit of positive and negative emotions. Here is where this new understanding of the brain is relevant to the analysis of politics: established circuits of empathy and fear constitute the very bases of fundamental moral and ideological differences (Lakoff 2008: 103; Rifkin 2010).

Political parties, political leaders and social movements promote continually contending political programmes and images of society but also *counter-emotions* or even, on certain occasions, *subversive counter emotions*. We should insist that emotions can be as functional or dysfunctional for action as reasons and interests can be. For instance, emotions such as cynicism, fear or resignation are demobilizing, while indignation, empathy or fraternity can be highly mobilizing (Gamson 1992: 31).

Finally, the new "performative approach" should be also mentioned, that is, the analyses of "contentious performances" (Klandermans 2009) and "ritual performances" (Alexander 2006; Eyerman 2005). Klandermans, for example, considers classic instrumental and ideological variables in order to explain the motivation of individual agents who participate in demonstrations. But he also considers another factor disregarded by Tilly (2003), *group anger*, which plays also a crucial role, according to his argument. Eyerman claims that the narrative structures of cognitive frames appear within a wider rhetorical and emotional matrix from which they cannot be separated. In this way, according to his argument, a sense of continuity is provided, as well as connections to past references and to the future, shared emotional experiences are amplified, and so too is the collective significance of the event. Moral empathy, feelings of belonging, affective ties and bonds of solidarity are also some of the fundamental elements of the collective identities of social movements, social groups and political parties. These considerations lead to the conclusion that a broadened notion of *discourse* should be used in political analysis, i.e. one that refers to narratives consisting not only of words but also of protest repertoires, gestures and symbolically charged expressions (assemblies, demonstrations, celebrations, myths, flags, statues, emblems and so on). In summary, "performance theory adds a new dimension to the study of social movements in linking cognitive framing, narration and discourse with the practice of mobilization, and thus emotion" (Eyerman 2005: 49).

The Return of Passions to Political Theory

The aforementioned insights gained in the fields of neuroscience, social-psychology, epistemology of the social sciences and sociology have greatly influenced contemporary political theory. In this regard, they have forced it to revise its rationalistic axioms and to take up an argument that can be traced back to Aristotle's *Rhetoric*, but that has been marginalized until recently by utilitarianism and rational choice theory.

It should be noted from the outset that: *1)* the hyperrationalist approach to politics is a modern phenomenon. It has rested upon the displacement of the classical meaning of *emotion* by its modern meaning – i.e. the conception of *emotion* as unintentional, "visceral" and non-cognitive (Dixon 2003: 250) –, and upon a partial and restrictive interpretation of certain classic literature (Hobbes, Descartes, Hume, Madison and so on). This interpretation has been promoted mainly by utilitarianism and by the economic accounts of politics that prevailed during the last third of the 20th century. *2)* This foundational exclusion of passion from political theory – in other words, the construction of politics as the unpolluted realm of reason – is but a normative project that has not been fully accomplished by any theoretical approach, neither a classic nor a contemporary one, not to mention politics itself (incidentally, in this respect this normative project is similar to many others, e.g. the exorbitant ambition to monopolize power associated to the notion of *sovereignty,*). The many reformulations of this normative project have always ended up showing inconsistencies, generating normative and motivational deficiencies that have even been acknowledged by the own authors of these reformulations. On occasion, authors have even revised, explicitly or implicitly, the rationalist logic underlying their accounts. In this regard, I shall remind the reader of Hobbes' ambivalence not only toward *fear* (a concept that binds tightly together reason and emotion) but also toward ambition or desire for power, which can be, according to Hobbes, destructive or constructive. Moreover, these feelings are held to be even indispensable to the progression of knowledge and to happiness (James 1997). Even Kant, an authoritative reference of this rationalistic tradition, changed his point of view after his Third Critique – in particular, this change is evident in Kant's *Opus Postumum* –, giving passions greater consideration at the expense of moral action and acknowledging their inevitable and productive character. In this way, Kant paved the way for the subsequent romantic conception of emotion (Kahn et al. 2006).

The *Federalist Papers* constitute another significant example. To be sure, they are the *locus classicus* of an approach preoccupied with restraining passions. This goal does not only characterize the conception of *politics* advanced by the *Federalist Papers*, but it also serves as the basis for justifying the conception of State developed in these manuscripts. Passions are supposed to be blind, unruly and dangerous forces that overburden politics, promote sectarian attitudes and hamper negotiation and compromise. Nonetheless, at the same time emotions are constantly reintroduced in the discourse and presented as positive, even necessary, elements of politics: They are thought of as a kind of "democratic energy" that fuels the entire system of checks and balances (*Federalist*

Paper nº 45), as public-spiritedness (*nº 10* and *51*), as "veneration" of the legitimate government (*nº 49*), et cetera.

The same holds true for many other classic texts of modern political theory. One of them is *De l'Influence des Passions sur le Bonheur des Individus et des Nations* by Germaine de Staël (1796), which is of great interest in this context, though has been largely disregarded in the literature. Still in the tradition of radical Enlightenment, a tradition that de Staël herself revised some years later, in the advent of the German romanticism, passion is conceived of as "the impulsive force that drives men with independence of their will" and as "the greatest difficulty of governments." Furthermore, this conception is accompanied by the chimeric and rationalistic hope of "imagining that political science might someday acquire geometric evidence" (Staël 1796: 61). However, though Madame de Staël introduces the notion of interest as an explicit alternative to emotion, she also acknowledges, though without further elaboration, that "there is something grand in passion," that "the love for study has all the characteristics of a passion," and finally that "the veneration of the republic is, in its pure form, the highest feeling that a man can conceive" (Staël 1796: 67).

Many examples can be given, though it is compulsory to focus, in particular, on an author who has played a crucial role in establishing the modern hyperrationalist canon of politics; namely, Max Weber. In his classic work *The Protestant Ethic and the Spirit of Capitalism*, more precisely in his discussion of Pietism, Weber, who is influenced in this respect by Descartes and Kant, introduces first the culture/nature dualism, which then gives rise to the (more radical) reason/passion dichotomy. The German sociologist regards passions as irrational forces, i.e. impulses that disturb reason and the self-control that is necessary for modern life and modern forms of work. In his much famous critical analysis of Pietism, he censures the "greater emphasis of Pietism on the emotional side of religion," as well as its "weakening of the inhibitions which protect the rational personality." In this regard, Weber opposes Pietism to Calvinism, whose greater rationality and aversion to the emotional side of religion, i.e. "the anti-rational, emotional elements" (Weber 1920: 165), foster the worldly asceticism that triggers, in turn, progress of the capitalist civilization. Nonetheless, as has been shown by classic (Mitzman 1971) and contemporary (Barbalet 2008) studies, there is a conspicuous move of Weber's thought "away from the initial unqualified celebration of ascetic rationalism." His personal experiences and maturity drew him to a different perspective on reason and passion, and Weber finally acknowledged in his discussion of the notion of *Beruf* the undeniable importance of emotion for social action. He finally assumed "that emotions cannot be eliminated from human affairs and they also have a positive role in clarifying intentions and ordering action" (Barbalet 2008: 69).

Something very similar happens with contemporary political theorists. We have seen already that Rawls ended up reintroducing a secondary paradigm in his work, notwithstanding his arguments on reason and reasonableness, public reason and non-public reason, though without being systematic or revising the original rationalistic paradigm. This secondary paradigm articulates without prior notice "thought and feeling" (Rawls 1971: 587), and it is expressed by notions such as "moral sensitivity," "sense of justice," "moral feelings" et cetera. The same holds true for Habermas and his reflections on the "ideal speech situation" and "the public sphere." In order to achieve a purer proceduralism than Rawls, but also a more deliberative theory of democracy, Habermas tries to purge all normative content from the procedures of justification advanced by his theory. By doing so he attempts to maintain the principles of justice free from any (ethical) idea of the Good, which would be inevitably partial. This implies – as Habermas himself acknowledges – a "motivational deficit," which owes to the fact that moral rationality in Habermas' account tends to disregard, by differentiating too strictly between morality and conceptions of the good life, the affective bonds and desires that usually induce action. But then again, emotions reappear, though in an unsystematic manner, in Habermas' argumentation of the need for solidarity and empathy in real-world deliberation. Although Habermas' thought is potentiality well-suited to integrate passion, since his theory of communicative action does not rest upon semantics but on the pragmatics of speech-acts, said reintroduction of emotion remains under-theorized in his work. A similar argument can be advanced regarding the exaggerated emphasis that Habermas places on consensus in his initial account. Accordingly, he disregards the role played by passion in political confrontations between conflicting collective projects and identities, which constitutes the very essence of the political (Mouffe 2000). Habermas' account in his book *Between Facts and Norms*, biased by a Parsonian perspective, falls apart to some extent, because he fails to consider that the capacity for moral judgement rests upon the indissoluble connection between cognitive operations, on the one hand, and emotional dispositions and attitudes, on the other. No affectively neutral normative justification can be possible, if (the feeling of) self-affirmation on the part of the participants in a deliberative process constitutes an essential component of normative justifications. In this regard, it should be noted that according to Habermas a deliberative process should consist of real deliberation between real citizens, unlike Rawls' account of the original position and the veil of ignorance. In summary, social and political action, but also real deliberation, require of passion and affects. In other words, "neither human agency nor practical reason can be abstracted entirely from affective concerns. Any theory of justice that fails to account for this fact faces not only a motivational deficit but also a normative one" (Krause 2008: 46).

Within the field of political theory two authors – Remo Bodei and Martha Nussbaum – should be credited for initiating a systematic reintroduction of the topic of political passions. In his insightful book *Geometria delle Passioni*, Bodei advances a systematic critique of the reason/passion dichotomy. He suggests that passions prepare, preserve, memorize and re-elaborate the "reactive meanings" that are immediately attributed to objects, persons and events that human beings encounter in specific settings. Therefore, "to gain knowledge of passions is nothing else but to analyse reason itself though against the grain, illuminating reason with its own alleged shadow" (Bodei 1991: 12). Going beyond the myth of "the cancer of reason," Bodei proceeds, by revising a vast literature, from Aristotle to the Stoics, from Spinoza to the Jacobins, to show the classic connections and ruptures between reason and passion. This leads to a renewed appraisal of Spinoza (agreeing in this respect with Damasio 2003: 169) – though also with Tocqueville (in accordance with Elster 2009) – since Spinoza did not demand from individuals, for the first time in many centuries, self-sacrifice and the sacrifice of their passions in the name of God or in the name of the State. This is because Spinoza did not consider passions (love, hate, anger, compassion, fear and hope) as vices but as intrinsic properties of the human nature. To put it in his own terms, he conceived them as "imaginative knowledge." Indeed, Spinoza rejected any clear-cut distinctions between knowledge and passion, between soul and body and altruism and self-interest. Within the history of ethics, he is undoubtedly the thinker that has distanced himself most from these dichotomies. For Bodei, Spinoza's attempt to go beyond *fear* and *hope* is especially interesting, for it gives rise to a whole new perspective, which is different from that of realist thinkers (Hobbes), who accept the given order of things, but also from that of utopian thinkers (Aquinas), who take the world just as it should be. Spinoza did not accept either the notion of "calm passion," i.e. those types of passions initially introduced by Hobbes and then more fully elaborated by Hume. Nevertheless, these authors established with his notion of "calm passion" the indissoluble bond between moral appreciation, on the one hand, and pride, shame, love or hate, on the other one (Martínez Marzoa 2009: 68). These emotions would later be postulated as those emotions (e.g. the pursuit of profit) most suited to be rationalized and transformed (through domination, channelling or weakening) into interests, which are objects of calculation and negotiation (Hirschman 1977).

For her part, Martha Nussbaum has advanced certainly the most fully-fledged and substantive philosophical account of passions, and has provided many insights to political theory in particular. As early as 1994, in her book

Therapy of Desire she embarked on a systematic effort to take up the theme of passions studied by Aristotle, the Stoics and the Epicureans, whose philosophical accounts had been largely disregarded by contemporary ethics and political theory. According to Nussbaum, Aristotle should be credited for arguing against the conception of passions as blind animal forces. On the contrary, he depicted passions as having definitely cognitive and perceptive qualities, which are associated to certain types of beliefs. Precisely this image of emotions explains the current popularity of a normative theory that considers passions as indispensable elements of the good life, thus arguing for its education, as they constitute a *conditio sine qua non* of virtuous action. Thus, a citizen having *phronesis* will not only manage a concrete situation in accordance with reason, but also in an *emotionally adequate manner*. Nussbaum points out certain key aspects of the Aristotelian conception of passions that resonate with present philosophical, psychological and neuroscientific insights on this topic: *1)* passions are *intentional* forms of consciousness (i.e. they are 'about' something); *2)* that are closely linked to *beliefs*; *3)* and can be characterized as rational or irrational, true or false; in other words, they are not always correct, similarly to beliefs and actions,. *4)* Passions can be modified by changing the beliefs, and thus they can, and should, be educated in accordance with an adequate conception of the Good life. Nevertheless, for Nussbaum the Hellenistic thought developed by the Stoics and the Epicureans is richer and analytically sounder than that of Aristotle; in particular, regarding the way it conceives the relations between emotions and beliefs, its image of the evaluative dimension of emotion and the connection that it establishes between emotional life and (a tragic) *Weltanschauung* (Nussbaum 1994: 514).

In her book *Upheavals of Thought*, Nussbaum develops further this conception of emotion as an integral part of ethical thinking and thus as a crucial substantive component of moral philosophy. In this book, she highlights particularly the cognitive and evaluative dimensions of emotions and their role in making value judgements. In this regard, emotions can be useful or misleading for the task of making ethical decisions, but they have to be considered – so the argument goes – as one of the *basic human capacities* (in the sense attributed to this expression by Amartya Sen and Martha Nussbaum herself). Hence, she advances a concept of emotion that is based upon three interrelated dimensions: *(1)* the *cognitive evaluation* of an object, *(2) eudaimonia*, i.e. personal development and flourishing; *(3)* the assessment and appraisal of external objects that are important for one's goals and happiness. Moreover, Nussbaum addresses an Aristotelian topic that remained underdeveloped in *Therapy of Desire*; namely, the irreducible *social* dimension of emotions – also highlighted by other authors (Gross 2006: 41) –, which she discusses together with their *evaluative* dimension. This leads to a constructivist conception of emotions that regards them as determined by specific norms, cultural elements, language and social structure. Accordingly, she advances a crucial argument concerning the links between passions, capacities and conceptions of the good life: "in an ethical and socio/political creature, emotions themselves are ethical and socio/political, part of an answer to the questions, 'What is worth caring about?' 'How should I live?'" (Nussbaum 2001: 149)

These and further reflections have definitely had an impact on the discipline of political theory; in particular on current debates on *deliberative democracy*, triggering an "affective turn" hand in hand with an "incremental inclusion of empathy" (Morrell 2010: 84). These reflections by Nussbaum resonate with concerns previously raised within that paradigm. More specifically, they have contributed to temper partially the hyperrationalist and argumentative bias that characterized the first theories of deliberation, which were too focused on consensus. It should be recalled in this context that the model of deliberative democracy is claimed to be an improvement not only over representative but also over participatory models of democracy, since both representative and participatory models regard citizens' preferences as given and thus as exogenous, i.e. as pre-political. Preferences should be aggregated or expressed directly, according to these models. In contrast, deliberative democracy opposes to this idea the notion of *endogenous preferences,* that is to say, a conception of democracy in which preferences are politically produced through uncoerced debates among equal participants. However, though this image of democracy in which preferences can be endogenously transformed through public egalitarian discussion remains attractive, it is evident that it is strongly influenced by a notion of reason that, to a large extent, rests upon the reason/passion dichotomy that we have already discussed here. Hence it can be argued that: *(1)* the neglect of the affective components of deliberation is nothing else but *(2)* the other side of dissensus and conflict inherent to politics. This is the unavoidable consequence of a rationalist image of deliberation that underlies expressions such as "the force of the better argument" (Pellizioni 2001), "reasoned argument for the purpose of resolving political conflict" (Knight and Johnson 1994: 285) or "epistemic conception of democracy" (Cohen 1986; Gutmann and Thompson 1996) – not to mention the overestimation of the chances of reaching a "rational consensus" (Habermas 1996).

If we consider the work of J. Elster, *Deliberative Democracy*, to take just an example, we will notice that the "pathologies" of deliberation mentioned in this volume are always closely related to emotional biases (e.g. manipulation, adaptation, distortions of preferences) (Elster 1998). In Fishkin's book *Democracy and Deliberation*, demagogy is always associated to unbounded emotions ("aroused publics," "stirring up" and so on) that undermine the equanimity of a deliberative process (Fishkin 1991). The same holds true for Cohen's essay in the compilation *Deliberative Democracy* by Bohman and Rehg (1997). The notion of *reason* is continuously mentioned without considering the emotional context in which reasons are given and accepted, or considering this emotional context just marginally, without any theoretical elaboration.

To our aims, the problem lies in an image of deliberation too influenced by scientific epistemology and its standards of objectivity (Lynch 2000: 47); or to put it another way, in a conception of the political debate that is scarcely pragmatic and informal and excessively logic-rationalist. Indeed, an increasing number of theorists of deliberative democracy, even some of the most decisive for the development of this theory, are censuring, and arguing against, this hyperrationalist image of deliberation. Bohman, for example, discussing Habermas' approach criticizes the Kantian hyperrationality resulting from translating the standards applied to scientific or philosophical knowledge to the political realm. At an early stage of the theory's development, he formulated a sophisticated critique of Habermas' account arguing for the need to pay more attention to the perlocutionary speech acts (irony, metaphors, art…), with preference to those illocutionary, in the emancipatory discourse, and thus for the necessity for retrieving the disregarded, or even proscribed dimension of rhetoric (Bohman 1988 and 1996). Gutmann and Thompson consider the affective modes of consciousness as a crucial catalyst for deliberation – though this argument does not alter the rationalist image of deliberation held by both authors, who nevertheless reject the "dichotomy between reason and passion" (Gutmann and Thompson 1996: 50).

However, the claim that emotions cannot be the leading factor of deliberation and, in contrast, that only those expressions that can be explicitly formulated in a speech act should be taken into account, cannot lead to ignoring that emotions, *empathy* for example, play a crucial role in deliberation. In other words, empathy and other relational emotions must be considered the own soul of democracy (Rifkin 2010: 165), they are necessary factors that foster communication, reciprocity and motivate citizens to participate; furthermore they fuel a pluralistic and tolerant antagonism that constitutes the very basis of any debate (Morrell 2010). Emotions like *empathy* constitute a key factor for the egalitarian inclusion of certain social groups in a deliberative process, while other emotions, *disgust* for example, exclude other groups from deliberation. In short, positive and relational emotions and sentiments are required to "assist the epistemic value of the process of argumentation" (Nino 2003: 175).

The criticisms advanced by authors working outside the theory of deliberative democracy are even more fundamental. Thus, for example, from the field of empirical research, Marcus highlights, considering the latest advances in the fields of neuroscience and psychology, the untenability of an "application of deliberative reason that necessarily excludes emotion" (Marcus 2002: 7). On the contrary, emotions provide "an intermediate link between biology and norms," implying social morality is not a mere choice but a *disposition* that guarantees a successful coordination between citizens. Emotions, hence, constitute the condition of possibility of any public ethic (Ovejero 2008: 266).

Within the field of political theory, Iris Marion Young in her formulation of an inclusive democracy deconstructs the hyperrationalist notion of "impartiality" (1990: 175). She argues for alternative forms of judgement, namely for forms that incorporate emotions, and criticizes compellingly the notion of (a "dispassionate and disembodied" form of) *speech* deployed by the early theory of deliberation (Young 2000: 39). Ernesto Laclau and Chantal Mouffe have been even more radical in their critique. According to them, collective identities cannot be explained relying solely on the argumentative and symbolic nature of reality. In contrast, emotions are crucial to account for them (Mouffe 2000 and 2002; Laclau 2005). From a psychoanalytic perspective, both these authors establish a close link between two topics: *(1)* the key function of rhetoric in the process of meaning-creation, which is conceived of as a permanent contamination of literality and grammar (i.e. the logical) by metaphor and synecdoche. This, in turn, requires *(2)* the concurrence of emotions so as to make political signification possible. In other words, what is required is the indissoluble articulation of cognitive and emotional components. Hence, emotions should be conceived not only as associated to *expressive* functions (expression of preferences or identities) but as *constitutive* of the political itself. Stressing the relevance of rhetoric as support for empathy, as Morrell has argued, is really key to a better approach to "the interconnections among affect, cognition and reason and provides a better understanding of how a deliberative democracy will likely function than those theories that rely upon unrealistic, cognitive understandings of rationality" (Morrell 2010: 149).

Recently, making use of the notion of "passionate utterance" and the Emersonian model of *adversative democracy* formulated by Stanley Cavell (Cavell 1990 and 2005), Aletta Norval has maintained that it is necessary to relate language and passion (a classic topic of psychoanalysis) in order to re-imagine deliberative democracy and integrate emotional expressions (Norval 2007). However, it is in the crucial books by Martha Nussbaum, Sharon Krause (and Michael Morrel) that we find two path-breaking and promising attempts to integrate systematically passion into the theory of deliberative democracy.

Developing further a research strand already discussed in this chapter, Nussbaum presents in her book *Hiding from Humanity,* the only available systematic (and controversial) analysis of the functionality and adequacy of different passions to deliberation. Summarizing, her argument brings together: *(1)* her Aristotelian thesis that beliefs and emotions are closely linked, that emotions are evaluative and can be evaluated, and *(2)* her capability approach: We all have certain necessities and basic capabilities, though we are also handicapped in different ways and to varying degrees, for we all lack to some extent certain "functionings" that are essential to flourishing as human beings. Acknowledging the evaluative function of emotions (in terms of the benefits and costs that follow from a particular decision), as well as the need for assessing emotions themselves, Nussbaum raises the following question: Which emotions are relevant to political deliberation? In this regard, her subtle analysis leads her to the conclusion that anger and compassion, for instance, are crucial for a deliberative process, as well as fear, grieve, love and gratitude. On the other side, however, shame and repugnancy should be in principle expelled from the public sphere, since they tend to exclude certain individuals and social groups from public discussion (Nussbaum 2004). In her recent manifest *Not for profit* Nussbaum concretizes further her previous theory of moral and anti-moral emotions. From her perspective of an "Education for Democracy," *disgust* merits special critical scrutiny due to 1) its nature not merely visceral, provided its "strong cognitive component;" and 2) its capacity in involving self-repudiation and "the displacement of self-repudiation onto another group" fuelling dangerous stereotypes and exclusionary dichotomies pure/impure, we/they, friend/foe. Very differently, *compassion* develops the necessary capacity for empathy, to see the world from the viewpoint of other people and, in this way, for looking at another person as and end and not merely as an instrumental means (Nussbaum 2010).

Finally, in her book *Civil Passions,* Sharon Krause provides an innovative "new politics of passion" inspired upon the philosophical tradition of moral sentiment (from Hume to Bernard Williams) and on the latest insights provided by neuroscience and neuropsychology, aimed at providing a theoretic and systematic place for passions in public deliberation. Her main goal is to overcome the normative and motivational deficit of the classic version of deliberative theory which, by distinguishing too sharply between 'reasons' and 'passions', fails to integrate the motivations of the participants into the process of deliberation. To this aims, Krause argues for a new ideal of "impartiality" that is reformulated as "a reflexive sensitivity to the sufferings and the joys of others," understood as the feeling of respect for others as morally significant persons (Krause 2008: 5). In summary, an "affective engaged impartiality" that is supposed to go beyond the endemic motivational and normative deficit of deliberative theory without ignoring the task of providing judgement and deliberation with standards of impartiality.

First, Krause reformulates the notion of public reason by defining it as a heterogeneous group of "common concerns" or "shared horizons of concerns" within which public discussions combine sensitivity, "care" and reflection. Thus, a "politics of civil passion" manages not to fall back into the aforementioned motivational deficit, since it succeeds in linking moral sentiments and impartiality to the affective sources that promote the participation of citizens in public deliberation. It should be noted, however, that this links operates in two ways: the contents of moral sentiments are fluid, socially constructed and thus subject to revision, since passions themselves depend upon deliberation and the outcomes of deliberation. Hence, the relation between moral sentiments and democratic deliberation is decisive: By providing the political conditions of equality, which in turn increase attentiveness to the sentiments of others, and by allowing the integration of a wide range of sentiments in the public sphere, deliberative democracy manages to broaden with unique efficacy public imagination and to educate the moral sentiments of the citizens. Second, Krause provides a coherent criterion for determining normatively which emotions are admissible in the public sphere; namely, only those that can be accepted from a moral point of view that is consistent with the principles of public reason (Krause 2008: 163). Third, from this point of view, social norms are intrinsically, and not contingently, connected to the diverse human motives; practical reason incorporates affective elements and the moral sentiment incarnates this unalienable connection.

Thus, in the present state of the debate, moving beyond the classic reason/passion dichotomy and its corollary (i.e. the exclusion of emotions from political theory and political science) requires a growing interdisciplinarity and, in particular, taking into account the insights gained by neuroscience, social-psychology and the epistemology of the social sciences. Far from promoting a pendulum-like movement between the two extremes of the binary code, that is, far from arguing for 'more passion' in politics – as some catchphrases suggest, e.g. 'new politics of passion', 'central role of passions' et cetera –, what is required is to re-think the articulation between emotional and cognitive elements in politics. This is necessary in order to analyse the irreducible dimensions of decision-making: social mobilization, public contestation and the conflicting relations between collective identities. Acknowledging that emotions do play a crucial role in politics does not undermine, however, the significance of strategic interaction between political actors. Indeed, one of the most promising areas of research in political science is to analyse the mutual relationships between strategic behaviour and emotions, for example by resorting to game theory (Lupia and Menning 2007; Elster 2007).

Current and certainly solid research from multiple disciplines demonstrates emotion is: *(1)* a necessary *explicative* variable of political reasoning – this forces us to reconsider the boundaries of rationality, even of broadened and bounded notions of rationality –, as well as *(2)* a valuable autonomous *normative* concept that accounts for an indispensable and crucial dimension of politics – this requires nuanced theoretical critique of the diverse roles of different emotions (fear, disgust, empathy, compassion etc.). In any case, however, we have just begun to clarify how emotions intervene, together with reason, in public deliberation, moral judgement, public mobilization and decision-making. Moreover, we have just begun to elucidate an even deeper conundrum; namely, which are the mechanisms that determine preference formation.

References

Alexander, Jeffrey (2006). *The Civil Sphere*. New York: Oxford University Press.
Baertschi, Bernard (2009). *La neuroéthique. Ce que les neurosciences font nos conceptions morales*. Paris: La Découverte.
Barbalet, J.M. (2001). *Emotion, Social Theory, and Social Structure: A Macrosociological Approach*. Cambridge: Cambridge University Press.
Barbalet, Jack (2008). *Weber, Passion and Profits: 'The Protestant Ethic and the Spirit of Capitalism' in Context*. Cambridge: Cambridge University Press.
Ben-Ze'ev, Aaron (2000). *The subtlety of Emotions*. Cambridge: The MIT Press.
Bodei, Remo (1991). *Geometria delle Passioni*. Milano: Feltrinelli.
Bohman, James F. (1988). Emancipation and Rhetoric: The Perlocutions and Illocutions of the Social Critic. *Philosophy and Rhetoric* 21 (3), 185 – 204.
Bohman, J. (1996). *Public Deliberation: Pluralism, Complexity and Democracy*. Cambridge: The MIT press.
Bohman, James and William Rehg (eds., 1997). *Deliberative Democracy: Essays on Reason and Politics*. Cambridge: The MIT Press.
Brader, Ted (2006). *Campaigning for Hearts and Minds*. Chicago: Chicago University Press.
Campbell, Angus, Philip E. Converse, Warren E. Miller and Donald E. Stokes (1960). *The American Voter*. Chicago: The University of Chicago Press.
Cassino, Dan and Milton Lodge (2007). The Primacy of Affect in Political Evaluations. In Russell Neuman, George E. Marcus, Ann N. Crigler and Michael Mackuen (eds.), *The Affect Effect: Dynamics of Emotion in Political Thinking and Behaviour*. Chicago: Chicago University Press.
Castells, Manuel (2009). *Comunicación y Poder*. Madrid: Alianza.
Cavell, Stanley (1988). *Conditions Handsome and Unhandsome: The Constitution of Emersonian Perfectionism*. Chicago: Chicago University Press. 1990.
Cavell, Stanley (2005). *Philosophy the day after tomorrow*. Cambridge: Harvard University Press.
Clarke, Simon, Paul Hoggett and Simon Thompson (eds., 2006). *Emotion, Politics and Society*. Basignstoke: Palgrave.
Cohen, Gerald A. (1978). *Karl Marx's Theory of History. A Defence*. Oxford: Oxford University Press.

Cohen, Gerald A. (2000). *If You're and Egalitarian, How Come You're So Rich?* Cambridge: Harvard U. Press.
Cohen, Joshua (1986). An Epistemic Conception of Democracy. *Ethics* 97(1), 26 – 38.
Cornelius, Randolph R. (1996). *The Science of Emotion: Research and Tradition in the Psychology of Emotions*. Upper Saddle: Prentice Hall.
Damasio, Antonio (1994). *Descartes' Error. Emotion, Reason, and the Human Brain*. New York: Putman's.
Damasio, Antonio (2003). *Looking for Spinoza: Joy, Sorrow, and the Feeling Brain*. New York: Harcourt.
De Sousa, Ronald (1987). *The Rationality of Emotion*. Cambridge: The MIT Press. 1990.
Dixon, Thomas (2003). *From Passions to Emotions: The Creation of a Secular Psychological Category*. Cambridge: Cambridge University Press.
Dryzek, John (2000). *Deliberative Democracy and Beyond*. Oxford: Oxford University Press.
Elster, Jon (ed., 1998). *La Democracia Deliberativa*. Barcelona: Gedisa. 2001.
Elster, Jon (1999a). *Alchemies of the Mind*. Cambridge: Cambridge University Press.
Elster, Jon (1999b). *Strong Feelings*. Cambridge: The MIT Press.
Elster, Jon (2007). *Explaining Social Science*. Cambridge: Cambridge University Press.
Elster, Jon (2009). *Alexis de Tocqueville: The First Social Scientist*. Cambridge: Cambridge University Press.
Evans, Dylan (2001). *Emoción. La ciencia del sentimiento*. Madrid: Taurus. 2002.
Evans, Dylan and Cruse, Pierre (eds.). (2004). *Emotion, Evolution, and Rationality*. Oxford: Oxford University Press.
Evers, Kathinka (2009). *Neuroéthique: Quand la matière s'éveille*. Paris: Odile Jacob.
Eyerman, Ron (2005). Emotions and Social Movements: How Social Movements Move. In Flam, Helena and Debra King (eds.), *Emotions and Social Movements*. London: Routledge.
Fishkin, James S. (1991). *Democracy and Deliberation: New Directions for Democratic Reform*. New Haven: Yale University Press.
Flam, Helena (1998). *Mosaic of Fear*. New York: Columbia University Press.
Flam, Helena (2002). *Soziologie der Emotionen*. Konstanz: UVK.
Flam, Helena and Debra King (eds., 2005). *Emotions and Social Movements*. London: Routledge.
Frank, Robert H. (1988). *Passions within Reason: The Strategic Role of Emotions*. New York: Norton.
Frijda, Nico H. (1986). *The Emotions: Studies in Emotion and Social Interaction*. Cambridge: Cambridge University Press.
Gamson, William A. (1992). *Talking Politics*. Cambridge: Cambridge University Press.
Goodin, Robert E. (1995). *Utilitarianism as a Public Philosophy*. Cambridge: Cambridge University Press.
Goodwin, Jeff, James M. Jasper and Francesca Polletta (eds., 2000). *Passionate Politics: Emotions and Social Movements*. Chicago: Chicago University Press.
Greco, Monica and Paul Stenner (2008). *Emotions. A social science reader*. London: Routledge.
Gross, Daniel M. (2006). *The Secret History of Emotion*. Chicago: Chicago University Press.
Gutmann, Amy and Dennis Thompson (1996). *Democracy and Disagreement*. Cambridge: Harvard University Press.
Habermas, Jürgen (1996). *Facticidad y Validez: Sobre el derecho y el Estado democrático de derecho en términos de teoría del discurso*. Madrid: Trotta.
Hall, Cheryl (2005). *The Trouble with Passion: Political Theory beyond the Reign of Reason*. London: Routledge.
Hetherington, Kevin (1998). *Expressions of Identity: Space, Performance, Politics*. London: Sage.
Hirschman, Albert O. (1977). *The Passions and the Interests: Political Arguments for Capitalism before Its Triumph*. New Jersey: Princeton University Press.

Holmes, Stephen (1995). *Passions and Constraint: On the Theory of Liberal Democracy*. Chicago: Chicago University Press.
Huddy, Leonie, Stanley Feldman and Erin Cassese (2007). On the Distinct Political Effects of Anxiety and Anger. In Neuman, Russell, George E. Marcus, Ann N. Crigler and Michael Mackuen (eds.), *The Affect Effect: Dynamics of Emotion in Political Thinking and Behaviour*. Chicago: Chicago University Press.
James, Susan (1997). *Passion and Action: The Emotions in Seventeenth-Century Philosophy*. Oxford: Oxford University Press.
Jasper, James (1997). *The Art of Moral Protest: Culture, Biography, and Creativity in Social Movements*. Chicago: Chicago University Press.
Kahn, Victoria, Neil Saccamano and Daniela Coli (eds., 2006). *Politics and the Passions 1500-1850*. Princeton: Princeton University Press.
Kahneman, Daniel and Amos Tversky (1979). Prospect Theory: An Analysis of Decision under Risk. *Econometrica* 47(2), 263 – 291.
Kahneman, Daniel and Amos Tversky (1992). Advances in Prospect Theory: Cumulative Representation of Uncertainty. *Journal of Risk and Uncertainty* 5(4), 297 – 323.
Klandermans, Bert (2009). Contentious Performances: The Case of Street Demonstrations. Keynote Address, *Jornadas Internacionales: Homenaje a Charles Tilly. Conflicto, poder y acción colectiva: contribuciones al análisis sociopolítico de las sociedades contemporáneas*. Madrid, May 2009.
Knight, Jack and James Johnson (1994). Aggregation and Deliberation: On the Possibility of Democratic Legitimacy. *Political Theory* 22(2), 277 – 296.
Koziak, Barbara (2000). *Retrieving Political Emotion: Thumos, Aristotle, and Gender*. Pennsylvania: PennState University Press.
Krause, Sharon R. (2008). *Civil Passions: Moral Sentiment and Democratic Deliberation*. Princeton: Princeton University Press.
Nardulli, Peter F. and James H. Kuklinsky (2007). Testing some Implications of Affective Intelligence Theory at the Aggregate Level. In Neuman, Russell, George E. Marcus, Ann N. Crigler and Michael Mackuen (eds.), *The Affect Effect: Dynamics of Emotion in Political Thinking and Behaviour*. Chicago: Chicago University Press.
Laclau, Eernesto (2005). *La Razón Populista*. Buenos Aires: Fondo de Cultura Económica.
Lakoff, George (2008). *The Political Mind: Why You Can't Understand 21st-Century American Politics with an 18th-Century Brain*. New York: Viking.
LeDoux, Joseph (1996). *The Emotional Brain: The Mysterious Underpinnings of Emotional Life*. New York: Simon & Schuster.
Lupia, Arthur and Jesse Menning (2007). Politics and the Equilibrium of Fear: Can Strategies and Emotions interact? In Neuman, Russell, George E. Marcus, Ann N. Crigler and Michael Mackuen (eds.), *The Affect Effect: Dynamics of Emotion in Political Thinking and Behaviour*. Chicago: Chicago University Press.
Lynch, Michael (2000). Against Reflexivity as an Academic Virtue and Source of Privileged Knowledge. *Theory, Culture and Society* 17(3), 26 – 54.
Mackie, Diane M. and Leila T. Worth (1989). Processing Deficits and the Mediation of Positive Affect in Persuasion. *Journal of Personality and Social Psychology* 57(1), 28 – 41.
MacIntyre, Alasdair (1981). *After Virtue*. London: Duckworth.
MacIntyre, Alasdair (1990). *Whose Justice? Which Rationality*. London: Duckworth.
Maffesoli, Michel (1988). *Le temps des tribus: Le declin de l'individualisme dans les societes de masse*. Paris: La Table Ronde, 2000.
Maffesoli, Michel (1992). *La Transfiguration du politique*. Paris: La Table Ronde. 2002.
Maffesoli, Michel (1996). *Éloge de la raison sensible*. Paris: La Table Ronde. 2005.
Maffesoli, Michel (2008). *Iconologies. Nos idol@tries postmodernes*. Paris: Albin Michel.
Maiz, Ramón (2007). *Nación y Revolución: la teoría política de Emmanuel Sieyès*. Madrid: Tecnos.

Marcus, George E., Russell W. Neuman and Michael Mackuen (2000). *Affective Intelligence and Political Judgement*. Chicago: Chicago University Press.
Marcus, George E. (2002). *The Sentimental Citizen*. Pennsylvania: PennState University Press.
Martínez Marzoa, Felipe (2009). *Pasión tranquila. Ensayo sobre la filosofía de Hume*. Madrid: Antonio Machado.
McDermott, R. (2004). The Feeling of Rationality: The Meaning of Neuroscientific Advances for Political Science. *Perspectives on Politics* 2(4), 691 – 706.
Mitzman, Arthur (1971). *The Iron Cage: An Historical Interpretation of Max Weber*. London: Blackwell.
Morrell, Michael E. (2010). *Empathy and Democracy. Feeling, Thinking, and Deliberation*. University Park, Pennsylvania: The Pennsylvania State U. Press.
Mouffe, Chantal (2000). *The Democratic Paradox*. London: Verso.
Mouffe, Chantal (2002). *Politics and Passions. The Stakes of Democracy*. London: CSD, Westminster.
Neuman, Russell, George E. Marcus, Ann N. Crigler and Michael Mackuen (eds., 2007). *The Affect Effect: Dynamics of Emotion in Political Thinking and Behaviour*. Chicago: Chicago University Press.
Nino, Carlos S. (2003). *La constitución de la democracia deliberativa*. Barcelona: Gedisa.
Norval, Aletta J. (2007). *Aversive Democracy*. Cambridge: Cambridge University Press.
Nussbaum, Martha C. (1994). *The Therapy of Desire*. Princeton: Princeton University Press.
Nussbaum, Martha C. (2001). *Upheavals of Thought. The Intelligence of Emotions*. Cambridge: Cambridge University Press.
Nussbaum, Martha C. (2004). *Hiding from Humanity: Disgust, Shame, and the Law*. Princeton: Princeton University Press.
Nussbaum, Martha C. (2010). *Not for Profit: Why Democracy Needs the Humanities*. Princeton: Princeton University Press.
Oatley, Keith (2004). *Emotions: A Brief History*. London: Blackwell.
Ovejero, Félix (2008). *Incluso un pueblo de demonios: democracia, liberalismo, republicanismo*. Buenos Aires: Katz.
Parrott, W. Gerrod (ed., 2001). *Emotions in Social Psychology: Key Readings*. Ann Arbor: Edwards.
Pellizzoni, Luigi (2001). The Myth of the Best Argument: Power, Deliberation and Reason. *British Journal of Sociology* 52(1), 59 – 86.
Petersen, Roger Dole (2002). *Understanding Ethnic Violence: Fear, Hatred, and Resentment in Twentieth Century Eastern Europe*. Cambridge: Cambridge University Press.
Rawls, John (1971). *A Theory of Justice*. Cambridge: Harvard University Press.
Rawls, John (1993). *Political Liberalism*. New York: Columbia University Press.
Reed, Jean-Pierre (2004). Emotions in context: Revolutionary accelerators, hope, moral outrage, and other emotions in the making of Nicaragua's revolution. *Theory and Society* 33(6), 653 – 703.
Reddy, William M. (2001). *The Navigation of Feeling: A Framework for the History of Emotions*. Cambridge: Cambridge University Press.
Rifkin, Jeremy (2010). *The Empathic Civilization: The Race to Global Consciousness in a World in Crisis*. Cambridge: Polity.
Rosenblum, Nancy L. (1987). *Another Liberalism: Romanticism and the Reconstruction of Liberal Thought*. Cambridge: Harvard University Press.
Sandel, Michael (1982). *Liberalism and the Limits of Justice*. Cambridge: Cambridge University Press.
Sludds, Kevin (2009). *Emotions: Their Cognitive Base and Ontological Importance*. Berna: Peter Lang.
Solomon, Robert C. (1993). *The Passions: Emotions and the Meaning of Life*. Indianapolis: Hacket.
Spragens, Thomas A. (1981). *The Irony of Liberal Reason*. Chicago: Chicago University Press.
Spragens, Thomas A. (1995). *Reason and Democracy*. Durham: Duke University Press.

Staël, Germaine de (1796). *Essai sur les fictions suivi De l'influence des passions sur le bonheur des individus et des nations*. Paris : Ramsay. 1979.

Sunstein, Cass R. (2005). *Laws of Fear: Beyond the Precautionary Principle*. Cambridge: Cambridge University Press.

Tilly, Charles (2003). *The Politics of Collective Violence*. Cambridge: Cambridge University Press.

Trepel, Christopher, Craig R. Fox and Russell A. Poldrack (2005). Prospect Theory on the Brain? Toward a Cognitive Neuroscience of Decision under Risk. *Cognitive Brain Research* 23(1), 34 – 50.

Turner, Jonathan H. and Jan E. Stets (2005). *The Sociology of Emotions*. Cambridge: Cambridge University Press.

Turner, Jonathan H. and Jan E. Stets (2007). *Handbook of the Sociology of Emotions*. London: Springer.

Walzer, Michael (2004). *Politics and Passion*. New Haven: Yale University Press.

Weber, Max (1920). *Die protestantische Ethik und der Geist des Kapitalismus*. München: Verlag C.H. Beck. 2006.

Westen, Drew (2007). *The Political Brain*. New York: Public Affairs.

Williams, Raymond (1977). *Culture and Society: 1780 – 1950*. London: Penguin.

Young, Iris Marion (1990). *Justice and Politics of Difference*. Princeton: Princeton University Press.

Young, Iris Marion (2000). *Inclusion and Democracy*. Oxford: Oxford University Press.

Zajonc, Robert B. (1980). Feeling and Thinking: Preferences Need No Inferences. *American Psycologist*, 35(2), 151 – 175.

Methodological Issues

The Influence of Affective States on the Depth of Information Processing

Brad Verhulst and Mary-Kate Lizotte

Politics are rife with emotions. During campaigns, candidates frequently use advertisements to induce emotional responses. To evoke negative emotions toward their opponent, candidates pair discordant music with their rivals' policy proposals. When the campaign advertisement transitions to their own policy positions, the music expediently becomes harmonic and soothing. In the 2008 presidential election, the Grand Old Party (GOP) strategy appeared to revolve around anxiety, be it from a threat of another terrorist attack or fears about the impending recession.[1] By contrast, the Obama campaign focused on positive emotions, epitomized by the Iconic "Hope" Poster. Given the omnipresence of emotions in politics it is essential to ask how emotional states influence how people think about politics and how these affective states alter the political decisions that people make?

In this chapter we review the extant literature regarding the influence of emotions on how carefully people think about information with a specific focus on how emotionally induced styles of thinking relates to politics. The majority of this literature is firmly rooted in social psychology and has yet to fully penetrate theoretical models of political cognition. One goal of this chapter is to illustrate opportunities to incorporate these findings into our understanding of political emotions. In doing so we examine several different models of affect, moods and emotions on information processing, and examine the existing empirical support for the relationship between affective states and how carefully people think about information relevant to political attitudes and behaviors. To illustrate how the psychological theories of emotions related to the central political questions that we are ultimately interested in, we refer to the 2008 presidential election between Senators Barack Obama and John McCain.

---

[1] None of the literature that we review throughout this chapter explicitly draws on the 2008 Presidential election between Senators Barack Obama and John McCain. As such, the direct references to the 2008 Presidential election are based on generalizations that extend the findings within the existing literature to the specific Obama-McCain context.

Emotion and Affect

The terms emotion and affect have been used interchangeably in much of the literature, especially within political psychology. Herein we use the term affect as an all-inclusive umbrella term referring to both mood and emotional states. This does not imply that mood and emotion are interchangeable constructs. Rather, emotions are intense, targeted affective states while moods are diffuse, untargeted states (Forgas 1995; Robinson and Clore 2002). Further, emotions are associated with a definite object or event, and consequently, are experienced viscerally. Moods, on the other hand, are not necessarily triggered by a specific object or event, and as such are experienced as more diffuse and less intense than emotional states (McDermott 2004). Moreover, because they are unconnected to a specific precipitating event, mood typically has a longer duration. It is important not to over emphasize these differences, however, as moods and emotions do share several key features. Notably, both emotions and moods vary in their pleasantness or even their more discrete dimensions. For example, people can be anxious about a specific event, like an election, or they experience an anxious mood. In most situations, the implications for information processing are the same.

The theoretical conceptualization of the structure of affect has considerable implications for the basic questions researchers ask and therefore, the data concerning the influence of affective states on information processing. By assuming affective states vary along a single positive or negative dimension, one misses the nuanced influence of different discrete emotions of the same valence on information processing. More insidiously, this theoretical framework does not motivate researchers to collect data that would test a multidimensional theory of emotions. Conversely, a focus on discrete emotions risks ignoring the similarities between emotions of the same valence and emphasizing minor empirical variations. We discuss findings from both lines of research and acknowledge that by no means is this chapter an exhaustive review.

For the current chapter, the essential feature is that people experience both emotions and moods as temporary affective states. While there are individual differences in baseline levels of emotionality, our focus is on the effect of affective states on the way people think about information with the primary point being that the affective state in particular motivates people to process information in a distinct way (Izard 1971; Tomkins 1962, Frijda 1986; Lazarus 1991). Specifically, affective states motivate people to think about information more or less carefully and subsequently engage in various behaviors. The important point is that the emotional state changes how people think about information. People who are chronically anxious engage in the information processing strategies promoted by experiencing anxiety more often than people who are rarely anxious. Importantly, when people who rarely experience anxiety feel anxious, they will engage in the same information processing strategies when they feel anxious as chronically anxious people do when they feel anxious.

These basic assumptions allow us to examine how political campaigns can manipulate emotions in an attempt to alter the way voters think about the candidates and what information they bring to bear on their vote choice. Specifically, what emotions will be effective in changing how voters think that will maximize the probability that the voter incorporate the message into their attitudes toward the candidate?

Information Processing

Because our review of the literature revolves around the way emotional states influence the way people behave, the way they think about or process information plays an integral role in these behaviors. Therefore, a brief discussion of information processing provides the necessary backdrop for understanding the connection between affective states and behaviors.

The literature on information processing focuses on the effort or depth of thinking that a person is motivated to engage in with the ultimate goal of illuminating how differential depth of thinking influences subsequent behaviors, attitudes and preferences. There are two prototypical modes of information processing (Chaiken 1987; Petty and Cacioppo 1986): an in depth, systematic style of information processing that requires high levels of cognitive effort and a low effort, superficial style of information processing that relies on cognitive short cuts. These prototypical styles of thinking fall under the heading of dual process models of information processing (see Chaiken and Trope 1999 for an in depth review of a variety of dual process models of information processing).

More specifically, Dual Process Models assume two conflicting motives are constantly present when people think about any information. The first is the accuracy motive. Other things equal, people would like to be accurate. The second is the efficiency motive, whereby people are assumed to be cognitive misers and think only as carefully as is necessary given the situation. When the accuracy motivation trumps the cognitive efficiency motivation, individuals are highly motivated to hold accurate preferences. This motivates them to think about the information carefully and systematically, pay attention to the inherent strengths of the arguments presented within the information and spend longer processing the information. Conversely, when the efficiency motivation trumps the accuracy motivation, people are not motivated to think carefully. Accordingly, people who lack the motivation to process information in a careful, systematic manner rely heavily on stereotypes, accessible informational cues such as the credibility of the source of the information, and establish cognitive short cuts or heuristic devices that simplify the information.

The influence of variations in how carefully people process information has already been applied to politics (Lupia 1994; Lau and Redlawsk 2001). Consistent with the findings from dual process theories in social psychology, these studies demonstrate that when people are unable or unwilling to think carefully about a decision, they latch onto informational shortcuts. Our assertion is that different emotional states either accentuate or attenuate the motivation to engage in systematic thinking or rely on these cognitive shortcuts within the political domain. Candidates who can most effectively motivate voters to think about the information that is most optimal to their campaign will likely receive more votes on Election Day, and manipulating voter's emotions offers one vehicle for achieving that goal.

The Direct Influence of Positive and Negative Affective States on Behaviors and Judgments

Affective states influence the judgments and decisions people make in two distinct ways. Affective states may directly alter an individual's favorability toward an object by making their evaluations more affectively congruent. Alternatively, affective states can indirectly influence attitudes and decisions by altering how people think about the information. In this section we focus on the direct influence of affective states on judgments and in the following sections we elaborate on the indirect ways affective states influence judgments.

Early work investigating the role of affect on attitudes and decisions focused on the direct influence of affect on judgments. Specifically, research on affective valence – positive or negative affect – demonstrates that affective states influence decision making by biasing a person's judgments consistent with the positivity or negativity of the person's affective state (Schwarz and Clore 1983; Clore *et al.* 1994; Forgas 1995; Schwartz and Clore 1996). Positive affective states make people generally more positive. This leads them to express greater liking for people, more favorability to ideas, and increased satisfaction with their lives (Clore *et al.* 1994; Forgas 1995; Schwartz and Clore 1996). This direct influence of affect on behavior is epitomized by the Affect-As-Information hypothesis and Affect Infusion model (Schwartz and Clore 1983; Forgas 1995). In the Affect Infusion Model (AIM), affect acts as a heuristic or cognitive short cut, influencing one's response to unfamiliar stimuli (Forgas

1995; Clore and Parrott 1991; Schwarz and Clore 1988). These subjective affective experiences are sources of information independent of the semantic information people simultaneously process (Schwarz and Clore 2003). The impact of the affective state is felt outside the boundaries of conscious awareness. As such, emotions or moods directly influence evaluations without any explicit knowledge of the reasons underlying one's judgments. Affective states are particularly influential for judgments that require evaluations, like those routinely made in politics. Because evaluations have an affective component – attitudes can be understood as one's affective evaluation of a target – contemporaneous feelings are easily integrated into judgments (Schwarz and Clore 1996).

It is not a giant leap to extrapolate the direct effect of affect on decisions onto more traditional concepts within political science. In particular, the direct effect of an individual's affective states on her attitudes towards political candidates is completely compatible with the literature in psychology on the direct effect of affect on other judgments people routinely make (McDermott 2004). Accordingly, flag waving, up-beat, patriotic music, and positive imagery can directly heighten positive evaluations of candidates and in turn increase the likelihood an individual will vote for that candidate. As such, Obama's message of hope, a positive emotional state, may have simply made voters feel more pleasant, and therefore more amenable to his ideas and even more positive toward him. This latent positivity may have been, in part, offset by the negativity of the Republican's electoral strategy of fear about Obama's policies.

Understanding the Direct Influence of Affect

The direct influence of affect on information processing is particularly pronounced when people are unable to accurately attribute the cause of their affective state to its source. People are relatively poor at distinguishing affective states, which are the direct result of interacting with a relevant object or event, from incidental, unrelated affective states that are evoked by an irrelevant object or event. Failing to discriminate between affective states that are either relevant or irrelevant to the decision at hand leads people to unwittingly incorporate incidental affect into their evaluations. Errors in accurately attributing the affective state to the actual cause can results in overly positive or negative attitudes towards a secondary object. For example, happy people attribute their happiness to the attitude object under evaluation – I feel happy because I like Obama – but they are unaware that their happiness is completely unrelated to the judgment. More realistically, their positive evaluation is caused by their affective state – I like Obama because I am happy (Griffitt 1970; Zanna, Kiesler and Pilkonis

1970). This judgmental bias is eliminated or reduced if the affective state is attributed, accurately or otherwise, to another source. For example, on a rainy day, if people are reminded of the weather, they attribute their negative demeanor to the rain rather than to the attitude object under judgment (Schwarz and Clore 1983). If such attributions are not made, the affective state biases subsequent evaluations (Schwarz and Clore 1983 and 2003). As a result, incidental moods are more influential when they remain outside a person's awareness (Schwarz and Clore 1983). Increased cognitive engagement fails to attenuate the influence of incidental affect on later evaluations. Instead, when a person's affective state remains outside his awareness, intense cognitive effort exacerbates the effect of an individual's affective state on his attitudes and judgments (Fiedler 1991; Forgas 1995). When people think carefully about a problem, subsequent judgments are more biased by an unnoticed affective state. Consistent with the automatic incorporation of affective information into a person's evaluation, Verhulst, Lodge and Taber (2008) demonstrate that affective subliminal primes, presented outside an individual's awareness, alter individuals' evaluations of candidates. Across two separate studies, participants primed with positive words like sunshine and rainbow were more likely to evaluate the candidate positively than participants primed with negative words like cancer and cockroach. Because the primes were presented outside of the participants' conscious awareness, participants were unable to intentionally alter their evaluations of the candidates. Thus, the affective subliminal primes spontaneously altered participants' evaluations of the candidates.

Although in actual political campaigns, subliminal primes inspire political outrage, as was observed with the RNC's infamous "Rats" ad where the word "rats" was presented immediately before the word "bureaucrats" (Weinberger and Westin 2008). The use of implicit cues, while not necessarily subliminal, is commonplace in politics. Such innocuous things such as celebrity endorsements undoubtedly make voters more favorable toward a political candidate in part because the endorser creates a sense of positivity in the voters that is subsequently transferred to the candidate. Barack Obama had a number of celebrity endorsers as well as endorsements from highly respected political individuals such as Colin Powell.

The Indirect Influence of Positive and Negative Affective States on Information Processing

While the prior section provides evidence of the direct effect of affect on evaluations, other findings suggests that affective states also indirectly influence attitudes and judgments by conditioning how people think about information. In the following sections, the evidence of this indirect influence is discussed within the two main conceptualizations of the structure of affect, valence and discrete emotions.

The Bipolar Conceptualization of Affect

The bipolar or valence conceptualization emphasizes a singular dimension of positive versus negative affective states. At one end of the continuum are positive affective states and at the opposite end, negative affective states. Thus, by definition, people only experience positive or negative affect at any given point in time. This conceptualization of positive versus negative affect circumvents the need to specify whether the affective state under consideration is a diffuse mood state or a more specific emotional state, like happiness or sadness. The important characteristic is whether the affective state is positive or negative. This parsimonious understanding has produced considerable evidence for the indirect influence of affect on information processing.

The majority of the evidence suggests people in negative affective states process information more carefully relative to when they are in positive affective states (Bless *et al.* 1990). Alternatively, individuals experiencing positive affective states are less likely to engage in systematic processing and instead rely on cognitive shortcuts. In dual process terms, positive affective states prompt people to process information heuristically while negative affective states lead people to processes information systematically (Eagly and Chaiken 1993; Petty and Cacioppo 1986).

In line with expectations derived from dual process theories of attitudes, the quality of the information is more influential for individuals in negative affective states than people in positive affective states (Bless *et al.* 1990; Armitage *et al.* 1999). Specifically, negative affective states motivate people to process information carefully, meaning they spend longer thinking about the information, spontaneously produce more task-relevant thoughts, are more influenced by the inherent strength of the arguments and therefore their subsequent attitudes are more influenced by the persuasive appeals that contain stronger arguments.

Alternatively, people in positive affective states are less motivated to process information carefully resulting in less attention to the content of the messages, and as such, being equally influenced by both strong and weak arguments (Armitage *et al.* 1999; Petty and Cacioppo 1981; Petty, Wells and Brock 1976). Moreover, people in positive affective states rely more heavily on heuristic cues, such as the expertise, attractiveness or likeability of the source, the length (rather than the quality) of the message, stereotypes or even more familiar products (regardless of quality: Bless *et al.* 1990). Importantly, these cues are much less influential when people think carefully about message.

The effects implied by the psychological literature are found in the existing political science literature. Specifically, voters confronted with information that evokes negative affective reactions are more likely to search for additional information (Brader 2005; Marcus, Neumann and Mackuen 2000). Apparently, the presence of negative information implies that there is a problem in the environment that requires systematic thought and attention. By contrast, voters experiencing positive affective states are less likely to engage in more in-depth processing such as information searches and learning but rather rely on the shortcut or heuristic of partisanship (Brader 2005; Marcus, Neumann and Mackuen 2000).

Accordingly, when Obama inspired people to feel hopeful, he likely promoted heuristic processing. Meanwhile when McCain made people anxious, he likely motivated them to think more carefully about the relevant issues. Neither strategy is globally preferable. Instead the effectiveness of the emotional state to induce the optimal information processing strategy depends on a wide variety of factors including the strength of the candidate's position and the likelihood that the new information will alter the individual's attitudes.

Therefore, the positivity inherent in Obama's message of hope may have lead people away from carefully considering the specific details of his proposals. This may have been highly effective, as Obama was criticized for making ambiguous campaign promises lacking any specific steps for actually turning the promises into policy. As such, because people were caught in the hedonistic glow of positive emotions, they may have failed to carefully scrutinize Obama's proposals. On the other hand, the negativity embedded in the RNC's election campaign may have undermined McCain's success by motivating voters to think more carefully about the issues. As the major electoral issue by November was the economy, motivating people to think carefully about the economy likely hurt McCain in the voting booth.

Understanding the Differential Influence of Positive and Negative Affect

Several potential explanations have been posited to explain why people process information more carefully when they are in negative relative to positive moods. First, according to the mood maintenance explanation, people in positive moods want to stay in positive moods. Maintaining their mood, therefore, reduces the motivation to carefully examine information unless the individual believes that the information they uncover will enhance or maintain their mood (Isen 1987). As searching often uncovers counter-attitudinal arguments which would detrimentally change their mood, positive affective states reduce the accuracy motivation. Conversely, because individuals in negative affective states are motivated to improve their moods, they are willing to risk encountering additional negative or counter-attitudinal information, and as such they are willing to process information more carefully.

The major limitation of the mood maintenance explanation for differential processing styles is that people can still process information carefully in positive affective states, but it takes more time and effort (Petty *et al.* 2004; Mackie and Worth 1989). Therefore, a second explanation for why people in positive affective states are less likely to process information carefully is that positive affective states erode available cognitive resources (Mackie and Worth 1989). Accordingly, the accuracy motivation must be stronger in order to surpass the efficiency motivation. Thus, in direct contrast to the mood maintenance hypothesis, people experiencing positive moods are still willing and able to process information carefully. The specific reason why cognitive resources are depleted in positive moods remains unclear.

The third explanation, the broaden-and-build hypothesis (Fredrickson 2001 and 2004), is consistent with both the cognitive depletion and the mood maintenance explanation for differential effect of positive versus negative emotional states. The broaden-and-build hypothesis posits positive moods or emotions motivate people to think about more information, and more diverse information, relative to negative affective states (Boucher and Osgood 1969; Bousfield 1944 and 1950; Isen 1984; Isen, Daubman and Gorgoglione 1987; Fredrickson 2001 and 2004). Because people access more information that is more variable in content when they are in a positive mood state, positive moods have been shown to greatly increase the creativity of the responses to a variety of problems (Fredrickson 2001 and 2004). In negative mood states people are much more task-oriented, leading to the dismissal of ideas not directly related to the immediate situation.

The final theoretical explanation for the differential impact of affective states on information processing can be gleaned from the Affective Intelligence theory (Marcus and Mackuen 1993; Marcus, Neumann and Mackuen 2000), which is the dominant theory of affect in the political psychology literature. According to Affective Intelligence, affective states serve as a cue signaling a need for increased attention and more in-depth processing or a reliance on existing predispositions like party identification (Gray 1986; Marcus and Mackuen 1993). Drawing on evolutionary explanations, Affective Intelligence argues that negative emotional states signal problems in an individual's environment necessitating careful attention and a disregard of habitual behavioral patterns or heuristics. Accordingly, emotional states such as anxiety evoke the surveillance system that carefully monitors the environment for threatening stimuli. On the other hand, positive affective states suggest relative safety, and therefore reduce the need to vigilantly monitor the environment. Accordingly, positive affective states evoke the dispositional system and suggest that it is acceptable to rely on habit, such as one's partisan disposition. In general terms, the surveillance system corresponds with careful, systematic processing while the disposition system corresponds with heuristic processing.

It is easy to derive hypotheses from these potential explanations that have direct implication for information processing in the political domain. As searching for and learning new information is one of the key indicators of systematic thinking, within politics people in negative affective states should be more willing to search for additional political information, and as such should be relatively better informed. This is confirmed by the fact that negative affective states predict attention to the political campaign and searching for additional information about the candidates as well as stimulate increased political involvement and decreased reliance on existing political habits or heuristics (Marcus and MacKuen 1993; Marcus et al. 2000; Brader 2005 and 2006). Alternatively, positive moods correlate with an increased reliance on previously learned information and habitual behaviors and increased confidence in one's existing beliefs (even though these beliefs are based on less accurate information). Importantly, these hypotheses as well as the empirical evidence apply to every explanation regarding why people process information more carefully in negative affective states. Therefore, the task of future research is to develop hypotheses that would enable them to disentangle which explanation is most plausible given additional empirical data. One way of doing this may be to focus on discrete affective states.

The Discrete Emotion Conceptualization of Affective States

Recent evidence suggests that this relatively simplistic conceptualization of the emotions as uni-dimensional overlooks the differential impact that emotions within the same valence can have on information processing. Conceptualizing emotions as discrete, though related affective states, allows specific emotions of the same valence to influence judgments and information processing strategies in different ways. Although the bipolar conceptualization of affect is parsimonious, recent work demonstrates that discrete emotions often differentially influence subsequent information processing and behavior (Lerner and Keltner 2000).[2]

One prominent theory of discrete emotions in the current literature is the Appraisal-Tendency approach (Lerner and Keltner 2000; Smith and Ellsworth 1985). According to the theory, the specific emotion people experience is a function of their interpretation of their environment along several relevant dimensions. This interpretation or appraisal of the environment happens automatically or pre-consciously: the individual is completely unaware that these appraisals occur. The six primary dimensions the Appraisal Tendency Framework theory delineates are pleasantness/unpleasantness, responsibility (self-responsibility, other responsibility), certainty/uncertainty, attention/inattention, effort, control (human control, situational control: Smith and Ellsworth 1985). For the emotions discussed here, the most important dimensions are certainty and control. These are the primary dimensions that distinguish between anger, anxiety and sadness. Angry individuals tend to perceive events as predictable and caused by others while anxious individuals tend to perceive events as unpredictable and caused by the situation (Lerner and Keltner 2000).

Centrally, the discrete emotions paradigm has demonstrated that different emotions of the same valence have different effects on the way people think about information. This literature undermines the general conclusion that positive affective states result in heuristic information processing and negative affective states result in systematic information processing. Instead this theory emphasizes the importance of discriminating between which specific emotion people experience when they are making judgments or stating their attitudes.

The majority of the work on discrete emotions has focused on the disparate impact of different negative emotions such as sadness, anger, and fear. Various studies demonstrate the differential influence of discrete negative emotions on risk assessments and depth of processing. Specifically, fearful individuals are more likely to make pessimistic risk assessments while those experiencing anger are more likely to make optimistic risk assessments (Lerner and Keltner 2000 and 2001); anger promotes risk seeking choices while fear results in risk averse choices (Lerner and Keltner 2001; Raghunathan and Pham 1999); and anger results in more superficial information processing than sadness and fear (Tiedens and Linton 2001). Within the political domain, in response to the September 11th terrorist attacks, fear increased perceptions of terrorism risk while anger decreased perceptions (Lerner *et al.* 2003). Other researchers have also

---

2   Discrete emotions refer to specific and distinct emotions, such as joy, pride, anger, sadness, fear, etc. It is important to note that these emotions are often correlated. Thus, people who report being angry often also report elevated levels of anxiety and sadness, and reduced levels of happiness.

found differences in anger and anxiety with respect to September 11th and terrorism (Huddy et al. 2005; Huddy, Feldman and Cassesse 2007; Lambert et al. 2010).

Furthermore, with respect to depth of processing, evidence to date finds substantial differences between anxiety, anger, and sadness. Anxiety results in greater depth of processing than anger (Lerner and Keltner 2000 and 2001), higher levels of information search, learning and attention (Marcus and MacKuen 1993; MacKuen et al. 2010; Marcus, Mackuen and Neuman 2000; Brader 2005 and 2006) and more responsiveness to the quality of the arguments in a persuasive message (Verhulst and Sohlberg 2009). Meanwhile, anger leads to greater reliance on preformed cognitive shortcuts (Lerner and Keltner 2000; MacKuen et al. 2010; Bodenhausen, Kramer and Shepard 1994; Lerner and Tiedens 2006; Verhulst and Sohlberg 2009; Valentino et al. 2009; Lerner and Tiedens 2006). Compared with anxiety, anger motivates people to process information more peripherally (Raghunathan and Pham 1999). Accordingly, angry people are less likely to search for additional information (Valentino et al. 2009; MacKuen et al. 2010), more likely to rely on cognitive shortcuts and stereotypes (Bodenhausen et al. 1994; Tiedens 2001b; Verhulst and Sohlberg 2009), and more likely to rely on dispositional attributions and ignore situational constraints on behaviors (Keltner et al. 1993; Goldberg et al. 1999).

The influence of sadness on information processing is more variable. In several studies, sadness acts as a middle ground between the processing characteristics typified by anger and anxiety. Sadness appears to have similar effects as anxiety (Bodenhausen, Kramer and Shepard 1994), but to a lesser extent (Raghunathan and Pham 1999). Compared with anger, sadness motivates people to process information more carefully (Bodenhausen, Kramer and Shepard 1994). With respect to welfare spending preferences, sadness results in increased amounts recommended for welfare spending and anger results in decreased amounts with this difference being the result of differences in depth of processing (Small and Lerner 2008).

Another line of evidence that underscores the importance of examining the specific emotion that people experience rather than the general affective valence demonstrates persuasive appeals are more effective when their emotional content matches the emotional state of the recipient. For example, DeSteno et al. (2004) find stronger persuasion effects when angry people read a persuasive message that evokes feelings of anger, relative to when angry people read a sad persuasive message. Thus, if the emotional overtones of a message match an individual's emotional state the message is more effective. They note, however, that if individuals are aware their emotional state might bias their judgments they correct for this and opposite effects are observed.

Understanding the Differential Influence of Discrete Emotions of the Same Valence

Appraisal theories provide a concise explanation for why differential effects arise among emotions of the same valence. Two appraisal dimensions appear to be central to this process. First, in accord with the approach avoidance dimension, emotions motivate a general approach or avoidance response. Second, emotions, associated with specific levels of certainty or control, affect one's confidence levels in turn influencing depth of processing.

The extant literature finds anger encourages approach tendencies, similar to the effect of positive affect discussed above, while anxiety and sadness encourages avoidance, consistent with the pattern of results observed for general negative affective states (Lerner and Keltner 2000 and 2001). According to appraisal theories, one of the primary dimensions that distinguish anger from anxiety and sadness rests on differences in perceived control. Angry people have high levels of agency and efficacy relative to anxious and sad people. Thus, anger motivates people to engage in actual behaviors, without necessarily thinking about the consequences of one's actions. Contrastingly, sadness and anxiety may be more likely to result in the avoidance of any tangible behaviors, therefore giving time to ruminate about potential behavioral options. Consistent with this expectation, angry individuals are more likely to engage in risky behaviors. Furthermore, this also accounts for why angry people engage in low effort processing while anxious individuals seek out more information and process information more carefully. Importantly, it is possible that sadness acts as a de-motivational state, resulting in lethargy. Accordingly, although sad people spend longer thinking about information, which is indicative of systematic processing, their subsequent judgments do not reflect this additional careful thought (Verhulst and Sohlberg 2009).

These findings on the effects of different discrete emotions may help explain the controversy over the effects of negative campaign advertising. Some research on negative political advertisements finds that they are demobilizing (Ansolabehere *et al.* 1994), while other research fails to find this demobilizing effect (Wattenburg and Brians 1999). Besides methodological differences (aggregate data versus cross-sectional data versus experimental data), it is possible that depending upon the negative emotions advertisements evoke a demobilizing or mobilizing effect may result. Accordingly, it is possible that the demobilizing effect is most prominent when the ads evoke anxiety or sadness, which promote pensiveness and decrease outwardly observable behaviors, rather than anger, which decreases systematic thinking and promotes action.

The second dimension that discriminates between sadness, anxiety and anger is the certainty inherent in the emotional state. Specifically, the low levels of certainty associated with anxiety and sadness reduces an individual's confidence in her judgments while the high levels of certainty associated with anger correspondingly increase judgmental certainty. As such, anxious and sad individuals pay more attention to current information to increase their confidence and therefore engage in more careful thinking (Roseman 1984; Smith and Ellsworth 1985; Tiedens and Linton 2001). Alternatively, anger reduces the motivation to expend time and effort searching for more information (Lerner and Tiedens 2006; Tiedens and Linton 2001; Bodenhausen, Sheppard and Kramer 1994; Valentino et al. 2009; Isbell et al. 2002 and 2006). For example, if a political issue makes someone anxious, his anxiety temporarily reduces his confidence. This motivates him to seek more information about the issue to increase his confidence and alleviate his anxiety. By contrast, angry individuals are confident and spend less time seeking out new information. A confident person is not motivated to bolster his confidence by thinking carefully or searching for more information. Instead, he simply makes a decision.

In the Obama-McCain election, the differential impact of discrete emotions can be seen in the debate over the Iraq war. Specifically, both the Democrats and the Republicans attempted to elicit anger over the war. The Obama campaign emphasized the misguided focus on Iraq rather than the 'more justified' War on Terror in Afghanistan. Alternatively, the McCain campaign argued that Obama's strategy was to 'cut and run' in Iraq, a strategy that would only 'embolden' the terrorists. In all likelihood, the anger created by both campaigns prevented in-depth, systematic consideration of the issue and reified the habitual partisan responses. Thus, in this case, anger gave each side superficial confidence in their beliefs and reduced the motivation to consider the benefits of the other camp's suggestions.

Issues of Measurement

Given the pervasive impact of emotions on information processing, it is essential that political scientists incorporate emotional constructs into their theories of political decision making (See McDermott 2004 for a similar conclusion). From this perspective, the obstacle becomes determining the best way to measure emotions. Several insights can be gleaned directly from the research in psychology that has dealt with these measurement issues. Some issues, however, are specific to research on political questions.

Semantic recollections of emotional experiences are notoriously inaccurate as well as self-reports of anticipatory emotions, known in the literature as affective forecasting. In other words, individuals are not able to accurately report how they felt in the past or predict how they will react to future events (for an extensive review see Loewenstein and Lerner 2003). People misestimate the duration and intensity of their emotional reactions to future events (Gilbert *et al.* 1998; Wilson and Gilbert 2005). This has been shown with respect to future food consumption (Gilbert *et al.* 2002), ending of a romantic relationship (Gilbert *et al.* 1998), and tenure decisions (Gilbert *et al.* 1998). This inability to accurately anticipate emotional responses even applies to electoral results. Gilbert and colleagues (1998) find that electoral results did not have a measurable influence on general happiness one month after the election. Specifically, individuals who voted for the losing candidate in a gubernatorial election were just as happy one month after the election as they reported being on the election day. Individuals forecasted that if the candidate they voted for lost they would be substantially less happy than they were on Election Day. These estimates were highly inaccurate and they were much happier than they expected even though the candidate they voted for lost the election. Interestingly, these effects – inaccurate forecasts of emotional reactions to electoral and all other events – appear to be asymmetrical in that one is more likely to overestimate the intensity and duration of negative events on future happiness than of positive events (Gilbert *et al.* 1998; Wilson and Gilbert 2005).

Furthermore, emotions research within political science should take note of the difference between actually experiencing emotions and semantic recalling previously experienced emotional states. The physical presence of an emotionally evocative object has enormous implications for the measurement of emotional responses to that object (Breckler 1984). Physiological, attitudinal, self-described emotional and behavioral responses to an attitude object differ depending on whether the object is actually present. When the object is present one's affective, cognitive, and behavioral responses are all distinct and fail to correlate highly. When the object is absent, the expected high correlations are found between these three responses. This finding radically limits the conclusions that researchers can draw based on semantic recollections of emotional experiences. If emotional states are measured on surveys (without any experimental emotional induction procedure), strong relationships between affective, cognitive, and behavioral responses would be expected. Importantly, the typical research question that researchers claim to answer relates more closely to the former scenario where the attitude object is actually present.

Other research shows that experiencing an emotion has different consequences on subsequent information processing than semantic activation of an emotion concept. Innes-Ker and Niedenthal (2002) find that subjects with induced emotional states evaluated later information in an emotionally congruent manner. Inducing an emotion and observing the effect of emotion on later cognitive processing, has successfully been done by asking subjects to recall an emotional autobiographical memory (Niedenthal *et al.* 2003). Recent work on the embodiment of emotions, finds that not only does the experience of emotions influence subsequent information processing but that embodying emotions also influences later processing. An individual's facial expressions and body postures that mimic those of individuals experiencing an emotional state lead to emotionally congruent information processing (Niedenthal 2007). Future research in political science should explore the applicability of this research for political attitudes.

Recent research on emotions within political science has also called into question the validity of traditional survey questions measuring emotional responses to political candidates. Affective Intelligence research has regularly relied on American National Election Study (ANES) data for supportive empirical evidence. The ANES routinely includes questions asking respondents how anxious, happy, angry, or proud each of the presidential candidates makes them. Ladd and Lenz (2008) provide compelling evidence that these questions do not actually measure emotional responses to the candidates but are rather purely evaluative indicators. Their findings suggest that if a respondent likes a candidate then they report positive emotional responses and dislike results in reports of negative emotional responses. Ongoing work in political science needs to further investigate the validity of current measures of emotions. Thus, in the absence of actually experiencing an emotional state at the time people give an emotional response, their emotional responses simply reflect their evaluation of the political persona.

Future Directions and Conclusions

The extant literature provides several insights into the influence of affect on information processing. Research indicates that affect, acting as a heuristic, can have a direct influence on information processing. Evidence also demonstrates an indirect influence with negative valence and/or negative discrete emotions such as anxiety and sadness leading to more in-depth processing compared to positive valence and/or anger, respectively.

There are several questions that arise, however, from this area of research. First, it is important to keep in mind that emotions of the same valence are often highly correlated. More often than not people do not feel anxious or sad, but rather anxious and sad. Research focusing on discrete emotions needs to account for other emotions of the same valence. For example, the differential effect of happiness and sadness can be explained either by their differing valences or their discrete emotional states. To disentangle the unique influence of happiness or sadness, the researcher should compare the emotional state to other emotional states of the same valence.

Second, other negative emotions have received much less attention than anger, anxiety and sadness. The influence of these other negative emotions on information processing remains unclear. Moreover, the differential impact of specific positive emotions deserves further inquiry. Existing evidence suggests that positive affective states expand the relevant information individuals entertain while evaluating information. This additional information absorbs cognitive resources (Mackie and Worth 1989), but it also leads to more creative solutions to problems (Fredrickson 2001 and 2004).

Alternatively, any election, especially those lasting over an extended period of time as was seen for the Obama-McCain election, voters experience multiple emotions. Some of these will be positive and some negative; some will be a function of the campaign and others will be a function of an individual's life more generally. In some situations, these emotional states will motivate people to think more carefully about the information while other emotional states will interfere with an individual's ability to process information. Future research that explores the effects of emotions on information processing strategies must begin to incorporate the longitudinal impact of emotional states on the utilization of information and how information presented in different affective states alters the impact of that information months later when individuals are in the voting booth.

Lastly, the effects of emotions at different levels of intensity remain understudied. For example, the empirical evidence is mixed with respect to anxiety. Some research finds anxiety leads to increases in information seeking and learning about politics (Marcus, Neumann and Mackuen 2000). Other work suggests that extremely high levels of anxiety actually prevent political learning (Huddy *et al.* 2005). In the laboratory, the ability to elicit extreme emotions is limited by ethical concerns about harm and distress. Accordingly, it is possible that investigations into the impact of emotional intensity must rely on observational studies of extreme events such as September 11th, or on clinical populations.

The literature on the impact of emotions on judgments, attitudes and the process of thinking about information has received increasing attention over the past three decades. The extant literature provides a general outline of the broad way that emotions can influence a variety of cognitive and behavioral political outcomes. This outline provides an excellent point for further, more nuanced explorations of the impact of emotions on our thoughts and actions. Clearly emotional states alter the way politicians such as Barack Obama and John McCain conducted their bids for the Presidency. Exploring the ways that these emotional appeals alter how voters form, change and maintain their attitudes about the candidates and subsequently decide who to support will add immensely to our understanding of the impact of both the cognitive and affective components of political campaigns.

References

Ansolabehere, Steven, Shanto Iyengar, Adam Simon and Nicholas Valentino (1994). Does Attack Advertising Demobilize the Electorate? *American Political Science Review* 88, 829 – 838.

Armitage, Christopher. J., Mark Conner and Paul Norman (1999). Differential effects of mood on information processing: evidence from the theories of reasoned action and planned behaviour. *European Journal of Psychology* 29, 419 – 433.

Bless, Herbert, Gerd Bohner, Norbert Schwarz and Fritz Strack (1990). Mood and Persuasion: A cognitive response analysis. *Personality and Social Psychology Bulletin* 16, 331 – 345.

Bodenhausen, Galen. V., Lori A. Sheppard and Geoffrey P. Kramer (1994). Negative affect and social perception: The differential impact of anger and sadness. *European Journal of Social Psychology* 24, 45 – 62.

Boucher, Jerry and Charles Osgood (1969). The Pollyanna hypothesis. *Journal of Verbal and Learning Behavior* 8(1), 1 – 8.

Bousfield W. A. (1944). An empirical study of the production of affectively toned items. *Journal of General Psychology* 30, 205 – 215.

Bousfield W. A. (1950). The relationship between mood and the production of affectively toned associates. *Journal of General Psychology* 42, 67 – 85.

Brader, Ted. (2005). Striking a responsive chord. *American Journal of Political Science* 49, 388 – 405.

Brader, Ted (2006). *Campaigns for Hearts and Minds. How Emotional Appeals in Political Ads Work*. Chicago: The University of Chicago Press.

Breckler, Steven J. (1984). Empirical Validation of Affect, Behavior, and Cognition as Distinct Components of Attitude. *Journal of Personality and Social Psychology* 47, 1191 – 1205.

Chaiken, Shelley (1987). The heuristic model of persuasion. In M. P. Zanna, J. M. Olson and C. P. Herman (eds.), *Social influence: The Ontario Symposium (Volume 5)*, Hillsdale, NJ: Erlbaum.

Chaiken, Shelley and Yacov Trope (1999). *Dual-process theories in social psychology*. New York: Guilford Press.

Clore, Gerald. L., Norbert Schwarz and Michael Conway (1994). Affective causes and consequences of social information processing. In R. S.Wyer and T. K. Srull (eds.), *The handbook of social cognition (2nd Ed)*. Hillsdale, NJ: Lawrence Erlbaum Associates.

Clore, Gerald and W. Gerrod Parrott (1991). Moods and their vicissitudes: Thoughts and feelings as information. In J. Forgas (Ed.), *Emotion and social judgment*. Oxford: Pergamon Press.

DeSteno, David, Richard E. Petty, Derek D. Rucker, Duane T. Wegener and Julia Braverman (2004). Discrete emotions and persuasion: The role of emotion-induced expectancies. *Journal of Personality and Social Psychology* 86, 43 – 56.

Eagly, Alice and Shelley Chaiken (1993). *The Psychology of Attitudes*. Fort Worth, TX: Harcourt Brace Jovanovich.

Fazio, Russell H., David M. Sanbonmatsu, Martha C. Powell and Frank R. Kardes (1986). On the Automatic Activation of Attitudes. *Journal of Personality and Social Psychology* 50(2), 229 – 238.
Fiedler, Klaus (1991). On the task, the measures, and the mood in research on affect and social cognition. In J.P. Forgas (ed.), *Emotion and social judgments*. Cambridge, UK: Cambridge University Press.
Forgas, Joseph P. (1995). Mood and judgment: The Affect Infusion Model (AIM). *Psychological Bulletin* 117, 39 – 66.
Fredrickson, Barbara L. (2004). Gratitude (like other positive emotions) broadens and builds. In Emmons RA, McCullough ME (eds.), *The psychology of gratitude*. New York: Oxford University Press.
Fredrickson, Barbara L. (2001). The role of positive emotions in positive psychology: The broaden-and-build theory of positive emotions. *American Psychologist* 56, 218 – 226.
Frijda, Nico H. (1986). *The emotions*. Cambridge: Cambridge University Press.
Gilbert, Daniel T., Michael J. Gill and Timothy D. Wilson (2002). The Future is Now: Temporal Correction in Affective Forecasting. Organizational Behavior and Human *Decision Processes* 88(1), 430 – 444.
Gilbert, Daniel T., Elizabeth C. Pinel, Timothy D. Wilson, Stephen J. Blumberg and Thalia P. Wheatley (1998). Immune neglect: A source of durability bias in affective forecasting. *Journal of Personality and Social Psychology* 75(3), 617 – 638.
Goldberg, Julie H., Jennifer Lerner and Philip E. Tetlock (1999). Rage and reason: the psychology of the intuitive prosecutor. *European Journal of Social Psychology* 29, 781 – 795.
Gray, Jeffery A. (1986). Anxiety, personality and the brain. In A. Gale and J.A. Edwards (Eds.), *Physiological correlates of human behavior: Vol. 3. Individual differences and psychopathology*. Orlando, FL: Academic Press.
Griffitt, William (1970). Environmental effect of interpersonal affective behavior: Ambient effective temperature and attraction. *Journal of Personality and Social Psychology* 15, 240 – 244.
Huddy, Leonie, Stanley Feldman and Erin Cassese (2007). On the Distinct Political Effects of Anxiety and Anger. In W. Russell Neuman, George E. Marcus, Ann Crigler and Michael MacKuen (eds.), *The Affect Effect: Dynamics of Emotion in Political Thinking and Behavior*. Chicago: University of Chicago Press.
Huddy, Leonie, Stanley Feldman, Charles Taber and Gallya Lahav (2005). Threat, Anxiety, and Support of Anti-Terrorism Policies. *American Journal of Political Science* 49, 593 – 608.
Innes-Ker, Ase and Paula M Niedenthal (2002). Emotion Concepts and Emotional States in Social Judgment and Categorization. *Journal of Personality and Social Psychology* 83, 804 – 816.
Isbell, Linda M. and Victor C. Ottati (2002). The emotional voter: Effects of episodic affective reactions on candidate evaluation. In V.C. Ottati, R.S. Tindale, J. Edwards, F.B. Bryant, L. Heath, D.C. O'Connell, Y. Suárez-Balcazar and E.J. Posavac (eds), *Developments in political psychology*. New York: Plenum Publishing Company.
Isbell, Linda M., Victor C. Ottati and Kathleen C. Burns (2006). Affect and politics: Effects on judgment, processing, and information selection. In D. Redlawsk (Ed.), *Feeling Politics*. Hampshire: Palgrave Publishing Company.
Isen, Alice. M. (1984). Towards Understanding the Role of Affect in Cognition. In Wyer, R. S. and Srull, T. K. (Eds.), *Handbook of Social Cognition*. Hillsdale, NJ: Erlbaum.
Isen, Alice. M. (1987). Positive affect, cognitive processes and social behavior. In L. Berkowitz (Ed.), *Advances in Experimental Social Psychology*. New York: Academic.
Isen, Alice. M., Kimberly A. Daubman, K. and Gary P. Nowicki. (1987). Positive Affect Facilitates Creative Problem Solving. *Journal of Personality and Social Psychology* 52, 1122 – 1131.
Izard, Carroll E. (1971). *The face of emotion*. New York: Appleton-Century-Crofts.

Keltner, Dacher, Phoebe C. Ellsworth and Kari Edwards (1993). Beyond simple pessimism: Effects of sadness and anger on social perception. *Journal of Personality and Social Psychology* 64, 740 – 752.

Ladd, Jonathan M. and Gabriel S. Lenz (2008). Reassessing the Role of Anxiety in Vote Choice. *Political Psychology* 29(2), 275 – 296.

Lau, Richard R. and David P. Redlawsk (2001). Advantages and disadvantages of cognitive heuristics in political decision making. *American Journal of Political Science* 45, 951 – 971.

Lambert, Alan J., Laura D. Scherer, John P. Schott, Kristina R. Olson, Rick K. Andrews, Thomas C. O'Brien, Alison R. Zisser (2010). Rally Effects, Threat, and Attitude Change: An Integrative Approach to Understanding the Role of Emotion. *Journal of Personality and Social Psychology* 98(6), 886 – 903.

Lazarus, Richard S. (1991). *Emotion and adaptation*. New York: Oxford University Press.

Lerner, Jennifer S. and Larissa Z. Tiedens (2006). Portrait of the angry decision maker: How appraisal tendencies shape anger's influence on cognition. *Journal of Behavioral Decision Making* 19, 115 – 137.

Lerner, Jennifer S. and Dacher Keltner, (2000). Beyond valence: Toward a model of emotion-specific influences on judgment and choice. *Cognition and Emotion* 14, 473 – 493.

Lerner, Jennifer S. and Dacher Keltner (2001). Fear, anger, and risk. *Journal of Personality and Social Psychology* 81(1), 146 – 159.

Lerner, Jennifer S., Roxana M. Gonzalez, Deborah A. Small and Baruch Fischhoff (2003). Effects of fear and anger on perceived risks of terrorism: A national field experiment. *Psychological Science* 14, 144 – 150.

Lerner, Jennifer S. And Larissa Z. Tiedens (2006). Portrait of the angry decision maker: How appraisal tendencies shape anger's influence on cognition. *Journal of Behavioral Decision Making (Special Issue on Emotion and Decision Making)* 19, 115 – 137.

Loewenstein, George and Jennifer S. Lerner (2003). The role of affect in decision making. In R. Davidson, K. Scherer and H. Goldsmith (Eds.), *Handbook of Affective Sciences*. New York: Oxford University Press.

Lupia, Arthur (1994). Shortcuts Versus Encyclopedias: Information and Voting Behavior in California Insurance Reform Elections. *The American Political Science Review* 88(1), 63 – 76.

Mackie, Diane M. and Worth, Leila T. (1989). Processing deficits and the mediation of positive affect in persuasion. *Journal of Personality and Social Psychology* 57, 27 – 40.

MacKuen, Michael, Jennifer Wolak, Luke Keele and George E. Marcus. (2010). Civic Engagements: Resolute Parisanship or Reflective Deliberation. *American Journal of Political Science* 54(2), 440 – 458.

Marcus, George E., W. Russell Neuman and Michael MacKuen (2000). *Affective Intelligence and Political Judgment*. Chicago: University of Chicago Press.

Marcus, George E. (2003). The Psychology of Emotion and Politics. In D.O. Sears, L. Huddy, and R. Jervis (Ed.), *Oxford Handbook of Political Psychology*. New York: Oxford University Press, Inc.

Marcus, George E. and Michael MacKuen (1993). Anxiety, enthusiasm, and the vote: The emotional underpinnings of learning and involvement during presidential campaigns. *American Political Science Review* 87, 672 – 685.

McDermott, Rose (2004). The Feeling of Rationality: The Meaning of Neuroscientific Advances for Political Science. *Perspectives on Politics* 2(4), 691 – 706.

Niedenthal, Paula M. (May 18, 2007). Embodying emotion. *Science* 316, 1002 – 1005.

Niedenthal, Paula M., Anette Rohman and Nathalie Dalle (2003). What Is Primed by Emotion Concepts and Emotion Words? In J. Musch and K.C. Klauer (Ed.), *The Psychology of Evaluation: Affective Processes In Cognition and Emotion*. Mahwah, New Jersey: Lawrence Erlbaum Associates.

Petty, Richard E. and John T. Cacioppo (1986). *Communication and persuasion: Central and peripheral routes to attitude change*. New York: Springer-Verlag.
Petty, Richard E. and John T. Cacioppo (1981). *Attitudes and persuasion: Classic and contemporary approaches*. Dubuque, IA: William C. Brown.
Petty, Richard E., Derek D. Rucker, George Y. Bizer and John T. Cacioppo (2004). The elaboration likelihood model of persuasion. In J. S. Seiter and G. H. Gass (Eds.), *Perspectives on persuasion, social influence and compliance gaining*. Boston: Allyn & Bacon.
Petty, Richard E, Zakary Tormala and Rucker, Derek D. (2004). Resisting persuasion by counterarguing: An attitude strength perspective. In J. T. Jost, M. R. Banaji and D. A. Prentice (Eds.), *Perspectivism in social psychology: The yin and yang of scientific progress*. Washington, D.C.: American Psychological Association.
Petty, Richard E., Gary L. Wells and Timothy C. Brock (1976). Distraction can enhance or reduce yielding to propaganda: Thought disruption versus effort justification. *Journal of Personality and Social Psychology* 34, 874 – 884.
Raghunathan, Rajagopal and Michel Tuan Pham (1999). All Negative Moods are Not Equal: Motivational Influences of Anxiety and Sadness on Decision Making. *Organizational Behavior and Human Decision Processes* 71(1), 56 – 77.
Robinson, Michael D. and Clore, Gerald L. (2002). Episodic and semantic knowledge in emotional self-report: Evidence for two judgment processes. *Journal of Personality and Social Psychology* 83, 198 – 215.
Roseman, Ira J. (1984). Cognitive Determinants of Emotion: A Structural Theory. In P. Shaver (Ed.) *Review of Personality & Social Psychology, Vol. 5: Emotions, Relationships, and Health*. Beverly Hills, CA: Sage.
Schwarz, Norbert and Gerald L. Clore (1983). Mood, misattribution, and judgments of well-being: Informative and directive functions of affective states. *Journal of Personality and Social Psychology* 45, 513 – 523.
Schwarz, Norbert and Gerald L. Clore (1988). How do I feel about it? The informative function of mood. In K. Fiedler and J. Forgas (Eds.), *Affect, cognition, and social behavior*. Toronto: C.J. Hogrefe.
Schwarz, Norbert and Gerald L. Clore (1996). Feelings and Phenomenal Experiences. In Tory Higgins and Arie W. Kruglanski (ed.), *Social Psychology: Handbook of Basic Principles*. New York: Guilford.
Schwarz, Norbert and Gerald L. Clore (2003). Mood as Information: 20 Years Later. *Psychological Inquiry* 14, 296 – 303.
Small, Deborah A. and Jennifer Lerner (2008). Emotional policy: Personal sadness and anger shape judgments about a welfare case. *Political Psychology* 29, 149 – 168.
Smith, Craig A. and Pheobe C. Ellsworth (1985). Patterns of cognitive appraisal in emotion. *Journal of Personality and Social Psychology* 48(4), 813 – 838.
Tiedens, Larissa Z. (2001). Anger and advancement versus sadness and subjugation: The effects of negative emotion expressions on social status conferral. *Journal of Personality and Social Psychology* 80, 86 – 94.
Tiedens, Larissa Z. and Susan Linton (2001). Judgment under emotional certainty and uncertainty: The effects of specific emotions and their associated certainty appraisals on cognitive processing. *Journal of Personality and Social Psychology* 81, 973 – 988.
Tomkins, Silvan S. (1962). *Affect, Imagery. Consciousness, (Vol. 1)*. New York: Springer Publishing Co.
Valentino, Nicholas A., Krysha Gregorowicz and Eric W. Groenendyk (2009). Efficacy, Emotions and the Habit of Participation. *Political Behavior* 31(3), 307 – 330.
Verhulst, Brad, Milton Lodge and Charles Taber (2008). The Effect of Unnoticed Affective Cues and Cognitive Deliberation on Candidate Evaluation. Paper presented at the *66th annual meeting of the Midwestern Political Science Association*, 4 April, 2008: Chicago, Ill.

Verhulst, Brad and Jacob Sohlberg (2009). Information Processing Strategies and Negative Emotions. Paper presented at the *67th annual meeting of the Midwestern Political Science Association*, April 5, 2009.

Wattenberg, Martin P. and Craig Leonard Brians (1999). Negative Campaign Advertising: Demobilizer or Mobilizer? *The American Political Science Review* 93, 891 – 899.

Weinberg, Joel and Drew Westen (2008). RATS, We Should Have Used Clinton: Subliminal Priming in Political Campaigns. *Political Psychology* 29(5), 631 – 651.

Wilson, Timothy D. and Daniel T. Gilbert (2005). Affective forecasting: Knowing what to want. *Current Directions in Psychological Science* 14, 131 – 134.

Zanna, Mark P., Charles A. Kiesler and Paul A. Pilkonis (1970). Positive and negative attitudinal affect established by classical conditioning. *Journal of Personality and Social Psychology* 14, 321 – 328.

Barack Obama and the Political Science of Hope

Andrew J.W. Civettini

The role of emotions in political behavior has been the subject of a substantial amount of recent research in political science. Perhaps the most well known argument about the role of emotions in shaping political behavior is Marcus, Neuman, and MacKuen's Affective Intelligence and Political Judgment (2000). Marcus and colleagues develop a theoretical perspective of the way that two basic emotions, anxiety and enthusiasm, drive attention to the political environment and shape political judgments. Anxiety, by alerting us to threat-ening stimuli in the environment, leads us to react to the environment by considering our options consciously and learn new information. Enthusiasm lets us know when our standing dispositions serve us well so that we can continue voting for whom we vote for, write checks to our regular interest groups and candidates, and basically leave politics out of our conscious considerations. Much of political behavior, however, seems not to be reactionary but action oriented. People desire something from government, set about a plan to secure that good or service, and (often relentlessly) execute that plan. Something other than anxiety must be causing this action-orientation. I argue that we must consider the role of hope in not only shaping political behavior but how politicians attempt to motivate citizens to vote, volunteer, and organize, among other civic activities. Political struggles are often about what is likely to happen rather than what has happened and this should cause us to consider how political behavior is prospectively oriented. Prospective emotions, or emotions about things that are expected to happen, likely hold the key to understanding political action more than current state emotions. Because hope concerns future goals and the plausibility of achieving those goals, it is an ideal candidate for understanding action oriented political behavior.

Barack Obama and the 'Politics of Hope'

If you asked a thousand voting citizens what words best describes the 2008 U.S. Presidential election, I have no doubt that a common word would be 'hope'.

Barack Obama began setting his theme of hope as early as the 2004 Democratic National Convention in Boston, when he asked delegates, "Do we participate in a politics of cynicism or a politics of hope?" (Obama 2004). He would hone this message, but also importantly given the scientific literature on hope I will detail below, he began to talk not only about goals but also about agency. This agency was captured clearly in his campaign rally cry, "Yes we can". In a speech on the night of winning the Iowa caucuses, Obama said, "Hope is the bedrock of this nation; the belief that our destiny will not be written for us, but by us; by all those men and women who are not content to settle for the world as it is; who have courage to remake the world as it should be (January 3, 2008)." This statement clearly illustrates that hope requires not only a desired goal but agency to achieve that goal. But Obama is not the first politician in the United States to invoke hope. Jesse Jackson made hope a defining rhetorical feature in his campaign speeches in 1988, ultimately telling supporters to "keep hope alive" in his speech at the 1988 Democratic national convention (Jackson 1988). Democrats do not have a monopoly on hope, either. Republicans also appeal to hope. Richard Nixon told the crowd gathered at his first inaugural address that, "What kind of nation we will be, what kind of world we will live in, whether we shape the future in the image of our hopes, is ours to determine by our actions and our choices (Nixon 1969)." Nixon, like Obama nearly forty years later, understood that agency was a crucial component of the hope concept. It is not merely enough to dream, but to have plans to achieve those desired goals and the belief in our agency that we can achieve them.

What is Hope? Defining the Concept

Eliot (2005) considers the varied meanings that hope carries in theology, philosophy, politics, medicine, literature, and others. She concludes that although hope is a rich and complex construct, there are two primary constants across all conceptualizations of hope: significance and power. All constructs of hope view it as a significant force culturally and a primary component of the essence of humanity. Moreover, hope is accorded a sort of basic power – a power that can 'change lives' and can be harnessed personally, interpersonally, as well as communally (perhaps through great oratory). Dauenhauer (2005) contemplates the place of hope in the power struggle between unity of people and the nature of rulers and the ruled. He argues that hope unifies people, subverting the ruling function to the unifying function and resulting in responsible political practice. Responsible governmental systems, then, are those that foster hope and "power-in-common". While the idea that good governments are those that foster hope might arouse debate among social scientists, it likely would not engender much controversy to suggest that hope is part of the essence of humanity, culturally important, and can be a driving force in human lives. Yet, it may still not be clear that hope can help us understand political behavior. Can we discern a reliable concept of hope that would enable us to test its importance in igniting political activity or is the personal and subjective nature of hope reason to suspect that as an emotion hope is ill-suited to any use in rigorous empirical political science?

Reading (2004: 5) defines hope as a "pleasurable subjective state that arises when individuals expect that a desired future goal is realistically achievable, and that expectation energizes them to initiate activities they believe will help them attain it." This conceptualization of hope has two main components. First, an individual must have desired future goals. While some may take issue with the idea that citizens have desired policy preferences and desired directions for government activity due to low levels of citizen knowledge about government, it is likely that most, if not all, individuals hold some idea about what general direction they prefer government to take with respect to overall policy. The second key component of Reading's definition is the expectation that the goal is reasonably achievable. This belief leads to the pleasurable subjective state and energizes the individual to initiate actions to achieve the goal. Thus, Reading's definition requires two central components, goals and expectations about those goals.

Reading (2004: xii) points out that "one of the reasons science has had such a difficult time coming to grips with hope is that doing so requires understanding how something merely imagined and yet to occur can cause something else to happen." Essentially, it is because we believe we can attain something that causes us to do what is necessary to attempt to attain it. For Reading, hope is more than just a positive emotion experienced when imagining a future event or set of circumstances, but an encompassing emotional state that involves pleasure, energy, motivation, and goal-directed behavior. Reading refers to what he calls *future-oriented behavior*, which he calls "the behavioral signature of hope" (2004: 6). *Future-oriented behavior* is behavior that focuses on goals and costs that are well beyond the immediate. Passing on the hot dog vendor to get a gyro the next street over is not future oriented behavior, but passing on lunch out to save for retirement is geared toward a future benefit that can not be tangibly enjoyed in the present or near present time.

The components of goals and expectations of Reading's conception fit well with the primary conception of hope in the scientific literature espoused by Snyder (1994; 2000). Snyder's (2000: 8-13) definition of hope has three main components: goals, pathways, and agency. Much like Reading's definition, goals are necessary to the development of hope. Without goals there can be no hope. Pathways refer to the imagined path or sequence of events that get a person from the present state to the goal, while agency refers to perceiving that it is possible to follow those pathways. In this way, hope exists when an individual sees a path toward a desired goal and believes he or she can follow that path. This is the essence of the difference in the two conceptions. For Reading, hope is the positive emotional state that is experienced when a goal itself is considered attainable, leading to behavior that leads the individual toward attainment of the goal. For Synder, however, it is in seeing the path of behavior that can lead to attainment, and in believing that the individual can follow the path of behavior to the goal, that is the crux of hope. Whether hope generates energy and motivates an individual to find pathways to goal attainment or the existence of pathways makes hope for the goal possible is no small disagreement however. Let's suppose an interest group wants a particular policy (and personify the interest group, for simplification). In Snyder's configurations, the group would need to have the goal, see pathways to achieving that goal, and believe the organization can follow one of those pathways to achieve the goal. When the group believes the pathway can be followed, it experiences hope. For Reading, however, hope is experienced if the group expects it can achieve the goal, regardless of having any concrete idea of pathways to goal attainment. Thus, Reading's definition allows more for the possibility of blind or false hope. Snyder's conceptualization provides a fuller elaboration of when hope is possible, and how to measure it. For these reasons, I believe Snyder's conceptualization of hope to be superior for considering hope as a motivating force in political behavior.

Snyder's conception is by definition individual hope. But the concept has been extended beyond the individual. Drahos (2004), for example, distinguishes between what he sees as three types of hope: private, collective, and public hope. Private hopes are those held by individuals, while collective hopes are shared by many individuals across, in Drahos' conception, a society. Public hope, on the other hand, "is hope that is articulated or held by actors acting politically in relation to societal goals." (Drahos 2004: 20) Public hope is, Drahos argues, dangerous. Leaders may rouse followers' emotions to support a goal by creating public hope even when that goal is understood poorly by those followers. As a result, followers have little ability to judge the realistic achievement of the hoped-for goal. Without reassessment of the probability of goal attainment, public hope could lead to negative consequences. Drahos' example of the failure of Indian negotiators demonstrates this possible consequence of public hope.

Collective hope has also been implicated in explaining collective action. Braithwaite (2004b) argues that sustainable collective action is dependent on hope. Individuals must, in Braithwaite's (2004b: 129) words, "'sign on' to the collective hope process". Individual goals become shared ideas about what society should be like and those goals are pursued because of the combined individual agency and the pathways inherent in social networks and institutions. Braithwaite cautions that the ingredients of collective hope, shared individual goals for society, widespread personal efficacy, and access to social institutions, may be less available in some societies than others. Collective hope may not therefore be a possibility in the case of totalitarian society. Braithwaite's findings, based on a 2001 survey, show that "the *positive emotions* of collective efficacy and trust are critically important" to the achievement of hoped-for-goals (Braithwaite 2004b: 144, emphasis mine).

Hope, it seems, consists of the components of goals, pathways, and agency. So conceived, it seems less like an emotional construct and more like a formula for rational behavior. Goals are the payoffs for reaching an end state. Pathways are exactly that, the various paths to reach that particular end state of the game. What's missing really is the understanding of costs associated with those pathways, which may be accounted for by whether an individual (or collective) believe they can efficaciously follow any given pathway. Yet hope is more than simply these components because the agentic belief that one can follow a pathway engenders a positive emotional state that *itself* can sustain goal-directed behavior. Thus, the emotion that results from believing an individual can follow a given path to a goal causes the individual to be able to stay on the path.

A Little of What We Know So Far about Positive Political Emotions

Hope is a positive emotion, and considering its impact on political behavior means putting aside notions of emotion based solely on emotional valence. While most work on the effect of discrete emotions and political behavior focus on negative emotions, some authors have begun to examine the role of discrete positive emotions. Just, Crigler, and Belt (2007) examine the impact of voters' emotional responses to candidates on candidate evaluations and trait appraisals. They find that hope and enthusiasm drive those evaluations and trait appraisals up. Conversely, anger, anxiety, and worry decrease those evaluations and appraisals. Hope and not enthusiasm was found to have some effect in generating higher levels of political interest, in some cases. When a favored candidate is ahead in the horse race, hopeful feelings toward that candidate increase news viewership. Hope in a sense then is an emotional trigger to motivated reasoners that watching the nightly news will more likely confirm than deny the previous evaluation of the preferred candidate.

Gross, Brewer, and Aday conducted a panel study in the fall of 2001 and summer of 2002, measuring individuals' levels of confidence in government institutions. What they found was that hope and pride were both positively related to confidence in government. While their data do not permit a test of causal direction, they do indicate a likely link between the emotions of hope and pride and citizen confidence in government, with hopeful citizens less likely to decrease in confidence. Since hope may be as much (if not more of) a trait emotion as it is a state emotion, this finding has implications for confidence in government overall. High-hope individuals would likely be more confident in government institutions and perhaps more likely to vote for incumbents.

Brader's (2006) examination of the effect of emotional appeals in political ads tell us more about the impact of the positive emotion enthusiasm. Enthusiasm led to increased *desire* to participate in the political process, from voting to volunteering to general interest in the campaign. Brader cautions about the intensity and duration of effects of ads, but his results clearly show a short term increase in civic participation intention when cued by enthusiasm. However, Brader also presents evidence that enthusiasm merely serves to strengthen reliance on previous attitudes, not generate learning. In this work and more likely to follow, we see positive emotions having distinct political effects. Moreover, we see hope leading to greater interest as well as confidence in government.

A Political Science of Hope

In the concluding chapter of *The Handbook of Hope*, Snyder and Feldman (2000) offer what they call a social agenda for hope. They reject the notion that the hope construct is another individual-differences psychological measure merely helpful for individual assessment, counseling, and personal betterment. Rather, they speculate about ways in which hope may be more broadly understood in a societal context. Government is especially important in this formula, they argue, because government can create pathways to the successful attainment of collective goals of society. Snyder and Feldman argue that governments that foster individual advancement on the basis of merit and effort alone create high levels of hope in society, whereas governments that hinder personal growth create a cycle of hopelessness that leads to low levels of growth and poor consequences for society, like higher rates of suicide. While their normative goals are worthy, I believe a first step in understanding the role of hope in political behavior is in applying the individual-differences measure to assess how high hope individuals differ in their engagement in political activities, and in assessing the impact of political rhetoric on citizens' preferences and how that might differ for high and low hope individuals.

Hope and Campaign Rhetoric

Candidates do a lot of things – kissing babies, shaking hands, and speaking to crowds, to name a few. With those speeches, which are now as likely to end up on the evening news as any other story that day, candidates try to move undecided voters, firm support among followers, and perhaps even convert opponent's followers. It is commonly held that President Obama is perhaps one of the best campaign orators of not only our time, but all time. Atwater (2007) contemplates the origins of Obama's rhetoric of hope, examining the ways in which the President's core values and personality contribute to his rhetoric. The article focuses more on what Obama means by hope and the American dream more than what hope is and how Obama uses it as a rhetorical tool. Obama's rhetorical abilities only accentuated the ways in which he cultivated a rhetoric of hope because he made it easier for people to see pathways and believe goals were attainable. But can we think of ways that emotions, including hope, might be instrumental to understanding the effect of campaign rhetoric?

Jerit, Kuklinski, and Quirk (2009) separate political rhetoric into three forms: party value reinforcement, fact-based descriptive rhetoric, and predictive rhetoric. It is with predictions about future outcomes that politicians likely have the most success in swaying unaligned voters to their side in a campaign. The key to understanding how and why unaligned voters choose which candidates to support lies in their emotional reactions to those predictions of future outcomes. Hope might provide a particularly interesting construct for analyzing the ability of candidates to win undecided voters. The positive emotional state of hope comes from the agency of believing that available pathways can be followed to achieve a goal.

In the case of campaign rhetoric, candidates need to draw on collective goals (though the best orators would likely be able to convince their audience of the worth of a given goal), show their audiences the pathways available to achieve the goals, and make them believe that the pathways are clear and attainment is possible. Thus the ability of candidates to win undecided voters may rest on their ability to *raise hope* of those voters. To test such an implication, we would need measures of hope that can change over time, or a measure of hope as an emotional state.

Hope and Voters

An obvious relationship between hope and voting may be that individuals likely would vote for the candidate that makes them the most hopeful. A quick analysis of the individual affect questions in the American National Election Studies would bear this out, but what does it mean? Candidates may make voters feel more hopeful when they share their goals for society, or when they highlight pathways that voters are supportive of (a national referendum, e.g.). Candidates may heighten voters sense of efficacy and agency leading to greater hope, or some combination of goals, pathways, and agency. Or voters may be more hopeful the more likely their candidate is to win, resulting in the appearance that voters are choosing candidates based on a feeling of hope when in fact the greater levels of hopefulness for the winning candidate were caused by the likelihood of that candidate's victory. So predicting elections based on how hopeful the voters are is likely no better than using the latest Gallup poll. An answer to how hope can help us move forward in understanding voter behavior likely lies in examining the differences in political behavior between high and low hope individuals. By this, I don't mean voters who are contemporaneously hopeful about their preferred candidate, but rather voters who are predisposed to being hopeful. The hope contruct as formulated by Snyder (1994) can be applied to discern high hope individuals from low hope individuals by understanding hope not as an emotional state but as a dispositional trait. Some people are more likely to feel individual agency, be able to articulate goals, and see pathways to achieve their goals. High hope individuals are less likely to be deterred by threat-related stimuli (Michael 2000). This is an important consideration because the theory of affective intelligence, which much of political science research on the role of emotions takes as a starting point, treats threatening stimuli (and the resultant anxiety) as the most important component of understanding the role of emotions in political decision making. Yet some people, high hope people, are less deterred by threat related stimuli. This means they would be less likely to be impacted by negative campaign advertising or conflicting information about their preferred candidate. Thus an initial step in examining the role of hope in voter decision making would be to look at differences in voter decision making strategies and behavior between high and low hope individuals.

Hope and Staffers, Volunteers, and Activists

In addition to exhibiting differences in voting behavior, high hope individuals are likely to be more active in other forms of political participation. High hope individuals feel more confident about and inspired by life goals (Snyder *et al.* 1991). When those goals are collective goals, high hope individuals are likely to translate that confidence into public action by pursuing public pathways to collective goals. Moreover, high hope people make higher estimates of the probability of attaining their goals (Snyder *et al.* 1991). Political activists and those who volunteer their time need to not only have goals for their organizations or candidates, but believe that those goals are attainable. Thus, high hope individuals are probably more likely to be joiners and even policy entrepreneurs. Those same high hope individuals are more likely to experience success in translating pursued goals into attained goals because they are better at managing the *process* of goal attainment. High hope people are more likely to segment goal attainment into smaller, more manageable steps (Snyder 1994). Thus, I argue that high hope individuals are more likely to be political participants than low hope individuals, more likely to start political organizations or initiate political movements or causes, and more likely to be successful at achieving stated political goals. Hope is the stuff of successful political action. Another reason high hope individuals may have more success in pursuing collective or political goals is that high hope individuals may have more extensive social networks (Cheavens, Michael and Snyder 2005). Thus, they have a greater wealth of the most crucial resource in politics, sheer numbers. Yet none of these findings of high versus low hope have been directly applied to political action, but rather have been tested in terms of patient treatment and illness management. The first step in understanding the role of hope in political participation and activism would be an analysis of the dispositional levels of hope for a sample of individuals and a subsequent analysis of their levels of political activity.

A Note on Measuring and Testing 'Political Hope'

In order to develop some assessment of the role of hope in generating political behavior and structuring the interactions of elites, activists, and the mass public, we need some way of accounting for hope when we see it. For behavioral implications of hope and hoping, we can turn to the psychological measurement literature on hope. To measure hope, C.R. Snyder and researchers developed the Adult Dispositional Hope Scale (DHS) to introduce a common metric for hope (Snyder *et al.* 1991). The DHS consists of twelve items, four each to measure the key concepts of agency and pathways and four filler items. The scale was shown to be valid and reliable. Subsequent research has shown the scale to be generally unidimensional, with separate treatment of Pathways and Agency resulting in little additional explained variance (Brouwer *et al.* 2008). Hope measured through the DHS is a trait emotion: high hope individuals would on average over time score consistently high, while low hope individuals would score low. Yet for some purposes a state scale, developed by Snyder and colleagues, would be appropriate. If we return to the idea of understanding the way campaign rhetoric persuades undecided voters by creating a sense of hope, we could measure state hope before and after campaign speeches.

The Hope Scale is simple, reliable, and methodologically easy to administer. Yet hope as a state or trait emotion may vary across life domains, such that hopefulness in one's family life does not translate to hopefulness in one's social life. Sympson (1999) applied the Dispositional Hope Scale to six life domains: social, academic, family, romance/relationships, work/occupation, and leisure activities. The resulting Domain Specific Hope Scale was consistent and valid and the six distinct domains were corroborated by factor analysis. While the social domain seems as the best categorical fit for political hope, its items measure social life as an individual interactive domain more so than measuring broad societal hope. Thus, though the Domain Specific Hope Scale provides guidance in possibility developing a measure of political hope, none of the domains themselves are directly translatable to political activity and political hope. While a political domain seems ultimately worth pursuing, it is not readily clear what would be constituted by 'political hope' that would be different than other domains, except to say that political hope would be more squarely focused on collective goal attainment than personal goal attainment.

An Agenda for Political Hope

This essay outlines what I feel is an important emotion to consider in advancing our understanding of political behavior, hope. Hope is defined as combining goals, agency, and pathways, and can be measured reliably through the Dispositional Hope Scale, the State Hope Scale, and the Domain Specific Hope Scale. I outline some brief considerations of where to go next in the consideration of political hope. First, we must begin to understand the ways that high hope individuals differ with respect to voting, volunteerism, activism, and other forms of political participation and decision making. Next, we must consider the ways in which politicians use hope as a rhetorical tool to sway undecided voters and win support for favored policies by looking at what impacts the emotional state of hope. In doing so, we can begin to explore the role of hope as a dispositional trait and emotional state in shaping political behavior and political rhetoric.

References

Atwater, Deborah F. (2007). Senator Barack Obama: The Rhetoric of Hope and the American Dream. *Journal of Black Studies* 38(2), 121 – 129.
Braithwaite, Valerie (2004). The Hope Process and Social Inclusion. *The ANNALS of the American Academy of Political and Social Science* 592(March), 128 – 151.
Brader, Ted (2006). *Campaigning for Hearts and Minds: How Emotional Appeals in Political Ads Work*. Chicago: University of Chicago Press.
Brouwer, Danny, Rob R. Meijer, Anke M. Weekers and Joost J. Baneke (2008). On the Dimensionality of the Dispositional Hope Scale. *Psychological Assessment* 20(3), 310 – 315.
Chaevens, Jennifer S., Scott T. Michael and C.R. Snyder (2005). The Correlates of Hope: Psychological and Physiological Benefits. In Jaklin Eliott (ed.), *Interdisciplinary Perspectives on Hope*. New York: Nova Science Publishers.
Dauehauer, Bernard P. (2005). The Place of Hope in Responsible Political Practice. In Jaklin Eliott (ed.), *Interdisciplinary Perspectives on Hope*. New York: Nova Science Publishers.
Drahos, Peter (2004). Trading in Public Hope. *The ANNALS of the American Academy of Political and Social Science* 592(March), 18 – 38.
Eliott, Jaklin (2005). What Have We Done With Hope? A Brief History. In Jaklin Eliott (ed.), *Interdisciplinary Perspectives on Hope*. New York: Nova Science Publishers.
Gross, Kimberley, Paul R. Brewer and Sean Aday (2009). Confidence in Government and Emotional Responses to Terrorism After September 11, 2001. *American Politics Research* 37(1), 107 – 128.
Jackson, Jesse (1988). *Speech to the Democratic National Convention*. July 19, 1998. Omni Coliseum, Atlanta, Georgia.
Jerit, Jennifer, James H. Kuklinski and Paul J. Quirk (2009). Strategic Politicians, Emotional Citizens, and the Rhetoric of Prediction. In Eugene Borgida, Christopher M. Federico and John L. Sullivan (eds.), *The Political Psychology of Democratic Citizenship*. New York: Oxford University Press.
Just, Marion R., Ann N. Crigler, and Todd L. Belt (2007). Don't Give Up Hope: Emotions, Candidate Appraisals, and Votes. In W. Russell Neuman, George E. Marcus, Ann N. Crigler and Michael MacKuen (eds.), *The Affect Effect: Dynamics of Emotion in Political Thinking and Behavior*. Chicago: University of Chicago Press.
Marcus, George E., W. Russell Neuman and Michael MacKuen (2000). *Affective Intelligence and Political Judgment*. Chicago: University of Chicago Press.
Michael, Scott T. (2000). Hope Conquers Fear: Overcoming Anxiety and Panic Attacks. In C.R. Snyder (ed.), *Handbook of Hope: Theory, Measures, and Applications*. New York: Academic Press.
Obama, Barack H. (2004) *Remarks of State Senator (IL) Barack Obama to the delegates of the Democratic National Convention*. Fleet Center, Boston, Massachusetts.
Obama, Barack H. (2008). *Remarks of Senator Barack Obama: Iowa Caucus Night*. January 3, 2008. HyVee Hall, Des Moines, Iowa.
Reading, Anthony (2004). *Hope and Despair: How Perceptions of the Future Shape Human Behavior*. Baltimore: The Johns Hopkins University Press.
Snyder, C.R. (1994) *The Psychology of Hope: You Can Get There From Here*. New York: Free Press.
Snyder, C.R. (2000). Hypothesis: Is There Hope. In Snyder, C.R. (ed.), *Handbook of Hope: Theory, Measures, and Applications*. New York: Academic Press.
Snyder, C.R. and David B. Feldman (2000). Hope for the Many: An Empowering Social Agenda. In C.R. Snyder (ed.), *Handbook of Hope: Theory, Measures, and Applications*. New York: Academic Press.

Snyder, C.R., Cheri Harris, John R. Anderson, Sharon A. Holleran, Lori M. Irving, Sandra T. Sigmon, Lauren Yoshinobu, June Gibb, Charyle Langelle and Pat Harney (1991). The Will and the Ways: Development and Validation of an Individual-Differences Measure of Hope. *Journal of Personality ad Social Psychology* 60(4), 570 – 585.

Sympson, Susie C. (1999). *Validation of the Domain Specific Hope Scale: Exploring Hope in Life Domains*. Doctoral dissertation, University of Kansas, Lawrence.

Perspectives on Politics & Emotions
The Obama Phenomenon

Suspending Disbelief

Obama and the Role of Emotions in Political Communication

Oliver Escobar

By January 2009, Barack Obama had become the most popular leader in the world, restoring the USA's global image and crystallising a wave of European fascination that remains unchanged (Pew Research Center 2009; Harris 2009a 2009b; Transatlantic Trends 2008; 2009). Two years earlier, he was virtually unknown in his own country, let alone Europe. How did the Obama phenomenon flourish in an era of political cynicism? How can we interpret Obama's success in terms of communication and emotional appeal? In order to suggest some answers, I have studied audiovisual materials up to January 2009 – many of which can be accessed by following the links provided – and drawn on cross-disciplinary literature to flesh out my interpretation of the findings from a small-scale qualitative research project.[1]

Obama's campaign managed to embody American history in a personal story, and turned a personal story into American history. This was achieved by effectively blending old and new communication strategies. Accordingly, the campaign was embedded in a multilayered architecture of meanings, as well as underpinned by carefully crafted communication, and the synergetic use of grassroots mobilization, media technologies and symbol-building master narratives. My main focus is to reflect on the emotional and communicative fabric of Obama's transatlantic appeal. I will argue that a key component of this phenomenon was Obama's steady transformation into the kind of symbol that many were longing for.

---

[1] I am deeply indebted to everyone who took part in the conversations, interviews and focus groups that have broadened the scope of my own experience and interpretation of the Obama phenomenon. There were 24 participants from 8 countries: UK (10), USA (5), Poland (4), Bahrain, Canada, Ireland, Germany and Spain. They currently live in Scotland, and vary in ages and backgrounds. Of course, the sample is not intended to be representative in any way, but to add flesh to the bones of statistics and arguments from secondary sources. The purpose was to underpin the essay with qualitative data regarding perceptions, meanings and self-reported feelings. The research took place between December 2009 and March 2010.

Emotions in Political Communication

For Aristotle, human virtue depends on the harmonious dance between reason and emotion (Sokolon 2006; Koziak 2000). Similarly, David Hume (1739: 312-313) argued that emotions power moral actions, and that reason by itself is "utterly impotent". Darwin (1890) explained the key adaptive role that emotions play in communication. Despite this intellectual heritage, however, political science has been dominated by an overly rationalistic view of the human mind (Fischer 2009: 272-273). Emotions in politics have often been depicted as mere drivers of irrationality, demagoguery and dangerous mass arousal. These assumptions are now challenged by cross-disciplinary political science (i.e. Marcus *et al.* 2000; Goodwin *et al.* 2001; Brader 2006) that transcends the unhelpful theoretical antagonism of emotion versus reason.

In the traditional view, emotions hinder rationality, and thus individuals must subordinate emotions to the dictates of instrumental reason. The problem, however, is that this view misrepresents how our brains work. Neuroscience, cognitive science and political psychology show that reason and emotion are intimately intertwined and share joint responsibilities (i.e. Damasio 1994; Ledoux 1996; Lakoff 2009; Lakoff and Johnson 1999; Marcus 2002; 2000). In other words, emotions are an essential component of reason's mechanism, and hence an integral part of human intelligence (Nussbaum 2001). The fact that emotion is indispensable in enabling reason to operate has profound consequences for understanding political communication. For instance, it deepens our comprehension of information-processing and political motivation, and it invites us to move beyond the rational choice era.

Our brain receives far more information that our conscious reason is able to process (Marcus 2002: 62). Thanks to efficient evaluative functions performed by emotion, our lives are not paralysed by permanent indecision. Indeed, cognitive and emotional systems not only intersect but also reinforce each other; without emotional motivation, reason is unlikely to drive us to act (Damasio 1994). Long before the latest breakthroughs in neuroscience, Edelman (1972: 58-9) argued that emotions underpin our ability to understand the world, and hence our political behaviour. Emotions motivate us to engage in politics (Goodwin *et al.* 2001) and assist us in swiftly processing information for our participation in public deliberation (Marcus and MacKuen 1993: 672). However, communication is more than message-transmission and information-processing. As Penman (2000: 1) puts it, "communication is the observable practice of a relationship". Such a relationship, as we will see, depends on affective elements as well.

In the conversations that underpin this essay I found that, unsurprisingly, charismatic politicians like Obama inspire a wide range of simultaneous feelings[2]: enthusiasm, excitement, hope, inspiration, compassion, empathy, satisfaction, elation, pride, anxiety and fear. They do so, as we will later argue, by establishing an intimate relationship with their publics. Candidates do not choose between inspiring feelings or dealing with policy issues, they often integrate both by employing emotional appeals that enhance the effectiveness of their substantial message (Brader 2006: 179). Accordingly, by using narratives, metaphors, images and symbols they strive to establish and modulate specific cognitive frames and to activate and reinforce their neurological networks (Lakoff 2009).

Marcus (1991) finds that voting preferences depend more on affective responses to candidates than on assessments of ideological positions (see also Glasser and Salovey 1998). Westen (2007: 115) points out that we can predict 80 percent of voter's judgements about policy issues by analysing emotional alliances (i.e. partisan sentiment). Subsequently, eliciting the right feelings, rather than presenting the best arguments, seems crucial for electoral success (p.125). However, emotion and cognition are in a permanent feedback loop, and thus it is difficult to make conclusive claims on causality and impact (Mutz 2007). In any case, I take the Aristotelian view that powerful political communication combines *ethos* – personality and stance; *pathos* – emotional arousal; and *logos* – coherent argumentation (Cockcroft and Cockcroft 1992). This essay refers to aspects related to *ethos* and *pathos*.

In retrospective, we may assume that Obama understood the importance of building the campaign on emotionally compelling communication. However, his quasi-professorial take on issues during the first stage of the primary elections threatened his prospects of success (Westen 2007: 433). It was only when his signature policies were embedded in emotionally laden narratives that the seeds of the global phenomenon were sowed. When most participants in my research were exposed to Obama for the first time, his branding machinery had already been attuned and his campaign had become something of a movement. In this essay, rather than understanding exposure to the Obama phenomenon in terms of message-reception, I look at communication as the process of co-creation of

---

[2] Emotions are "specific sets of physiological and mental dispositions triggered by the brain in response to the perceived significance of a situation or object" (Brader 2006: 51). Feelings are the subjective awareness and experience of emotions (Damasio 1994: 133). My arguments are based on self-reported feelings, which poses clear research challenges. However, a more nuanced analysis of emotions and feelings is beyond the scope of this interpretive essay. For a useful discussion see Brader (2006).

meanings. The key question here is not what Obama says, but *how* Obama means[3].

The Medium is the Message: Emotional Architectures of Meaning[4]

Obama started the campaign as an individual and finished it as a collective symbol. That is, a flexible "signifier" (Edelman 1988: 119) capable of evoking multiple cross-cultural meanings. As Edelman argues (1967: 6), "condensation symbols" are able to encapsulate a wide range of "anxieties, remembrances of past glories or humiliations" and "promises of future greatness". Multiple dynamics intervene in the configuration of a symbol. Among other things, it is the product of communication processes in which, paraphrasing McLuhan (1967), the message and the medium become one. However, MacLuhan understands the medium in technological terms, whereas I use *medium* to refer to the conduit of symbolism. An example would be how Mandela is the compelling symbol of the end of South Africa's apartheid. In our case study, the message and its emotionally charged medium constitute the same entity: Obama is Obama's message.

It is important to understand that meanings reside not in the symbols, but in society (Edelman 1967). I take this process of collective co-creation of meanings to be at the core of political communication. In this view, electoral campaigns are fought in the battleground of meanings, and the message is only part of the ammunition. The communication strategies of the Obama campaign were substantially different in the primary and national elections. Democrat candidates have often approached communication with a dispassionate mindset and a rationalistic take on policy (Westen 2007). This explains Obama's focus on issues to seek support from the Democratic Party in the caucuses[5]. In the election, however, issues and passions became more subtly intertwined: Obama embedded the issues in emotionally laden narratives[6].

So, *how* did Obama mean along this process? In a nutshell, from early 2007 he started meaning through words and images compounded in uneven performances[7]. During the course of 2008, speeches and images steadily turned into seamless parts of complex personal and historical narratives. By October 2008, those master narratives were part of a *global symbol* (see Gallup 2008c) whose multilayered meanings could be evoked by a simple sound bite or image.

---

3 Yanow's (1996) interpretive method focuses on *how* policy means.
4 Both expressions are borrowed from McLuhan (1967) and Yanow (2000), respectively.
5 E.g. Iowa, 10.11.2007. http://www.youtube.com/watch?v=tydfsfSQiYc
6 E.g. Denver, 28.08.2008. http://www.youtube.com/watch?v=yZCrIeRkMhA
7 See Westen (2007: 432-436).

To sketch out the communicative fabric of this process, I focus on narratives, archetypes, frames and the *mirror effect*.

Storytelling is at the heart of our cultural and biological life. Our brains naturally crave coherent stories (Westen 2007: 231). As Damasio (1994) has shown, many of the emotional reactions in our social life are triggered by *"systematic connections between categories of objects and situations, on the one hand, and primary emotions, on the other"* (Damasio 1994: 134; emphasis in original). Narratives serve to structure those connections, and can create and reinforce compelling associations in our minds. Much of the emotional power of political communication stems from effectively shaping and activating such associations. In the brain, "neural binding" allows the combination of simple narratives into more complex ones (Lakoff 2009: 25), which operate as neurological "building blocks" (p.21) and play a central role in the creation of emotional experiences (p.27).

Narratives are also building blocks in our cultures. For instance, the narrative frames 'Rags-to-Riches' or 'Pull-Yourself-up-by-Your-Bootstraps' are American icons themselves (Lakoff 2009: 29). Although every culture has specific master narratives, we share many of them. Think of those classic fairy tales, novels or dramas that – anchored in compelling archetypes – transcended borders long before globalisation. Apparently, our minds naturally search for stories with a particular kind of structure that makes them rhetorically powerful. Such structures are similar across cultures (Westen 2007: 146). The Obama story has that type of structure. Its potency is magnified by the overlapping of personal and historical narratives that are conflated in the production of a powerful symbol. In Obama, the personal is historical, and vice versa.

There are some interrelated master narratives that, apart from being central in Obama's performances, emerged most prominently in my research. Firstly, Obama is the symbol of a *double American redemption*. The first one concerns the USA's redemption in terms of race politics. Here Obama appears as the symbolic culmination of the anti-slavery and civil rights movements. Race is, without doubt, what attracted most of my research participants – even those disengaged from politics – to follow the 2008 election. For instance, a participant recalls vividly how emotional it was to hear Obama saying "I was raised by white grandparents but my wife has slave blood in her veins". Expressions like this had the power to evoke in our minds myriad images from our collective imaginary. They walked us along the allegedly teleological line that Obama traced between himself, King, Kennedy and Lincoln. By wrapping himself in a series of "historical hot-button associations" (Hill 2009: 63) he shaped, activated and reinforced his own symbolic meaning. This was not only done through language, but also by managing the narrative power of space, time and objects;

for instance, the choice of Lincoln's Springfield to launch the campaign, the nomination acceptance on the anniversary of King's "I have a dream", or the presidential oath over Lincoln's bible. This kind of invocation provided countless subtexts that contributed to feed the story-hungry cycles of the media. The narrative pointed the spectator to 'this defining moment', a cathartic mantra that Obama repeated constantly. In the process, he became a "synecdoche for the African American journey" (Darsey 2009: 95), and functioned as a magnifying lens for a reinvigorated teleological – progressive – view of American history.

The second redemption concerns the USA in the world scene. Here, Obama is not only seen as the antithesis of, but the antidote to, the Bush era. Nothing defines a hero better than the perfect antagonist. By November 2008, the contrast in popularity between Bush and Obama was staggering (Gallup 2008e), with Bush being amongst the most unpopular American presidents both at home (Gallup 2008a; 2009) and abroad (Pew Research Center 2009). Alongside race, the anti-Bush sentiment featured most prominently in the research participants' feelings. The American participants claimed that "Obama has made it easier to be an American abroad", "It was like a return to grace", and even "I can love America again!" The rest agreed on the direct impact of the USA's politics in their countries, and reported strong negative feelings towards the Bush Administration. In general, most participants encoded their views along the Obama/Bush stereotypical contrast outlined by Mitchell (2009: 129): smart/stupid, eloquent/inarticulate, flexible/rigid, modest/arrogant, mixed-raced cosmopolitan/white Texas cowboy, subtle and complex/simplistic and reductive, collaborative and deliberative/unilateral and aggressive. I found also a general tacit acceptance of the USA as the world's 'leading beacon', and thus a lack of critique of the 'American exceptionalism' narrative that pervaded Obama's campaign (Ivie and Giner 2009). It is perhaps understood as part of the unavoidable patriotic ritual of the candidacy, and hence seemingly irrelevant from a transatlantic perspective.

Finally, of course, my research brought up the centrality of the master narrative of the American Dream, used by Obama as a structuring theme for his best campaign performances[8] and his most sophisticated adverts[9]. In this narrative, the USA is a land of romance and opportunity where hard-working citizens succeed. However, Obama recasts it as the American Promise, a more communitarian frame grounded on social justice and equality. In this sense, he not only pledged to restore the American Dream, but he embodied it. Here we enter the realm of biography politics that has been so instrumental in forging the Obama

---

8   E.g. Denver, 28.08.2008. http://www.youtube.com/watch?v=yZCrIeRkMhA
9   See *American stories, American solutions* (2008).

phenomenon. Granted, many politicians capitalise on aspects of their autobiographies, but Obama took it to another level. He had been distilling publicly the quintessence of his life-story for a long time[10]. Anyone who had read his bestsellers (Obama 1995; 2006) was familiar with the well-rehearsed personal stories that would sustain the architecture of meanings of his campaign. They condensed the archetypal epic journey of trial, error, tribulation, self-discovery, and success. As Darsey (2009) argues, Obama's use of the archetypal metaphor of the journey underpins much of his communication success. It does so by creating one of those narrative structures that our brains crave, and it becomes emotionally compelling through the conflation of personal and collective struggles[11]. This metaphor was constantly used to rally his grass-roots movement[12].

At the crossroads of these narratives, Obama is capable of inhabiting many roles. As Mitchell (2009: 127) argues, "the key to Obama iconicity resides not in determinacy but ambiguity, not in identity but differential hybridity". By embodying the prospects of an unknown alternative future, he becomes a "virtual candidate" (Conley 2008: 309). His slogans – Change, Hope, Unity – function as "empty boundary objects" (Cetina 2009: 132), signifiers that different groups fill up with multiple meanings. However, Obama was not only a blank canvas, but a mirror in which different people could see themselves, for instance: the single-parent boy raised by grandparents, the indebted student, the young family man, the community organiser, the academic, the writer, the civil rights lawyer, the sportsman, the global citizen, the religious convert, the passionate preacher, the technology geek, and most prominently, the underdog[13]. When an archetype was missing, Obama incorporated it by telling the life story of others[14]. As Marshall (1997: 240) argues, media privilege the affective dimension in the construction of political personalities. In this context, as Hart (1999: 69) puts it, "the language of personality is expansionistic, it allows one person to become all persons, all archetypes". My research suggests that this sort of mirror effect can bolster identification and emotional attachment.

Lakoff (2009) argues that *framing* is the crucial battleground in politics. Obama's campaign was efficient at turning his potential weaknesses into strengths; for instance, his youthfulness became a guarantee of being an *uncon-*

---

10 E.g. Boston, 18.08.2004. http://www.youtube.com/watch?v=eWynt87PaJ0&feature=related
11 E.g. Berlin, 24.07.2008. http://www.youtube.com/watch?v=Q-9ry38AhbU&feature=related
12 See *By the people* (2010).
13 See, for instance *By the people* (2010), *God bless Barack Obama* (2010), or *American stories, American solutions* (2008).
14 The *Victory Speech* offers an example of masterful storytelling. Obama uses the centenary life of Anne Marie Cooper to encapsulate American history. Chicago, 05.11.2008. http://www.youtube.com/watch?v=jJfGx4G8tjo&feature=related

taminated politician. His executive inexperience was countered by the pledge of *relational leadership* (Yankelovich 1999), based on dialogue and deliberation. This underpinned two of his signature moves: the discursive dissolution of oppositions – i.e. religion/science, individualism/compassion, security/human rights, patriotism/shame (Conley 2008: 309) – and the recurrent theme of unity, not only as interconnectedness, but as interdependency (Ivie and Giner 2009: 372). In addition, although racial prejudice hurt his campaign (Piston 2010), being mixed-race strengthened his ability to embody a changing America where 40% of the population is non-white (Hill 2008: 83), as well as to be the face of globalisation's cosmopolitan project (Parameswaran 2009).

Most of my research participants did not watch any of Obama's speeches in full. Many did not follow much of the electoral race. Some ignored it completely. Almost none could recall the campaign's signature issues, besides foreign policy and health care. However, they were all familiar with the narratives, archetypes and frames hereby outlined, and they reflected on Obama's emotional appeal in reference to them. This suggests the fast pace at which Obama became a symbol beyond the realm of politics. In its symbolic versatility, Obama resembled Whitman's image of the ideal "leader of a democracy as the poetic inhabitor of all its varied lives" (Nussbaum 2001: 435).

The Intimate Crowd

Obama's oratorical skills are unquestionable. However, rhetoric does not explain the fascination that he produces among people who do not understand English, or who were only exposed to random headlines, sound bites or images. As Sullivan and Masters (1988: 362-363) have shown, watching brief excerpts can emotionally influence viewers' attitudes toward candidates. Furthermore, Kinder (2003) argues that political communication through the media can change citizens' priorities and preferences.

It is difficult to comprehend the full spectrum of elements and dynamics involved in communication. Although we think in images and half of our brain is devoted to visuals (Hill 2008: 11), most sensory information processed by our emotion systems never reaches our consciousness (Marcus 2002). As Lewicki (1986) has argued, emotional arousal can shape our cognition without us being aware. No wonder it is difficult to explain how we come to pass judgement on Obama after a few brief media experiences. Consider, for instance, some of the affective evaluations expressed by my research participants: *likeable, charming, mesmerising, enticing, charismatic, down-to-earth, feels very normal, engaging, attractive, personable, felt a degree of trust, felt uplifted, makes me feel hope, a man of a rare integrity, feels natural, feels authentic*. Although we can try to rationalise these perceptions, they are produced by the joint work of gut-feelings and cognition. Such feelings are triggered by evaluations swiftly performed by our emotion systems (Damasio 1994; Ledoux 1996).

When Obama's character 'feels authentic', the campaign's communication work lays on solid foundations. As Aristotle argued, the perceived credibility of the source determines the persuasiveness of the message (Teven 2008: 393). Subsequently, personality politics become crucial because campaigns "privilege the code of character to the point where all other types of information are either neglected or structured into the code" (Marshall 1997: 238). Media emphasise personality because it helps to build fluid narratives. Accordingly, politics is increasingly interwoven "with the domains of the personal and wired into the emotional circuitry of popular culture" (Richards 2004: 349).

In this context, Obama not only became a celebrity politician, but a global cultural star (Parameswaran 2009). This was the platform from where Obama reached out so far and so deep. Of course, celebrity culture is nothing new (Norris 2000:72-73); however, the media keep perfecting the experience and achieving new degrees of intimacy. Long ago, Horton and Wohl (1956) coined the term *para-social interaction* to refer to the intimate relationship between distant publics and media figures. In the case of Obama, the intensity of such relationship is striking, even from this side of the Atlantic. Adding more excerpts to the above, we can notice the familiarity and closeness with which many of the research participants spoke about Obama: "approachable", "it feels he is honest", "humoristic", "you feel charmed", "he is one of us but still powerful", "humble", "trust in him", "sense of confidence", "felt connected and related to him", "I was worried about him", "I'm proud of him", "I feared for him". Such degree of proximity seems remarkable, particularly considering that most participants only had brief *mediatised encounters* with him. The concept of 'curb appeal' seems useful here. It refers to the "emotional impression" that viewers get when they "drive by" a candidate a few times (Westen 2007: 294). Obama's curb appeal was, arguably, a central factor in attracting attention and follow up. Surely the genuineness that facial coders detect in Obama's body language (i.e. Hill 2008) played an important role in these short, albeit powerful, communication episodes.

On the other hand, there is also an oxymoronic visual quality to Obama that is immediately apparent in his performances. In Mitchell's (2009: 127) words, "he is a figure of both intimacy and monumentality, accessibility and reserve, enormous energy and casual relaxation". Indeed, while the crowd lingers in adoration, Obama appears "dignified, regal, and detached" (Hill 2008: 83). This ability to manage the tension between intimacy and detachment is part of the basic repertoire of celebrity politicians. Here, as ever, style conveys meaning. In particular, this form of public subjectivity is found in political leaders and film stars alike, as they "must provide evidence of familiarity while providing evidence of exceptionality and hierarchical distance" (Marshall 1997: 226-227). In the case of politicians, this is crucial in terms of building trust and credibility. Richards (2004: 348) argues that, as party traditions become weaker, trust becomes increasingly personalised and thus political leaders must present themselves as *persons* "to be trusted for their intrinsic qualities".

Trust and credibility are not only important as a basis for effective communication through the media, they are also crucial in terms of enthusing campaign volunteers. This is not necessarily confined within a country's borders. Indeed, an American interviewee reported his son's pro-Obama canvassing activities from Scotland. As Super (2009: 155-180) shows, grassroots participants endorse the candidate to their social networks, serving as physical representations of him, and translating campaign abstractions into pragmatic realities. In the process of this "boundary work" they establish a bond that enables the co-production of "thick linkage between elites and citizens" (Super 2009: 155). This activity of endorsing, representing and translating can perhaps be extrapolated to the context of social media networking that has been so instrumental in building the Obama brand (see Harfoush 2009). Even in transatlantic context, my research participants identified a blend of traditional and new crosscutting networks of *influencers*, ranging from journalists, pundits, bloggers and media figures, to *Facebook* contacts, workmates, relatives, friends and so on. Obama's personal and symbolic qualities provided those trusted sources with an endless pool of discursive resources.

It is difficult to overstate the ability of the media to provide "vicarious forms of participation" (Dayan and Katz 1987: 174) that foster *para-social interaction* in the era of the 24-hour-news-cycle and the multimedia frenzy. This context of myriad news-consumption opportunities enhanced the "technology of attraction" of the Obama campaign (Cetina 2009: 135). Nevertheless, in the light of the synergy between his online/offline strategies, it seems more appropriate to talk about a *technology of participation*, where people were invited to be part of the communication process, rather than only at the receiving end of it. Indeed, citizen-generated contents and efficient participatory interfaces bolstered engagement (Dadas 2008; Pollard *et al.* 2009). However, increasing opportunities to participate does not guarantee that people will. Accordingly, despite the maturity and sophistication of this new generation of worldwide Internet users, 'technolust' solely (Everett 2009) cannot explain the Obama phenomenon.

In any case, the synergies between new and old media contributed to Obama's *hypervisibility*, as most people have multiple and overlapping uses of different media (Norris 2000: 112). My research suggests that, in Scotland too, Obama was inescapably heard: newscasts, newspapers, TV programmes, headlines in email accounts, magazines across the board, *Facebook* groups, *YouTube* clips, *Google* links, blogs, etc. According to Norris (2000: 162-179), this fragmentation of the media system poses a challenge to the postmodern campaign. Political messages can no longer be easily controlled and packaged; they get edited, transformed, repacked and reinterpreted. They are then reproduced in myriad formats and outlets, and therefore it is difficult to keep them constant and coherent. Except, I would suggest, when the message is a symbol that is able to function as a unifying code. A symbol is more flexible, resistant and versatile than a message. It can travel faster, inspire and accommodate multiple versions, and deliver golden ratings for those media who understand that a powerful symbol can attract the attention of followers, bystanders and detractors alike.

As many have pointed out, the success of the campaign was underpinned by a blend of elements: sophisticated political marketing (Madden 2008; Harfoush 2009; Johnson 2009), record-breaking viral advertising (Kaid 2009), synergetic use of the media (Plouffe 2009; Pollard *et al.* 2009; Everett 2009), strategic grassroots canvassing (Myers *et al.* 2009; Plouffe 2009), rhetorical excellence (Shaffer 2009), viral iconography (Fairey and Gross 2009; Wert 2009), record-breaking fundraising (Plouffe 2009), pro-Obama media biases (Wenger and MacManus 2009), the financial crisis game-changer (Gallup 2008d), Bush's unpopularity, the ambiguities of the McCain-Palin ticket (Gallup 2008b), and so on. However, the global scale of the Obama phenomenon also invites anthropological reflection.

Obama and the Suspension of Disbelief

Coleridge (1817) coined the term "suspension of disbelief" to reclaim the place of fantasy in literature. Political cynicism is widespread, as we become more knowledgeable and critical (Norris 2000). There have been no moments of positive political catharsis, on a global scale, for a decade. The warlords have held us hostage, and many forces have converged in helping us to forget how it feels being part of a collective cause with political impact. Obama's journey to power, a phenomenon infused with "a human interest and a semblance of truth" (Coleridge 1817: 312), can be seen as a process of suspension of disbelief that reclaimed the place of collective imagination in politics.

I found an interesting contrast in my research. Those participants aware of the campaign from its early stages were generally more sceptical about Obama's prospects that those who only watched the end of the election. Race was the factor that engaged most of the early observers. They doubted that Obama stood a chance and that "America was ready". Many feared that he was powerless against the "Clinton machine" and "conservative America". They deemed it "unlikely" or "unfeasible" for him to succeed. A former Scottish minister made the following synthesis: phase one, "interesting guy, no chance"; phase two, "he could give a hard time to Hilary"; phase three, "potent candidate, electable". Another Scottish participant, who works in the construction industry, put it in these terms: "I was interested in the race since very early because of him being an African American... I thought it would come to nothing... the odds were against him... then I watched him gaining momentum more and more... later I started to see him as a real statesman with a lot of charisma. I didn't get that impression when I first saw him on TV. That sort of grew on me the more I saw him". In contrast with this steady process of suspension of disbelief, later observers were less incredulous and probably more susceptible to the final bandwagon effect.

Some British participants pointed out similarities with Blair's ascendance to power. Many felt "uplifted" and "hopeful" back then, although much disappointment followed. Admittedly, they acknowledged their mistrust of potentially deceiving "charming characters" and reflected on the swaying nature of this kind of phenomenon. Nevertheless, they were willing to believe that something different was happening now. Or at least, they were willing to suspend disbelief. There is nothing *irrational* about this; it is part of our natural make, for as neuroscience shows, "the brain wants to believe" (Gazzaniga 2005: xviii).

Many will analyse what Obama *did* to us. However, I empathise with those who prefer to focus on what Obama *meant*, and why we participated in co-creating such meanings. From this perspective, the important lesson is not what the Obama phenomenon tells us about political campaigning, but what it says about those who were emotionally engaged with the process. Obama embodied a powerful symbol that spoke to audiences across borders, and that functioned as a unifying code for causes such as the peace, social justice, participatory democracy, and environmental movements. In transatlantic perspective, I would suggest that policy substance was epiphenomenal; what mattered were the symbol and the functions it fulfilled. Although Obama's charisma is often mentioned as the x-factor in the equation explaining his achievements, it is important to remember Weber's take on this: "Unlike common-sense definitions of charisma, which see charisma as an intrinsic personality trait, and then wonder about the elusiveness of this trait, Weber derived charisma from the followers, from *a group and its needs*" (Cetina 2009: 131; emphasis added).

Obama's two-year long campaign excelled at focussing on the importance of *process* (i.e. grassroots movement, record-breaking small donations; Plouffe 2009). Moreover, it managed to transform *process* into a message with global reach. Take for instance the speeches *Our moment is now*[15] and *Yes we can*[16]. Here, Obama was still fighting for the primaries, trying to convert 'the cynics'. He rallied the campaign troops by calling for the suspension of disbelief. It was still early days. In the next months such calls became implicit; they became a subtext for what was unfolding, for what happened along the primaries, for the steady self-vindicating process that became a self-fulfilling prophecy. Even his emblematic slogan remained a mantra for the suspension of disbelief: Yes we can.

Those two speeches also contained the archetypal appeal that would pervade in the campaign. It capitalised on two emotions, namely, anxiety and enthusiasm. These two emotions are the most common in the communication between political leaders and their followers (Marcus 2002: 130). As Marcus and MacKuen (1993) show, enthusiasm and anxiety play a central role in motivating political involvement. In the first place, exposure to enthusiasm appeals increases citizens' interest and participation, and influences candidate preference (Brader 2006: 182). Enthusiasm was crucial in the turnout increase that favoured Obama (Gallup 2008b), as well as in forging his grassroots movement and global appeal. In the second place, anxiety is triggered by threat or novelty, which stimulate attention and discourage reliance on routines. In this sense, emotion becomes a catalyst for political learning (Marcus and MacKuen 1993: 672). As Marcus (2002: 105) explains, this function is performed by our "surveillance system", which helps us to answer the demands of political elections: "if each party nominates a conventional candidate and takes its usual positions, then habitual cues will do just fine (...) But if something unusual arises (...) then anxiety may open up the opportunity (...) Anxiety does not produce any specific judgement, but it does change the way people go about deciding (...) When people are anxious (...) they are more willing to consider alternatives outside the range of the familiar and comfortable. They will need to be persuaded that the new alternatives are worth adopting, and in the end they may not be persuaded, but they are open to the possibility".

---

15 Iowa, 27.12.2007. http://www.youtube.com/watch?v=jPtg-gvgWhE
16 New Hampshire, 09.01.2008.
    http://www.youtube.com/watch?v=Fe751kMBwms&feature=related

It could be argued that, from the outset of Obama's campaign, anxiety played an important role in attracting attention and scrutiny. Let us take just one example in which Obama managed to turn potential weakness into strength. It was the case of his association with Reverend Wright, whose inflammatory video clips were intensely broadcasted, provoking considerable public anxiety.[17] Obama took to the stage knowing that the *world* was watching because race was the central theme. Such media attention gave to a crosscutting audience the opportunity to witness Obama's rhetorical ability to tap into his life story in order to spell out the complexity of racism. In the process, a thorny issue was turned into an emotionally compelling narrative of American history. It was the famous *A more perfect Union*[18] speech. As one of my interviewees – still a Clinton supporter back then – puts it: "that speech sealed the deal in my heart and mind". Although the notion that anxiety favours political engagement may not be popular, its importance was clear to Seneca: "You will cease to fear, if you cease to hope" (Nussbaum 2001: 159).

Emotional arousal is not only the product of unidirectional communication. Interactivity plays a central role, and Obama seemed at ease modulating his body language from serene happiness to ignited declamation, from didactic seriousness to pondered indignation, and even from gratitude and pride to profound consternation[19]. However, there is another interesting aspect to the interactive dimension of feelings, namely, emotions are contagious. In my research I found that, in line with literature on the subject, watching other people getting emotional often moves people. Many remember, for instance, the emotionally compelling images of individuals and crowds attending Obama's *Victory Speech*[20], or the *Presidential Inauguration*[21]. Obama's infectious appeal, coupled with the contagious nature of emotions, constituted a powerful communication process.

As neuroscience suggests, when we watch others doing or feeling something, "neurons become active in the same regions of our brains as if we were doing those things" (Westen 2007: 288). In order to understand the feelings of the others, we "simulate their state of mind by activating our own emotional brain systems in the way we imagine theirs are activated" (Gazzaniga 2005: 104). Here the role of facial displays is central. Most emotional expressions are

---

17 See the broader context in *By the people* (2010).
18 Philadelphia, 18.03.2008. http://www.youtube.com/watch?v=zrp-v2tHaDo
19 Some research participants recalled vividly a poignant speech made when Obama's grandmother, a central character in his life story, passed away right before Election Day. North Carolina, 03.11.2008. http://www.youtube.com/watch?v=O5Lp9gRJUms
20 Chicago, 05.11.2008. http://www.youtube.com/watch?v=jJfGx4G8tjo&feature=related
21 Washington, 20.012009. http://www.youtube.com/watch?v=VjnygQ02aW4

"wired into the brain and face, allowing people from widely disparate cultures to recognise them" (Westen 2007: 70). Indeed, some consider that facial displays are "genetically encoded communication mechanisms" (Marcus 1991: 223).

These reflections not only apply to interpersonal contact; after all, "media experiences are, for the viewer, experiences" (Hart 1999: 145). As Dayan and Katz (1987) argue, the media do not only broadcast events, they *perform* them.[22] They construct the event by developing "an aesthetics of compensation" (p.175) that offers to the viewers "vicarious forms of participation" to compensate for their deprivation of direct engagement (p.174). In this sense, the Obama global phenomenon did not only unfold *through* the media, but *in* the media. As Nash (2008: 172) argues, popular media is the place where an imagined cosmopolitan community can be achieved. However, this does not imply that it was followed with distance. From small towns in Kenya to the US consulate party in Edinburgh; from a guesthouse in Malawi to a spontaneous congregation at the hall of a Scottish university; but mostly, from the comfort of their homes... many of my research participants attended memorable events of the Obama phenomenon, congregated around the ceremonial fire of the TV set.

Elections are made of symbols, myths and rituals (Edelman 1996: 104; 1967: 18). The horse-race electoral media coverage (Gastil 2008) keeps the narrative coherent and fluid as it progresses towards the climax. In this process, elections can release feelings of collective togetherness and belonging. They constitute "mediatized rituals" capable of forming "plural solidarities" (Cottle 2006: 411). Durkheim analysed the power of ritual in creating "collective effervescence": "a feeling of oneness or unity with something bigger than oneself, and a shared sense of community and identification with (...) collective symbols" (Westen 2007: 383). On a similar basis, Cottle (2006: 415) defines mediatised rituals as "those exceptional and performative media phenomena that serve to sustain and/or mobilize collective sentiments and solidarities on the basis of symbolization and a subjunctive orientation to what should or ought to be". Indeed, as Dayan and Katz (1992) argue, media events can create an "upsurge of fellow feeling" and offer moments of "mechanical solidarity" (p.196) in which technology seems to overcome social divisions (p.210).

Election night was a moment of such collective effervescence. A moment eagerly anticipated by the record-breaking audiences that never waned throughout the entire 2-year process (Wenger and MacManus 2009). All of my research participants agreed on the emotionality and/or "historical" significance of such

---

[22] At some point during the *Victory Speech*, the camera shows civil rights movement icon Jesse Jackson crying. The broadcaster did not rely only on Obama's words to contextualise the event. That kind of image was intended to encapsulate decades of struggle. In the words of a research participant, "it showed how far they had come".

"momentous occasion". For some of them it was so intense that "it went beyond politics and into an affirmation of humanity". That night Obama culminated his cathartic function as a political symbol. In anthropological terms, we entered a "moment in and out of time" (Turner 1969: 96), a *liminal phase* where social structure was overtaken by *communitas*. "Liminal phases" are characterised by performances that momentarily strip statutes, roles and structures (Turner 1987: 107)."Liminality" sets the "scene and time for the emergence of a society's deepest values in the form of sacred dramas" (p.102). *Communitas*, in Buber's (1947: 37) words, is "the being no longer side by side but with one another of a multitude of persons". In such occasions, as Dayan and Katz (1987: 194) have documented, the reality of everyday life is suspended for the ceremonial ritual: "Attendance takes place in small groups congregated around the television set, concentrating on the symbolic centre, keenly aware that myriad of other groups are doing likewise in similar manner, and at the same time." In its climax, it resembles ceremonial practices reported by anthropology: "Rituals *separated* (…) a group from everyday life, *placed them in a limbo* that was not any place they were in before and not yet any place they would be in, then *returned* them, changed in some way, to mundane life." (Turner 1987: 25; emphasis in original).

A research participant claimed that, after such an intense process, UK broadcasters are not "keeping us up to speed" with the aftermath of the Obama phenomenon. Indeed, the ubiquitous opportunity for vicarious participation vanished after the climax. This seems to be the nature of these unique processes. "Having performed the end of the event, having ritually declared it over, having organized the fall of the curtain, television assumed a new task. After stressing what was worth remembering, it organized forgetting" (Dayan and Katz 1987: 193).

In my view, for those of us who engaged emotionally with the Obama phenomenon, it became a medium of self-expression. We felt compelled by the possibility of projecting into politics not only frustrations but also hope, a longing for humanistic leadership in an inhuman system, and a desire to feel part of something momentous. Undoubtedly, Obama succeeded in galvanising a collective emotional 'us'. By means of communication, he elicited powerful emotions and turned himself into the receptacle for the mobilising energy projected by them. In this process, a symbolic bond was established. That bond fostered emotional attachment and invited suspension of disbelief.

Suspending disbelief in politics may ignite, as the Obama phenomenon shows, processes welcomed by many. Regardless of its aftermath, the arrival of Obama to the White House embodies incommensurable changes. He will remain an enduring symbol well after the dust settles over magazines and textbook covers. Have I succumbed to my own extreme process of suspension of disbelief? Perhaps I am still too young to understand the wisdom of previous transitional moments: sometimes some things change, so that everything else can remain the same.

References

American stories, American solutions. 2008. [TV Infomercial] FOX; NBC, CBS, 29.10.2008.
Brader, Ted (2006). *Campaigning for Hearts and Minds. How Emotional Appeals in Political Ads Work*. Chicago and London: The University of Chicago Press.
Buber, Martin (1947). *Between Man and Man*. London and New York: Routledge. 2002.
By the People: The Election of Barack Obama. 2010. [DVD] Alicia Sams & Amy Rice. USA: SONY PICTURES.
Cetina, Karin Knorr (2009). What is a pipe? Obama and the sociological imagination. *Theory, Culture & Society* 26(5), 129 – 140.
Cockcroft, Robert and Susan M. Cockcroft (1992). *Persuading people. An introduction to rhetoric*. London: Macmillan.
Conley, Donovan S. (2008). Virtuoso. *Communication and Critical/Cultural Studies* 5(3), 307 - 311.
Coleridge, Samuel Taylor (1817). *Biographia Literaria*. Edited by James Engell and W. Jackson Bate. New Jersey: Princeton University Press. 1985.
Cottle, Simon (2006). Mediatized rituals: beyond manufacturing consent. *Media, Culture & Society* 28(3), 411 – 432.
Damasio, Antonio (1994). *Descartes' Error: Emotion, Reason and the Human Brain*. London: Vintage. 2006.
Darsey, James (2009). Barack Obama and America's Journey. *Southern Communication Journal* 74(1), 88 – 103.
Dadas, Caroline E. (2008). Inventing the Election: Civic Participation and Presidential Candidates' Websites. *Computers and Composition* 25, 416 – 431.
Darwin, Charles (1890). *The expression of the emotions in man and animals*. London: John Murray. The Complete Work of Charles Darwin Online: http://darwinonline.org.uk/EditorialIntroductions/Freeman_TheExpressionofthe Emotions.html
Dayan, Daniel and Elihu Katz (1987). Performing media events. In: James Curran, Anthony Smith and Pauline Wingate (ed.), *Impacts & Influences. Essays on media power in the twentieth century*. London and New York: Methuen
Dayan, Daniel and Elihu Katz (1992) *Media Events: The Live Broadcasting of History*. Cambridge, MA: Harvard University Press.
Edelman, Murray (1967). *The Symbolic Uses of Politics*. Chicago: University of Illinois Press. 1985
Edelman, Murray, (1972). *Politics as Symbolic Action. Mass Arousal and Quiescence*. Chicago: Markham Publishing Company.
Edelman, Murray (1988). *Constructing the Political Spectacle*. Chicago: The University of Chicago Press.
Everett, Anna (2009). The Afrogeek-in-Chief: Obama and our New Media Ecology. *Journal of Visual Culture* 8(2), 193 – 196.
Fairey, Shepard and Jennifer Gross (Eds.) (2009). *Art for Obama: Designing Manifest Hope and the Campaign for Change*. New York: Abrams Image
Gallup (2008a). *Bush Job Approval at 25%, His Lowest Yet*. October 6th. Online: http://www.gallup.com/poll/110806/Bushs-Approval-Rating-Drops-New-Low-27.aspx [accessed 15.01.2010]

Gallup (2008b). *Gallup's Quick Read on the Election*. October 22nd. Online: http://www.gallup.com/poll/109759/Gallups-Quick-Read-Election.aspx [accessed 15.01.2010]

Gallup (2008c). *World Citizens Prefer Obama to McCain by More Than 3-to-1*. October 28th. Online: http://www.gallup.com/poll/111253/World-Citizens-Prefer-Obama-McCain-More-Than-3to1.aspx [accessed 15.01.2010]

Gallup (2008d). *Obama's Road to the White House: A Gallup Review*. November 5th. Online: http://www.gallup.com/poll/111742/Obamas-Road-White-House-Gallup-Review.aspx [accessed 15.01.2010]

Gallup (2008e). *Obama and Bush: A contrast in popularity*. November 10th. Online: http://www.gallup.com/poll/111838/Obama-Bush-Contrast-Popula rity.aspx [accessed 15.01.2010]

Gallup (2009). *Americans Expect History to Judge Bush Worse Than Nixon*. January 16th. Online: http://www.gallup.com/poll/113806/Americans-Expect-History-Judge-Bush-Worse-Than-Nixon.aspx [accessed 15.01.2010]

Gastil, John (2008). *Political communication and deliberation*. Thousand Oaks/London: Sage.

Gazzaniga, Michael S. (2005). *The Ethical Brain*. New York/Washington, D.C.: Dana Press.

Glaser, Jack and Peter Salovey (1998). Affect in electoral politics. *Personality and Social Psychology Review* 2(3), 156 – 172.

God bless Barack Obama? 2010. [TV documentary]. Mark Rossiter and Paul Yule. BBC2, 25.01.2010.

Goodwin, Jeff, James M. Jasper and Francesca Polleta (eds.) (2001). *Passionate Politics: Emotions and Social Movements*. Chicago: University of Chicago Press.

Harfoush, Rahaf (2009). *Yes We Did! An Inside Look at How Social Media Built the Obama Brand*. Berkeley, CA: New Riders.

Harris (2009a). *Obama by Far the Most Popular Political Leader in Europe and U.S.* Financial Times / Harris Poll. April 7th. Online: http://www. harrisinterative.net/news/FTHarrisPoll.asp [accessed 10.01.2010]

Harris (2009b). *Obama Most Popular Leader in Europe*. Financial Times/ Harris Poll. December 4th. Online: http://www.harrisinterative.net/news/FT HarrisPoll.asp [accessed 10.01.2010]

Hart, Roderick P. (1999). *Seducing America. How Television Charms the Modern Voter*. Thousand Oaks/London: Sage Publications.

Hill, Dan (2008). *Face Time. How the 2008 Presidential Race Reveals the Importance of Being on Emotion in Politics, Business, and in Life*. Edina, MN: Beaver's Pond Press.

Horton, Donald and Richard Wohl (1956) Mass Communication and Para-social Interaction. *Psychiatry* 19, 215 – 229.

Hume, David (1739). *A Treatise of Human Nature*. Kitchener, Ont.: Batoche. 1999.

Ivie, Robert L. and Oscar Giner (2009). American Exceptionalism in a Democratic Idiom: Transacting the Mythos of Change in the 2008 Presidential Campaign. *Communication Studies* 60(4), 359 – 375.

Johnson, Denis W. (2009). *Campaigning for President 2008. Strategy and Tactics, New Voices and New Techniques*. New York: Routledge.

Kaid, Lynda Lee (2009) Changing and Staying the Same: Communication in Campaign 2008. *Journalism Studies* 10(3), 417 – 423.

Kinder, Donald R. (2003). Communication and Politics in the Age of Information. In: David Sears, Leonie Huddy and Robert Jervis (ed.), *Oxford Handbook of Political Psychology*. New York: Oxford University Press.

Koziak, Barbara (2000). *Retrieving Political Emotion: Thumos, Aristotle, and Gender*. University Park: The Pennsylvania State University Press.

Lakoff, George and Mark Johnson (1999). *Philosophy in the flesh. The embodied mind and its challenge to Western thought*. New York: Basic Books.

Lakoff, George (2009). *The Political Mind. A cognitive scientist's guide to your brain and its politics*. London: Penguin.
Ledoux, Joseph (1996). *The Emotional Brain. The Mysterious Underpinnings of Emotional Life*. New York: Touchstone. 1998.
Lewicki, Pawel (1986). *Nonconscious social information processing*. Orlando, FL: Academic Press.
Madden, Mike (2008). Barack Obama's super marketing machine. Online: http:/www.salon.com/news/feature/2008/07/16/obama_data [accessed 20.04.10]
Marcus, George E. (1991). Emotions and politics: hot cognitions and the rediscovery of passion. *Social Science Information* 30(2), 195 – 232.
Marcus, George E. (2000). Emotions in politics. *Annual Review of Political Science* 3, 221 – 250.
Marcus, George E. (2002). *The sentimental citizen*. University Park: The Pennsylvania State University Press.
Marcus, George E. and Michael B. MacKuen (1993). Anxiety, enthusiasm, and the vote: The emotional underpinnings of learning and involvement during presidential campaigns. *American Political Science Review* 87(3), 672 – 685.
Marcus, George E., Russell W. Newman and Michael MacKuen (2000). *Affective Intelligence and Political Judgement*. Chicago: University of Chicago Press.
Marshall, P. David (1997). *Celebrity and Power. Fame in contemporary culture*. Minneapolis/London: University of Minnesota Press.
McLuhan, Marshall (1967). *Understanding media: the extensions of man*. London: Sphere Books.
Mitchell, W. J. Thomas (2009). Obama as Icon. *Journal of Visual Culture* 8(2), 125 – 129.
Mutz, Diana (2007). Political Psychology and Choice. In: Russell J. Dalton and Hans-Dieter Klingemann (ed.), *The Oxford Handbook of Political Behaviour*. New York: Oxford University Press. 2009.
Myers, Julian, Dominic Willsdon and Mary Elizabeth Yarbrough (2009). What Happened in Vegas. *Journal of Visual Culture* 8(2), 161 – 165.
Nash, Kate (2008) Global citizenship as show business: the cultural politics of Make Poverty History. *Media, Culture & Society* 30(2), 167 – 181.
Norris, Pippa (2000). *A Virtuous Circle. Political Communications in Postindustrial Societies*. Cambridge: Cambridge University Press.
Nussbaum, Martha C. (2001). *Upheavals of Thought. The Intelligence of Emotions*. Cambridge: Cambridge University Press. 2008.
Obama, Barack (1995). *Dreams from my father*. Edinburgh: Canongate Books. 2007.
Obama, Barack (2006). *The Audacity of Hope. Thoughts on Reclaiming the American Dream*. Edinburgh: Canongate Books. 2007.
Parameswaran, Radhika (2009). Facing Barack Hussein Obama. Race Globalization, and Transnational America. *Journal of Communication Inquiry* 33(3), 195 – 205.
Penman, Robyn (2000). *Reconstructing communicating: looking to a future*. Mahwah, NJ: Laurence Erlbaum.
Pew Research Center (2009). *Confidence in Obama Lifts U.S. Image in the World. The Pew Global Attitudes Project*. July 23rd. Online: http://pewglobal. org/reports/display.php?ReportID=264 [accessed 10.01.2010]
Piston, Spencer (2010). How Explicit Racial Prejudice Hurt Obama in the 2008 Election. *Political Behavior*, Published Online: http://www.springerlink. com/content/n71v6700m7282k76
Plouffe, David (2009). *The Audacity to Win: The inside Story and Lessons of Barack Obama's Historic Victory*. New York: Viking.
Pollard, Timothy D., James W. Chesebro and David Paul Studinski (2009). The Role of the Internet in Presidential Campaigns. *Communication Studies* 60(5), 574 – 588.
Richards, Barry (2004). The emotional deficit in political communication. *Political Communication* 21, 339 – 352.
Shaffer, Alan Kennedy (2009). *The Obama Revolution*. California: Phoenix Books.

Sokolon, Marlene K. (2006). *Political Emotions: Aristotle and the Symphony of Reason and Emotion*. De Kalb: Northern Illinois University Press.

Sullivan, Denis G. and Roger D. Masters (1988). Happy warriors: Leaders' facial displays, viewers' emotions, and political support. *American Journal of Political Science* 32, 345 – 368.

Super, Elizabeth (2009). *Everyday Party Politics: Local volunteers and professional organizers in grassroots campaigns*. The University of Edinburgh. Doctoral Thesis (unpublished).

Teven, Jason J. (2008). An Examination of Perceived Credibility of the 2008 Presidential Candidates: Relationships with Believability, Likeability, and Deceptiveness. *Human Communication* 11(4), 391 – 408.

Transatlantic Trends (2008). Europeans Back Obama but Not Necessarily His Policies. Spiegel Online, October 9th. Online: http://www.spiegel.de/international/world/0,1518,577449,00.html [accessed 10.01.2010]

Transatlantic Trends (2009). Survey Shows Huge Leap in European Support for US Foreign Policy. Spiegel Online, September 9th. Online: http://www.spiegel.de/international/world/0,1518,647954,00.html [accessed 10.01.2010]

Turner, Victor (1969). *The Ritual Process. Structure and Anti-Structure*. New York: Aldine de Gruyter. 1995.

Turner, Victor (1987). *The Anthropology of Performance*. New York: PAJ Publications.

Wenger, Debora Halpern and Susan A. MacManus (2009). Watching History: TV Coverage of the 2008 Campaign. *Journalism Studies* 10(3), 427 – 435.

Wert, Hall Elliot (2009). *Hope: A Collection of Obama Posters and Prints*. Minneapolis: Zenith Press.

Westen, Drew (2007). *The Political Brain. The role of emotion in deciding the fate of the nation*. New York: Public Affairs. 2008.

Yankelovich, Daniel (1999). *The magic of dialogue. Transforming conflict into cooperation*. New York: Simon & Schuster.

Yanow, Dvora (1996). *How Does a Policy Mean? Interpreting Policy and Organizational Actions*. Washington: Georgetown University Press.

Yanow, Dvora (2000). *Conducting Interpretive Policy Analysis*. Sage University Papers Series on Qualitative Research Methods, Vol. 47. Thousand Oaks, CA: Sage.

Persuading the Intractable

Charisma and Emotional Engagement within the Dialogue of Politics

Alan Sandry

Obama and 'Change'

President Barack Obama has probably had more column inches written about him than any other American politician since Richard Nixon. Why is that? Is it down to the public's increasing thirst for political knowledge and debate, or is it because there was a perceptible upsurge in interest within the United States, and worldwide, in the presidential race and its outcome? Or, in a less conventional sense, is it perhaps due to the fact that the media were merely reflecting our notions of identarian politics? Taking the third of these options as the most feasible explanation, it can be seen that we have, in Obama, a politician seeking high office who is identifiably different from the established norm of Harvard-educated lawyer, decorated soldier or Texan businessman. However, the realisation that he is indeed a Harvard-educated lawyer surely places him within, rather than outside of, the standard model. Notwithstanding this, the true reason why Obama draws so much public attention, and press scrutiny, is that his pigmentation differs from the vast majority of those who hunger for the Washington limelight. In a country that is still gradually, and at times painfully, evolving in regard to how it comes to terms with its segregationist past, Obama appears both comforting and triumphant at the same time; an avatar of Mandela and Martin Luther King, as his staunchest supporters might put it. Obama – with a radical guise but without, to date, the genuinely radical policies – certainly manages to tick all of the correct 'identarian' boxes. If he continues to play on this perception, which he has done very successfully so far, then he should not only retain presidential power until 2016 but he may also maintain the apparent air of 'change' that he presents as his hallmark; albeit that his eventual legacy may portray him as being far more conservative than radical when it comes to substantial transformation.

Despite the fact that Obama emphasised the concept of 'change', his approach towards modification was that it should be externally driven reform, conceivably 'bottom up', rather than any form of amendment that was centrally and hierarchically manufactured; one that would be 'top down', in effect. In his speech to the Democratic National Convention, in August 2008, Obama stated that "Change doesn't come *from* Washington. Change comes *to* Washington" (Obama 2008). Whilst sounding as if major restructuring of the political system and political practice was just around the corner – should Obama succeed in his quest to be elected – this statement is essentially superficial. It undoubtedly has an emotional rhetorical ring about it, as any talk of change gives the impression that that change will be 'change for the better', but, when put under exegesis, Obama is stating the obvious. A new president, and new presidential policies, by their very nature 'arrive' at Washington; Washington being the metonymy for political administration in the United States. So Obama, rather than instigating 'change', or leading a fresh political movement that was going to reshuffle the American body politic, was merely replicating the path, and sometimes the rhetorical and emotional style, of previous White House candidates and incumbents. Therefore, 'change', in its purest sense, it was unlikely to be, and it evidently has not proven to be so up to now!

Consequently rather than seeing the 44th President of the USA as a debonair revolutionary, or even as a radical reformer, for whom 'change' is a byword, we may now, and in the future, be considering Obama's tenure within the political world as one in which the politics of image, identity and emotional rhetoric were foremost. This will undoubtedly be seen by future historians as a missed opportunity, as the actual political deeds and commands that many progressives had hoped to have seen enacted will almost certainly fail to materialise.

Political Communicators

Nevertheless, in terms of communication alone, Obama displays a lucid rhetorical style that clearly captivated his listeners (and potential voters) in the run up to the poll of November 2008. According to Jack Shafer, even a battle-hardened journalist like the *New Yorker's* George Packer commented on how, just after the end of an Obama intervention, he was unable to recall precisely what Obama had said. But he noted that, "the speech dissolved into pure feeling, which stayed with me for days" (www.slate.com). The element of 'pure feeling' in Packer's remark is the key to unlocking that heightened sense of emotional engagement that can be conveyed through charismatic oratory, the like of which, admittedly, the current US President exudes. However, despite its indisputable charm and efficacy, Obama's charismatic oratory and leadership style is very far removed from the techniques demonstrated by iconic characters such as Che Guevara or Mohandas Gandhi, or even, in a mutually communicative and operational sense, by a group like the Communards. Individuals, like Guevara and Gandhi, led people, parties and movements to victory 'against all odds'. In so doing, their rhetoric, and use of emotion as a movement builder and political tool, was far more incisive and teleological than anything that Obama has so far conjured up.

Furthermore, whilst Guevara, Gandhi, and the Communards struggled with limited resources, and in the face of hostile hegemonic power structures, Obama's hundreds of millions of dollars election campaign, and his multi-millionaire backers, are less inclined to be stirred by the rhetoric of emotional politics, and talk of fundamental alterations to society, and more disposed towards rationally considered commercial and economic policies. For them, and for many with the professional political and economic classes, tawdry displays of excess take precedent over simplistic, but principled, human emotions and down-to-earth political desires and objectives. Admittedly, the 'identarian' politics surrounding Obama clearly succeeded in appealing to many American voters – both black and white – but the emotionally charged issue of striving for racial, and social, equality was never likely to have become the primary sociocultural and political motivator within a state system whose every move and internal focus is based on the prolonging, and advancement, of personal liberty through capitalist economics. Hence, financial considerations ultimately assume priority over the emotionally-loaded politics of ethnicity, race and culture.

Emotions, Identity and Politics

Even so, the politics of emotion – visibly expressed when it comes to matters of racial, ethnic and cultural inequality – cannot be completely ignored or sidelined; even by unrepentant capitalists, for whom economism is everything. To exemplify this, two seemingly unattached events have taken place in the USA in the past twelve months; namely the fact that Barack Obama has been elected and the realisation that Michael Jackson has unexpectedly passed away. Obama's victory and Jackson's death were both generally received throughout the world with a mixture of respect and joy, most evident in the former case, and shock and upset, primarily in the latter case; though both also witnessed some particularly exuberant scenes of celebration and mourning that could almost be labelled 'emotional hedonism'. In the face of these two developments, and especially given the 'identarian' nature of the two people involved, it could be contended, perhaps somewhat quixotically, that black and white humans appear to be more closely bound, through their communal emotions, than ever before. Whilst this may or may not turn out to be a superficial impression, what really needs to be explored, to a greater degree, is whether everything is quite so sanguine under the surface.

To take one salient case in point, at the 2009 European Elections a motley assortment of racists, xenophobes and Holocaust deniers – admittedly few in number but still exceedingly vociferous – were elected to represent countries ranging from France to Poland. In the United Kingdom, racism, in its overt and covert guises, has been given a fresh impetus with the election of two members of the British National Party (BNP) to the European Parliament. Running parallel to this, both in the UK and in other European states, is the casual daily verbal, and sometimes physical, attacks on refugees and people claiming asylum. Sadly, but not unexpectedly, for the perpetrators of these attacks, these two groups – refugees and asylum seekers – are associated with 'non-white' people; hence, to the distorted ideological eyes of the bigot, they are perceived as being 'not one of us'.

In all of this, whether there is a predisposition towards racist or anti-racist rhetoric, or racist or anti-racist symbols, gestures or body language, emotional engagement plays a significant part. The aforementioned Nelson Mandela, to produce a notable example, only had to walk a few metres and smile at the camera and people would pay attention and listen to his utterances. The passion he conveyed with his measured walk and his enlightening smile created an emotional engagement, which Mandela then methodically built upon through his rhetoric of social and political inclusion, and his forgiveness for those implicated in Apartheid's extremities.

An earlier example of this emotional engagement and 'presence' was visible in the actions of the Suffragettes, who at first glance appeared to be stereotypically meek and moderate women, but who, through their actions such as chaining themselves to railings whilst burly male law enforcers physically manhandled them, not only shattered their seemingly meek personas but also succeeded in their securing the moral high ground when it came to the struggle to attain female emancipation.

In another example, though one that is admittedly far more contentious and open to interpretation, Bobby Sands, an IRA prisoner at the height of the conflict in the north of Ireland, courted emotional engagement through his use of the hunger striker as a political weapon. The fact that Sands eventually died because of his steadfast belief in the protest only adds to raising the emotional aspect of the political scenario that was being played out at the time; an emotional intensity that was heightened even further by the fact that, whilst on hunger strike, Sands had been elected as a Member of the UK Parliament for the Fermanagh and South Tyrone constituency. These three examples span the spectrum of political activity and each one, in their own specific way, has created love / hate 'binary opposites'. Whilst, in all three, the emotional attachment of love and admiration comes through in different manifestations, the hate element is observable by the fact that Mandela was detested by white supremacists within South Africa and beyond, the Suffragettes were despised by misogynistic conservatives, and Sands was reviled by Ulster Loyalists and supporters of the English Crown.

Therefore, using these examples, and the emotional driver of 'hate', in particular, how can anybody persuade people who disagree with them to listen to, and accept, an alternative viewpoint or argument? Furthermore, what language, iconography, propaganda, coercion, and so forth can one use to achieve this conversion? Similarly, in a world in which identity and group affiliation is still deemed important, do we, whilst undertaking this art of persuasion, or coercive dialogue, attempt to create an 'individual' or a 'national consciousness?' in order to achieve some kind of level playing field from which discourse may emerge? On this point it is worth bearing in mind Frantz Fanon's warning that the latter form of consciousness, the 'national' one, "instead of being the all-embracing crystallization of the innermost hopes of the whole people. (...) will be (...) only an empty shell, a crude and fragile travesty of what it might have been" (Fanon 1961: 119).

If this is hard enough to traverse and to reconcile, there is also, evidently, a 'wall of intransigence' – wherein the public will not listen to politicians and, concurrently, politicians ignore *vox populi* – that has recently been exacerbated by the disingenuous approach, and occasional financially or carnally inappropriate behaviour, of some politicians. These misdemeanours have only added to the overall mood of civic disenchantment in the face of the global economic downturn. Thus, the two sides – public and politicians – are far apart; be it ideologically (a candid, often right-of-centre, populism versus a liberal democratic intelligentsia), in terms of everyday social and political narratives (the uncomplicated workplace conversations compared to the often convoluted discourse within government circles and academia) or rhetorically (the 'I dislike x or y' stance against the 'let us try to negotiate' approach). The question that requires addressing, therefore, is 'can emotion bring these contrasting forces closer together?' Or is there simply too much negativity, mistrust and apathy all around? If that is the case, then how can those detrimental attitudes be challenged and overcome?

Discourse and Emotional Engagement

Engagement at all levels would appear to be the key to a healthy political environment and discourse. Within that engagement, the outpouring of emotions will invariably act as a channel for conveying heartfelt or dramatic viewpoints. However, these cannot be undertaking as solo gestures, in any solipsistic sense, as "emotion must (...) be dialogically constituted: that is, it shapes and is shaped by our interactions with others (Crossley 1996: 46). Hence, we cannot be uncommunicative if we want to induce any reaction, be it from others or indeed from ourselves, as we seek reflection on our own thoughts and opinions. Thus, we have to co-operate with those around us, and we need to enthusiastically engage in social and political dialogue. Furthermore, we cannot simply be the receivers of information, be it via one-to-one conversations, or through reading or listening to the multifarious media outlets. We need, in effect, to collaborate in a 'right to reply' scenario; a conversation with other human beings, in the most undiluted and constructive ways possible. That conversation must, from time to time, be of an unambiguously political nature, and within that conversation expressions of emotion must be allowed – and indeed encouraged – to come to the fore.

Once this earnest process has begun, breakthroughs, and fresh levels of understanding, will invariably manifest themselves. Also, through the use of emotional political rhetoric, our values and ideological standpoints – which may have lain dormant – can be reified. One example of this, within the Welsh social and political glossary, is the use of the Welsh language term *hiraeth* to express 'longing' or 'desire', in a cultural, geographical, linguistic, emotional, and political sense. The term can also be used as a substitute for expressions of moderate forms of nationalism or patriotism, but not as a proxy for jingoism. *Hiraeth* therefore has a 'Communitarian' ring about it in that it identifies the individual within a communal setting; a setting in which that individual may find shelter but also one in which they may unearth emotional political engagement and ideological nourishment. *Hiraeth* also embraces collective historical memory, as well as the notion of integration, that becomes feasible due to the levelling out of the social stratifications under an umbrella of solidarity.

Arguably, alas, rather than promoting free political engagement through emotional and rhetorical practice, *hiraeth* could also be portrayed as evidence of the assimilation of 'thought-practices'; given the assumption that assimilation normally absorbs all of the peripheral voices into the ascendant communal ideology. The 'one voice, one movement' approach that *hiraeth*, and indeed Communitarianism, could fall into may hint at a totalitarian *modus operandi*. But, in reality, this method of incorporation is nothing out of the ordinary as it is already reflected in populist and democratic political movements worldwide. Nevertheless, it is important to remember that *hiraeth* is not a political movement, theory or ideology. It is an expression, an outpouring of emotion that binds people together; socially, culturally, linguistically but most of all emotionally. Thus, the tears flowing at the sound of a national anthem, or the sight of schoolchildren in traditional custom on their national day, would induce this emotion: this *hiraeth*.

Emotion and Political Concepts

Whilst it is fairly easy to understand how *hiraeth* and emotion may work on a cultural or linguistic level, how could this transfer to the world of politics and political rhetoric? For Michael Freeden, ideologies, and all forms of political rhetoric, have to contain a degree of emotion to communicate with the masses; that, for the most part, remain untrained in political philosophy or ideological analysis. Freeden talks of encouraging a "free mix of reason and emotion" (Freeden 1998: 30) but goes on to add that this combination is "intolerable to many philosophers, who do not regard emotive reasons for an argument as good ones" (Freeden 1998: 30). This 'open to all' political forum, nonetheless, is vital to the process of interaction, and people should not be dissuaded by any supposedly cerebral objections by political philosophers or elitists. Indeed, political discourse, and emotive engagement within that discourse, is a learning curve; with gaining knowledge of the dictionary of political terms being part of that educational process. Moreover, the use and misuse of concepts and terminology are a constant within politics, and therefore the shape of the dictionary, and its explanations, is forever shifting. For instance, whilst 'radical' suggests something exciting and 'conservative' hints at something staid or tedious, the reality is that political expressions are in constant flux, and are therefore never fully understood by either the user or the receiver. As Maurice Merleau-Ponty noted, "There is no longer a single word in our political vocabulary that has not been used to refer to the most different, even opposed, real situations: consider freedom, socialism, democracy, reconstruction, renaissance, union rights (Merleau-Ponty 2004: 80). To Merleau-Ponty's list we could comfortably add everyday terms such as 'politics', 'power', 'trust', and 'emotion'. What is the meaning of these terms? It may be fair to proffer that meanings vary for each and every individual and we each use, and abuse, them in a somewhat cavalier manner. Therefore, it is worth noting Arthur Schopenhauer's aphorism, which informs us that "as soon as our thinking has found words it ceases to be sincere or at bottom serious. When it begins to exist for others it ceases to live in us..." (Schopenhauer 1970: 201). If words cannot really reflect our opinions then possibly displays of emotion, and emotional engagement, are the only reliable ways to get across our political thoughts and perspectives. Emotion, given this scenario, may therefore turn out to be a far more significant player in politics, and specifically political rhetoric, that we had previously imagined.

So within in a democracy, the masses – who the politicians must convince in order to achieve a winning margin at election time – are vital components within this process. They therefore have to be inveigled into participating in a degree of political engagement, in a dialectic sense; despite their apparent lack of comprehension, previously alluded to, when it comes to the lexicon of political philosophy! R. G. Collingwood was one philosopher to expound upon this theme and direction. Relating our social discourse to our role within enlightened societies, Collingwood contended that "being civilized means so far as possible living dialectically, i.e. in the constant endeavour to convert occasions of non-agreement into occasions of agreement" (Collingwood 1992: 39.15). The desire for consensus in 'civilized' societies – societies that do not deny an unfettered avenue for the political dialectic, and polities that then develop these avenues by vigorously promoting a public dialogue – is what produces reasoned, rational debate.

The Political Masses and Empathy

But do the politicians and political leaders take the masses seriously? It is often the case that the 'non-political' or 'apolitical' men and women on the street, as they are somewhat disparagingly viewed as being, are regarded as nothing more than either ignoramuses or, at best, *bildungphilisters*, when it comes to matters of a political nature (Taleb 2008: 307). Taking the latter of these two invectives, *bildungphilisters*, it could be claimed that the political classes condescendingly regard some of the general public as possessors of a shallow knowledge of culture and politics; though those people may assume themselves to be fairly well versed in the subject-matter of politics. In the minds of the 'professional' political rhetoricians, therefore, the question that is asked is, "Is it possible to register, and reconcile, the ideas of our political strata with these people; these ignoramuses or *bildungphilisters*?" But what dogmatic thinking such as this merely succeeds in doing is exposing some of the conceptual and tactical weaknesses on the part of the political classes themselves; the very people who are making these value-judgements about others.

Instead of looking to further open up social and political fissures, it may be more useful for all of those who are seeking to reinforce political engagement between the different sectors to recall Richard Rorty's *Contingency, irony and solidarity*, with its observations on how emotion channelled through everyday life and popular culture enables us to embrace 'difficult' political and philosophical issues. Empathising with other human beings, especially those in crisis, is, as Rorty reminded us, "a task not for theory but for genres such as ethnography, the journalist's report, the comic book, the docudrama, and, especially, the novel" (Rorty 1997: xvi). Accordingly, while the masses may not understand all of the details of a government report, or they may not be able to cite quotes from famous politicians or theorists, they can, through emotional engagement with literature, music, arts, photography, and so forth, begin to comprehend, and form views about, detailed political situations and positions.

But how far is it realistic to calculate political rhetoric, discourse and dialectical progress using the 'empathy model? It is certainly true that the masses, through communal emotion, can engender empathy for major political concerns; the phenomenon of Live Aid, and its attempts to foster a sense of global repulsion at the images of hunger and malnutrition in the developing world, is a memorable example. Thus, it can be empirically proven that empathetic action, in terms of tears, embraces and charitable giving, genuinely outweighs the abstract concept of 'egalitarianism'. Obviously, the tears, embraces and donations are simply a practical manifestation of that concept. What they allow, however, is instant gratification and emotional attachment, whereas an exploration of egalitarianism, in its theoretical sense, would leave most people high and dry, and would not necessarily invoke a compassionate response. In any case, politicians and policy-makers should appreciate this. This is because an emotional politician – be that emotion real or staged – talking about humanitarian concerns, whilst comforting a baby who is suffering through AIDS, ticks all of the boxes – on the 'emotional empathy' model – whereas a theoretician sombrely discussing 'poverty', 'social justice' or 'inequality' tends to lose their audience within minutes.

Emotion and Transference

This still leaves us with the question of emotion and how that can transfer itself to actual political decision-making. It could be that emotionally-charged political rhetoric is essentially a veil which masks unfeigned political discussion and tangible political processes. Emotion could therefore be a smokescreen that allows an outpouring of grief – seemingly genuine – to supposedly reflect our views on a certain issue: I cry when I see the brutal imagery of mankind's actions on display at the Red Cross Headquarters at Geneva but how much, in all honesty, do I regularly donate to the Red Cross, or actively campaign for the eradication of poverty and conflict? An analogy could be made here to Isaiah Berlin's thoughts on difficult moral issues. As Berlin observed, "we escape moral dilemmas by denying their reality" (Berlin 1969: 80). Hence, it could be argued that emotion, in all its guises but certainly when used to address or, more likely, to deflect a political encounter, enables the user to avoid finding concrete solutions to the matters under consideration. As a result, we witness the avoidance of real life decision-making situations. The use of emotion, through actions or rhetoric, means that it becomes easier to hand over responsibility for political decision-making to someone else; usually the person or persons seen to be 'in power', or seeking power.

In a similar vein, though we may attempt to understand the methods and processes of political communication, and the art of persuasion, can people actually be converted from one point of view to another through the words or actions of another human? An existentialist take on this could declare that we are free to act in an independent manner, above and beyond determination by outside forces. Thus, we can only follow the path set out for us by the likes of Obama, Berlusconi or Sarkozy, or even Mao or Hitler for that matter, if we so choose. No amount of persuasion, coercion, or propaganda can negate our 'free determination'. That may prove to be fairly straightforward in sympathetic liberal democracies, for example, but it clearly presents greater difficulties when that choice of 'individual radical freedom' is articulated under totalitarian conditions. Nevertheless, whatever the consequences, and they may well be severe within anti-liberal autocratic societies, the principle of freedom of choice, and freedom from manipulation, remains. Ultimately, therefore, questions remain as to whether, if persuasion and coercion is the method chosen by politicians to 'buy our support', we are being true to ourselves if we fall for their charms? Conversely, are politicians acting ethically when they attempt to manipulate our thoughts and practices?

'Real' and 'False' Rhetoric and Actions

But in what environments – real, false, theoretical, political – are we operating? This has to be pondered as multi-faceted approaches to political rhetoric, and political actions and interactions clearly exist. Furthermore, is emotion a theoretically or practically honest stage within that process or interaction? In June

1997 Subcomandante Insurgente Marcos of the Zapatista Army of National Liberation, Mexico spoke of, "a world where many worlds fit, where all worlds fit..." (Vodovnik 2004: 277) A somewhat idealistic vision this may well be, but the words of the revolutionary, Subcomandante Marcos, are not that far removed from most mainstream political leaders who talk in terms of nurturing, and ruling over, multicultural, pluralistic societies; social and political inclusion being easier, in theory, to manage, and subsequently manipulate, than forms of exclusion. The difference between someone like the UK Prime Minister, Gordon Brown and Subcomandante Marcos is that whilst Brown emotes about Africa and debt relief – "we cannot excuse our inaction" (Richards 2004: 18) – then Marcos is engendering 'change' through insurgent political activity, cultivated from his own ideational development through his speeches and writings. Though cases in favour of both men, as purveyors of political rhetoric and emotion, could be made, when it comes to the 'soiled hands' approach to face-to-face political engagement, Brown remains primarily a theoretician – albeit an immensely powerful one – whilst Marcos has achieved praxis? 'Change' through emotional political activity, from a theoretical grounding, is the goal here. It comes down, eventually, to actions stemming from emotions. All of the ornate political rhetoric imaginable, crafted as it invariably is for dissemination through media outlets, cannot generate an atmosphere from which people will actually want 'to do' something rather than just hearing about what 'might' be done. Emotion, nevertheless, remains important. This is because it stirs the conscience and can lead to enduring political activity. In his poem *Stone Walls*, the Buddhist scholar and political dissident, Thich Tue Si, notes how "A lonely man stares at a flickering lamp; all history's words cannot describe these heartfelt emotions". (cited in Popescu and Seymour-Jones 2007: 111). Whilst Richard Rorty may have supported the sentiments behind Si's verse, emotion remains something of a conundrum when placed within the field of political activity. Does it enhance or does it obfuscate political discourse?

What Next for the 'Now' Agenda?

With Barack Obama now ensconced in office, large sections of the American public, delighted with the result, will have basked in the sunshine of a glorious victory and achievement. But within a short space of time they may well have been asking, just like Estragon in *Waiting for Godot*, "What do we do now, now that we are happy?" (Beckett 1965: 60) The problem for Obama, and for all other politicians who incite emotion through diatribe, and promise radical transformations of society, is that they themselves are victims of perpetual change, and are more often than not unable to adjust to that perpetuality. As Hegel noted, in his writings on the *Dialectic and Human Experience*, the idea of 'now', beloved by politicians and orators of every age, has in reality "already ceased to be when it is pointed out" (Weiss 1974: 59). The political orator, therefore, is mistaken if they feel that they can draw admiration on the basis of a 'now' agenda, and the synchronous emotional ties that some people believe exist.

So how do you ultimately persuade the intractable? Is it through mega campaigns, glossy television commercials or newspaper advertisements? Or is it a more subtle task, wherein gentle rhetoric overcomes the tub-thumping variety? As Gandhi remarked, when trying to appeal to people's better natures, "truth alone will endure; all the rest will be swept away before the tide of time" (Kalekar 2008: 153). Sadly, in this age of ever increasing political spin and media distortion, the question that each and every one of us has to face up to is "what is truth?" In the final reckoning, the use of emotion in our political rhetoric may be simply camouflaging that search.

References

Beckett, Samuel (1956). *Waiting for Godot*. London: Faber and Faber. 1965.
Berlin, Isaiah (1969). *Four Essays on Liberty*. Oxford: Oxford University Press.
Collingwood, Robin George (1942). *The New Leviathan*. Oxford: Oxford University Press. 1992.
Crossley, Nick (1996). *Intersubjectivity: The Fabric of Social Becoming*. London: Sage.
Fanon, Frantz (1961). *The Wretched of the Earth*. Harmondsworth: Penguin. 1973.
Freeden, Michael (1996). *Ideologies and Political Theory*. Oxford: Oxford University Press. 1998.
Kalekar, Archarya Kakasaheb (2008). *Thus Spoke Gandhi*. New Delhi: Gandhi Samadhi.
Merleau-Ponty, Maurice (1948). *The World of Perception*. London: Routledge. 2004.
Obama, Barack (2008). *Democratic National Convention speech August 28th 2008*, Mile High Stadium, Denver, Colorado.
Popescu, Lucy and Carole Seymour-Jones (eds.). (2007). *Another Sky*. London: Profile Books.
Richards, Steve (2004). Interview with Gordon Brown. *The Independent*. 20.12.2004.
Rorty, Richard (1989). *Contingency, irony and solidarity*. Cambridge: Cambridge University Press. 1997.
Shafer, Jack (2008). *How Obama Does That Thing He Does*. www.slate.com/id/2184480.
Schopenhauer, Arthur (1970). *Essays and Aphorisms*. London: Penguin.
Taleb, Nassini Nicholas (2008). *The Black Swan: The Impact of the Highly Improbable*. London: Penguin.
Vodovnik, Ziga (2004). *Ya Basta! Ten Years of the Zapatista Uprising: Writings of Subcomandante Insurgente Marcos*. Edinburgh: AK Press.
Weiss, Frederick (ed.). (1974). *Hegel: The Essential Writings*. London: Harper & Row.

"I'm Still Standing for Hope and Glory!"

Reflections on the Obama Phenomenon and the Politics of Resentment vs the Politics of Cosmopolitanism

Åsa Wettergren

The Obama phenomenon hit even remote corners of the world – like the small Swedish town where I caught myself for the first time ever watching an American president's inaugural speech – as a historically significant event.[1] It was remarkable not only because the new American president was black but also because he radiated the ambition to perform wise leadership. The question remains however: What is so hopeful about Obama? In this article I will explore this question through the concepts of resentment and cosmopolitanism in politics from an emotionsociological perspective. My discussion will draw on the Obama phenomenon (not his person) as it appears from this perspective and I will be using excerpts from Obama's Cairo speech as "clarifying depictions"(Goffman 1986). The Cairo speech is illustrative because it presents Obama's vision of global unity. I will start with a discussion of the role of emotions in politics and a critique of its displacement in the Western political tradition, to be followed by the politics of resentment and the politics of cosmopolitanism.

Emotional Politics

The last decades of research within neuroscience has shown that cognition and emotion are deeply intertwined and that one cannot exist without the other. Together they make up our consciousness and sense of self (Damasio 1999). Sociological research has found that emotions are as much products of social interaction and exchange as they are psychological phenomena inherent to the biographic memory of the person (as in patterns of emotional behaviour established in primary socialization). When I talk about emotion here I mean the

---

[1] The title of this chapter is borrowed from the refrain of Swedish singer Måns Zelmerlöv's song "Hope and Glory". Coincidentally, shortly after Obama entered on his duties as a president Zelmerlöv candidated to the Eurovision Song Contest 2009 with this song.

culturally and socially elaborated products of learnt emotional behaviour. No doubt, the capacity to feel is universal, yet there is a large variety of emotional regimes within and between cultures (Harré & Parrott 1996; Reddy 2001). Important for our understanding of emotion is therefore to study the feeling and expression rules (Hochschild 1983) that shape them, how they are used in social exchange and how we work on our emotions to meet others' expectations (Kemper 1990). Thus, although within neuroscience and neuropsychiatry it is often assumed that feelings are difficult to control, from a sociological perspective control is all there is. Not always conscious control however but control as incorporated adaptation to norms of conduct that we perform without reflection. Moreover, we are not alone in controlling our emotions. Our fellow interactants will be performing the emotion work for us if we fail (Goffman 1967; Goffman 1959). Shame functions as the self-reflecting social emotion that ensures conformity with the dominant emotional regime at any given occasion (*Ibid*, see also Elias 1982; Scheff 1990). Seen from this perspective the social spheres, institutions, roles and processes that we have been used to think of as non-emotional – i.e. bureaucracy, politics, public life in general – are not unemotional but governed by specific emotional regimes.

Emotions in politics are traditionally seen as exerting an irrational influence, as in extremism, populism, corruption, nepotism. Demertzis (2006) points out that even analysis of populism tends to avoid its emotional components, instead using concepts such as 'discontent', 'alienation' and 'antipathy' that connect to a dominant rational choice discourse where 'interests', 'preferences' and 'attitudes' serve to obscure the involvement of feelings in political action. Mouffe (2003) argues that in the post-Soviet 'politics of the Third Way' era there is an increasing tendency to postulate consensus-oriented political debate guided by absolute moral principles (of equality and justice). Antagonism and conflict according to Mouffe constitute ineradicable dimensions of politics, the suppression of which in deliberative democracy alienates people from politics, while leaving the door wide open to extremism. In a similar manner, Berezin argues that the separation of the public and private spheres and the "denial of emotion embodied in democracy's refusal to incorporate the sacred into its institutions" inherent to the liberal democratic model leads to its self-destruction (Berezin 2001: 88).

The failure of deliberative democracy to include passions and real alternatives is partly connected to its denial of corporeality as relevant to politics, and partly, as argued by Berezin and Mouffe, to the fundamental assumption of Western individualism that underestimates the importance of collective identities. In short, the agent of liberal democracy is a monad in a social vacuum. Given this point of departure, bodies, feelings and lived experiences brought into the political arena by carriers of alternative discourses are bound to be ridiculed or ignored. In addition, key signifiers such as democracy, freedom, justice, equality, human rights, and so on, have been fixed with a liberal democratic meaning, displacing truly alternative definitions. The issue of this asymmetry (and consequently exclusion of real political alternatives) is also raised by Cohen and Arato (1992) and Medearis (2005) who argue that it forces social movements to rely on extraordinary actions including the use of coercion[2] (Flam & Wettergren in press). Coercion increases the costs of the established routines and forces a response that eventually may lead to expansion of the democratic system. According to this radical democratic view, social movements and other non-parliamentary political actors are therefore vital to the learning-processes of democratic states by contribution to the continuous questioning and adjustment of its key concepts and principles (Cohen and Arato 1992).

As a consequence, the liberal democratic model also precludes the inclusion of non-Western political discourses and practices, i.e. those that can not be understood in terms of its own logic. Actions and experiences that are not framed in terms of autonomy and intentionality; collective action which can not be analysed in terms of representation; and political action which does not target the political institutions of the nation state, evade understanding and consequently inclusion (McDonald 2006).

The bottom line of this critique against deliberative democracy is that emotions (and bodies) matter in politics. *Not* primarily as a way to manipulate audiences but because emotion is an inextricable part of decision making. Emotions constitute and bind identifications and it is through our sensual orientation that we seek to reproduce the positive feelings of belonging and recognition that are essential for each one of us (Collins 2004; Honneth 2003). While patterns of emotional behaviour and thereby a propensity to favour some types of action choices rather than others may be established in early childhood we also keep transforming and learning about our own and others' emotions throughout life.

It follows that our emotional dispositions are bound to affect others, and more or less so depending on the reach of our actions. Leadership as a status position in which power (in terms of influence) is invested makes the connection between emotional dispositions and social/organizational change particularly clear. A leader must know his/her feelings, where they come from and how to use them or transform them. In other words, emotional maturity is a leader's responsibility and the sine qua non of exemplary leadership qua moral authority.

World leadership that aims beyond the limitations of the Western political imaginary must also be ready to learn from alternative discourses. Obama's

---

2   Such as infringement on property rights and civil disobedience.

Cairo speech contains numerous examples where he, although appealing to the Western deliberative understanding of democracy and human rights, also reaches out beyond it. For a start, he roots these Western values, Western science and Western civilization and progress in a Muslim tradition:

> It was Islam - at places like Al-Azhar University - that carried the light of learning through so many centuries, paving the way for Europe's Renaissance and Enlightenment. It was innovation in Muslim communities that developed the order of algebra; our magnetic compass and tools of navigation; our mastery of pens and printing; our understanding of how disease spreads and how it can be healed. (...) And throughout history, Islam has demonstrated through words and deeds the possibilities of religious tolerance and racial equality.

Obama here expands the horizon of Western self-understanding to an extent that rarely leaves the confinements of academic intellectual discourse. He also attempts to re-enchant politics by bringing myth into a narrative that focuses on the shared past of Christianity, Judaism and Islam:

> Too many tears have flowed. Too much blood has been shed. All of us have a responsibility to work for the day (...) when the Holy Land of three great faiths is the place of peace that God intended it to be; when Jerusalem is a secure and lasting home for Jews and Christians and Muslims, and a place for all of the children of Abraham to mingle peacefully together (...) as in the story of Isra, when Moses, Jesus, and Mohammed - peace be upon them - joined in prayer.

It may be objected that references to religion is hardly new to American politics. However, the sorts of references we have become familiar with are references to Christianity and sometimes to a sacred bond between American Christianity and Judaism. Obama instead asserts the bond between Islam, Christianity and Judaism, their origins and holy places and perhaps most importantly he invokes *shared suffering*, tears and blood. In a similar manner, to strengthen the narrative of shared suffering as a basis for unity, Obama invokes the memory and feeling of cultural trauma, one for each of the collective identities he addresses. He mentions "colonialism that denied rights and opportunities to many Muslims"; the "enormous trauma" of 9/11; and the Holocaust. Addressing the Palestinians he talks about "the daily humiliations - large and small - that come with occupation" and he mentions the African Americans' suffering "the lash of the whip as slaves and the humiliation of segregation."

The speech finally contains several examples where Obama evokes the feeling of his own embodied and personal experience. He talks about his childhood in Indonesia and most notably he offers his own embodied experience as a symbol of the possibility of reconciliation:

> I am a Christian, but my father came from a Kenyan family that includes generations of Muslims. As a boy, I spent several years in Indonesia and heard the call of the azaan at the break of dawn and the fall of dusk.

Obama invites the listener to hear and feel with the speaker and to sympathize with and trust his personal experience. He thereby invokes his own inescapable corporeality conveyed through his skin colour and his personal, multi-ethnic and cosmopolitan biography, through which he embodies the possibility of unity and the hope of a better world accessible not only to him but to everyone: *"My personal story is not so unique."*

The Politics of Resentment

Resentment is of interest here because it is an emotion that pertains to the potentially antagonistic relationship between collective identities; classes, status groups, ethnic groups, and so on. Resentment is defined by Meltzer and Musolf (2002: 241) as "a feeling of displeasure induced by being insulted, offended, or deprived" and Kemper (2001) classifies resentment as a response to the withdrawal of status from the subject. But as argued by Barbalet (1998) a personal experience and a direct relationship between perpetrator and victim is not necessary. Resentment is likely to appear where a person believes that a social injury, unjust or unfair treatment affects the group s/he identifies with. It may be a reaction to discrimination, stereotyping, racism, sexism and other kinds of verbal and/or physical abuse. Direct relationships and personal experience is however likely to intensify the feeling of resentment and to blend it with a desire for revenge (Barbalet 1998). As most potentially disruptive emotions, resentment is regarded with suspicion in late Western capitalism (Stearns 1994) but Barbalet points out that it is a key emotion behind many social movements' claim for their rights, dignity and recognition. "The active recognition that a person has been subject to intrusion, interference, and offense is precisely in their acting with moral anger, and in circumscribed manifestations of vengefulness and resentment" (Barbalet 198: 139).

Three points should be made here: First, the collective feeling of resentment does not automatically lead to mobilization and rights claims. 19th century philosophers like Nietzsche and Scheler considered resentment similar to the feeling of inhibited vengeance but as it was curtailed by power relationships and social subordination it settled for imaginary revenge instead (Meltzer and Musolf 2002). Demertzis (2006) develops this idea to suggest that resentment provides the fertile ground for political mobilization. Seen from this perspective, collectively felt resentment is 'powerless' as long as the social circumstances and power relations are generally seen as unchangeable, as *the way things are* (Barrington Moore 1978; Smith 2001). Changing political opportunities and/or the emotion work inherent in movement mobilization contribute to the transformation of resentment into moral anger and vengeance in terms of rights claims. Depending on the circumstances, such as the framing of movement actors, their media and communication strategies and so on, the expression of resentment in collective action may be met by sympathy by the public or resentfully rejected (Benski 2005).

The second point to be made is that not all movements are 'good' movements, i.e. engaged in the expansion of democratic values and resentment in movement is not always expressed in circumscribed ways. Connected to this is the third point: Contrary to the classic theories of resentment, Barbalet (1998) argues that resentment is *not* exclusively a feeling of the subordinate classes: "Resentment is not necessarily an emotion of subordination...rather it is an emotional apprehension of departure from acceptable, desirable, proper, and rightful outcomes and procedures." (*Op. cit.*: 138). Such an understanding of resentment opens up the concept for the obvious possibility that it may also be felt by privileged groups against those that challenge their norms and values. Resentment in this case is felt when the sacred symbols of a taken for granted order of things, and the status and privileges tied to this order, are threatened (Collins 2004). When resentment is unleashed in extremist movements, righteous anger and circumcised vengeance may instead be expressed as hatred and malevolence (Ahmed 2004).

The present conservative and extreme right wing movement against Obama's suggested reform of the United States health care system is a case in point. Paul Harris reports in the Observer[3] from a recent protest rally in California that Obama was depicted as Hitler and protesters carried posters reading "Death to Obama, Michelle, and two stupid kids". Referring to the general political climate, Harris continues:

> "Obama has been labelled as a threat to democracy and an anti-white racist by senior presenters on the TV Channel Fox News. Republicans (...) have called him a socialist who plans 'death panels' for the elderly. Rumours have circulated that Obama was not born in America and that he plans to ban firearms."

Resentment among white racist groups pertains to their continuous loss of privileges and status over blacks (and other 'strangers') during the 20th century (Ahmed 2004), crowned as it were by the election of a black president of the US. To these groups Obama is bound to symbolize a threat for the very same reason that

---

3   Sunday 16 August 2009

he symbolizes a promise and a hope of change to many structurally discriminated and oppressed groups who demand his recognition. Obama's task then, in order to reach the unity that is one of his trademarks, is to manage resentment.

In recalling suffering and trauma, the Cairo speech recognizes conflicts and expresses sympathy for the resentment felt by all the groups addressed. But it is circumcised resentment that is recognized, while "violent extremism in all of its forms" is fiercely rejected. The only true way to win full and equal rights is "peaceful and determined insistence" upon key democratic ideals. Importantly the speech contains promises to end also the violence committed by USA such as forms of torture, unlawful imprisonment, declarations of war without international support, and so on. There is both surreptitious and straightforward critique of previous American foreign policies; "[V]iolence is a dead end. (...) That is not how moral authority is claimed; that is how it is surrendered."

The Obama phenomenon is attached to the fact that Obama, like Simmel's stranger appears to be close and remote at the same time (Simmel 1971). His body and personal experiences bear witness of his involvement and offer a piece of something familiar to everyone, but also assert that he is committed to no one (except his formally patriotic duties as a president). It is this mix between distance and involvement that renders trustworthiness to his performance of leadership with 'moral authority'. But it is also what makes his Cosmopolitan stance position alien and suspicious to resentful local identities. We will now proceed to look at the cosmopolitan stance as a way to manage resentment.

The Politics of Cosmopolitanism

Cosmopolitanism generally denotes the idea of a global human community, based on moral, political, cultural, economic, or romantic principles and doctrines (Kleingeld 1999). Kleingeld shows how cosmopolitan ideas flourished during the Enlightenment but in the 19th century ceded way to nationalism. In the late 20th century, cosmopolitanism seemed to be resurging again, obviously entangled with the discourse and practice of modern globalization (Delanty 2000). While the definitions of the concept of cosmopolitan as well as the concept of local – which are traditionally taken to be opposites – are historically contingent, in today's debate cosmopolitan generally means global while the local is understood as the nation-state. The argument is that following globalization the nation state, national identities and national citizenship are becoming increasingly obsolete (Beck 2002; Delanty 2000; Nussbaum 1994). According to Beck (2002) while we already see a process of "cosmopolitization" from within driven by globalization, politics and social sciences are encumbered with "methodological nationalism" that is concerned with "future implications of a nationally shared past, an imagined past" (Beck 2002: 27). He contrasts this with the suggested paradigm shift into a "methodological cosmopolitanism" that engages with "the present implications of a globally shared future, an imagined future" (*Ibid*). The urgent imperative behind such a shift is based on the concern with universal risk and crisis that are the hallmarks of our time.

Cosmopolitanism as a stance and an identity per se is perhaps less tied to the context of globalization as it denotes a general orientation towards diversity and engagement with the Other (Hannerz 1990; Kleingeld 1999; Nowicka and Rovisco 2009). The cosmopolitan perspective in this sense is driven not only by a deeply felt attachment to the idea of equality and human community but, as argued by Hannerz, inherent to this disposition is also the celebration of tolerance and diversity and "a willingness to engage with the Other" as *different*: "It is an intellectual and aesthetic stance of openness towards divergent cultural experiences, a *search for contrasts rather than uniformity*" (emphasis added, Hannerz 1990: 239). The cosmopolitan perspective is thus premised on the existence of local cultures. Acquiring cultural codes and experiencing the world from an alien perspective contributes to the cosmopolitan's self-image and self-reflection. "Through cosmopolitan education, we learn more about ourselves" Nussbaum (1994: 4) says, and Hannerz argues that the cosmopolitan perspective contains a streak of narcissism; "the self is constructed in the space where cultures mirror one another" (Hannerz 1990: 240). Cosmopolitanism here implies physical mobility and temporary immersion into alien cultures that enable involvement without commitment. Free will, choice, the possibility to exit, appears to be key to its sustained open-mindedness and cultural curiosity.[4]

Globalization does however bring about alternative ways to cultivate a cosmopolitan stance. Whether we travel or not, we may reach the world through the media and the internet, and the world reaches us through international networks, international migration and the local expressions of a variety of cultures. Beck (2002: 28) talks about "banal cosmopolitanism" as an everyday experience of integrating the global into the local as a consequence of, for instance, youth cultures, the mass media, the Internet, food and so on. While the cosmopolitan perspective described above may seem inherently elitist, available to groups of people who move around by free will (e.g. diplomats, development aid workers)

---

4   As noted by Hannerz (1990) tourism and business travel do not necessarily bring a cosmopolitan perspective. Tourists tend to extend their local space by travelling (what Hannerz calls "home plus"), leaving their sense of local identities and its norms and values untouched but adding e.g. sunshine, nature, exoticism.The same, Hannerz argues, can be said about many migrant workers and refugees living in exile who travel by force and seek home plus work or home plus security.

banal cosmopolitanism seems to pertain more to a daily experience of globalization *potentially* available to all. It is not self-evident however that banal cosmopolitanism leads to cosmopolitanism as a stance. As a moral commitment and a conscious stance cosmopolitanism seems to require the level of self-reflexivity that comes with experience and/or education (Nussbaum 1994).

Globalization transforms the meaning of local. The inherent tension between local-cosmopolitan I suggest is thus not primarily tied to geographical spaces but rather to emotional regimes, abstract collective identifications and the production of solidarity. In this sense, "a local stance", as opposed to the cosmopolitan stance, means identification with a single collective above all others which produces "high conformity within the group, along with strong distrust of outsiders and alien symbols" (Collins 1990: 38). Carriers of a local perspective may well travel but do not necessarily deviate from their preferred group or learn something form the cultures they visit (Hannerz 1990). Of course, the cosmopolitan may also be oriented towards his/her own (cosmopolitan) community but in so far as cosmopolitanism stands for an orientation towards diversity and engagement with the Other the group is characterized by "relatively weak feelings of conformity to group symbols, emotional coolness of tone, and general trust in a wide range of interactions" (Collins 1990: 38). Thus cosmopolitanism neither *necessarily* implies physical mobility nor excludes attachment to particular places or communities. "Localism" is premised upon exclusive attachments to a group but this neither *necessarily* requires attachment to specific places nor excludes global networks.

In terms of emotional regimes, as already indicated, the cosmopolitan perspective tends to embrace ambivalence and non-conformity. The resentful reactions to violation of its sacred symbols (such as tolerance, open-mindedness etc) are cautious and tempered: "[P]ersons in these situations respond by amusement to minor ritual violations by others, and with embarrassment, contempt, and a desire to exclude perpetrators of more serious violations" (Collins 1990: 39). It does not mean that the cosmopolitan has no passion but that s/he manages and accepts tensions, conflicts, and ambivalences as part of his/her acquired multicultural competencies (Nussbaum 1994). According to Beck a central defining characteristic of a cosmopolitan outlook is "dialogic imagination" including: "The clash of cultures within one's life; globally shared collective futures (…); a sense of global responsibility (…); a commitment to dialogue against violence; and a commitment to (…) stimulate the self-reflexivity of divergent entangled cosmopolitan modernities" (Beck 2002: 35-36). Although also the cosmopolitan experiences resentment when his/her values/sacred symbols are violated, s/he will not respond with hatred and potential violent attacks, as will the 'localist' whose group attachment is exclusive and whose identity relies upon the rejection of ambivalence as well as of the Other.

We have already seen in the previous section examples of how the Cairo speech invokes Obama's personal cosmopolitan identity. The Cairo speech also clearly advocates a drive towards a cosmopolitan stance in the political and moral sense. It departs from the assumption of shared humanity and the principles "of justice and progress; tolerance and the dignity of all human beings." Obama declares that he is "firm in [his] belief that the interests we share as human beings are far more powerful than the forces that drive us apart." He refers to the globalization of risk – financial crisis, epidemics, nuclear weapons, violent extremism and genocide – as the imperative for partnership, and to a shared world and shared responsibility as the moral basis for unity. While remaining vague as to the concrete meanings of progress, partnership and unity, the speech does not deny or displace conflict but refers to the cosmopolitan future oriented imaginary:

> [H]uman history has often been a record of nations and tribes subjugating one another to serve their own interests. Yet in this new age, such attitudes are self-defeating. Given our interdependence, any world order that elevates one nation or group of people over another will inevitably fail. So whatever we think of the past, we must not be prisoners of it. Our problems must be dealt with through partnership; progress must be shared.

The suggested Other of the cosmopolitan unity is characterized by "the forces that drive us apart" and "violent extremism": "We will...relentlessly confront violent extremists who pose a grave threat to our security." Obama here narrows down the meaning of 'we' to denote 'the American people' referring to his "duty as President." However, he returns to the fact that terrorism is a globally shared threat "irreconcilable with the rights of human beings" that requires a unified effort to combat. He mentions partnership "of forty-six countries" against terrorism and particularly addresses the Muslim community: "Islam is not part of the problem in combating violent extremism - it is an important part of promoting peace."

Based on Obama's personal cosmopolitan stance the Cairo speech summons collective identities while skilfully manoeuvring their specific cultural codes. It appears that he also distances himself from the local stance of American patriotism. Thus balancing between the local/national and the cosmopolitan stance Obama may sacrifice local trust in his leadership in favour of building up trust in his cosmopolitan leadership. The balance act is a dimension of the management of resentment discussed above because Obama is vulnerable both to domestic resentful rumours that he is not *really* American and to international suspicions that he is executing the same old American politics in a cosmopolitan disguise.

Goffman (1959) mentions the importance of trustworthiness in the drama of social life; we must take care to perform the presentation of self as an *authentic* self. Successful performance here builds as much on cognitive coherence as on a convincing display of emotion. In the Cairo speech, Obama makes frequent reference to speaking the truth: "we must say openly the things we hold in our hearts", "I will try to (...) speak the truth as best I can, humbled by the task before us...". Summoning "the truth" can be understood as a way to strengthen Obama's authentic performance by distancing his politics from the previous American administration and by addressing those who suspect him for keeping hidden agendas or hidden resentment/qua revenge. Only if we believe that Obama can both be the American president and a cosmopolitan leader, both share the experiences of the Other and embrace Western democratic ideals and principles, only then can he escape the dilemma of the cosmopolitan stranger who is welcome everywhere but nowhere at home and whose mistakes are always taken to reveal his/her 'true' identity.

Conclusion

What is so hopeful about Obama? Obama instigates hope because almost everybody seems to get a share of the cake. Intellectuals and cosmopolitans recognize themselves in the way he masters emotions and promotes unity through the cosmopolitan imaginary, oppressed and structurally discriminated groups recognize his rise to power as their triumph and he offers to Muslims restored dignity and a place in history (albeit with Western frames). Obama brings this 'global' appeal to bear in a politics that is also hopeful: He merges his privately lived experience with the sacred of religious myths and with Western democratic ideas. He skilfully manages resentment by balancing the cosmopolitan and the local stances and he uses the cosmopolitan imaginary to show that recognition of conflict does not prevent dialogue and mutual respect. His performance of moral authority and wise leadership in this respect appears *authentic* insofar as he applies the principles of human and democratic rights to himself and to his own country by dismantling the politics of resentment and revenge that was the hall-mark of his predecessor. Finally, Obama may instigate hope worldwide because the particular historical context of his entering on his duties renders mythological dimensions to the event. It bears resemblance with the heroic saga of the return of the King at the time when the power of the dark Wizard seemed to have grown invincible. We all know that in order to succeed the King has to do the impossible, which is in many ways what Obama seems to be doing. It is an open-ended saga but so far Obama is indeed "still standing for hope and glory".[5]

References

Ahmed, Sara (2004). *The Cultural Politics of Emotion*. Edinburgh: Edinburgh University Press.
Barbalet, J.M. (1998). *Emotion, Social Theory, and Social Structure - A Macrosociological Approach*. Cambridge: Cambridge University Press.
Barrington Moore, Jr (1978). *Injustice: The Social Bases of Obedience and Revolt*. London: MacMillan Press Ltd.
Beck, Ulrich (2002). The Cosmopolitan Society and Its Enemies, *Theory, Culture and Society* 19 (1-2), 17 – 44.
Benski, Tova (2005). Breaching Events and the Emotional Reactions of the Public: Women in Black in Israel. In: H. Flam and D. King (eds.), *Social Movements and Emotions*. London: Routledge.
Berezin, Mabel (2001). Emotions and Political Identity: Mobilizing Affection for the Polity. In: J. Goodwin, J. M. Jasper and F. Polletta (eds.), *Passionate Politics - Emotions and Social Movements*. Chicago: University of Chicago Press.
Cohen, Jean L. and Andrew Arato (1992). *Civil Society and Political Theory*. Cambridge, Massachusetts: MIT Press.
Collins, Randall (1990). Stratification, Emotional Energy, and the Transient Emotions. In: T. D. Kemper (ed.), *Research Agendas in the Sociology of Emotions*. New York: State University of New York.
Collins, Randall (2004). *Interaction Ritual Chains*. Princeton: Princeton University Press.
Damasio, Antonio R (1999). *The feeling of what happens: body and emotion in the making of consciousness*. New York: Harcourt Brace.
Delanty, Gerard (2000). *Citizenship in a global age: society, culture, politics*. Open University Press.
Demertzis, Nicolas (2006). Emotions and Populism. In: S. Clarke, P. Hoggett and S. Thompson (eds.), *Power Passion and Politics*, London: Palgrave.
Elias, Norbert (1982). *The civilizing process*. New York: Pantheon Books.
Flam, Helena, and Åsa Wettergren (in press) Rule Breaking and Civil Disobedience. In: K. Fahlenbrach, M. Klimke and J. Scharloth (eds.), *Protest Cultures: A Companion*. Oxford: Berghahn Books.
Goffman, Irving (1967). *Interaction Ritual. Essays on Face-to-Face Behavior*. New York: Pantheon Books.
Goffman, Irving (1959). *The Presentation of Self in Everyday Life*. New York: Doubleday.
Goffman, Irving (1986). *Frame analysis: an essay on the organization of experience*. Northeastern Univ. Press Edition: Northeastern Univ. Press.
Hannerz, Ulf (1990). Cosmopolitans and Locals in World Culture. *Theory, Culture and Society* 7, 237 – 251.
Harré, Rom and W. Gerrod Parrott (eds.) (1996) *The emotions: social, cultural and biological dimensions*. London: SAGE.
Hochschild, Arlie Russell (1983). *The Managed Heart - Commercialization of Human Feeling*. Los Angeles: University of California Press.

---

5   This text was written in the summer of 2009.

Honneth, Axel (2003). *Erkännande: praktisk-filosofiska studier*. Daidalos.
Kemper, Theodore (2001). A Structural Approach to Social Movement Emotions. In: J. Goodwin, J. M. Jasper and F. Polletta (eds.), *Passionate Politics - Emotions and Social Movements*. Chicago: University of Chicago Press.
Kemper, Theodore (1990). *Research agendas in the sociology of emotions*. New York: State University of New York Press
Kleingeld, Pauline (1999). Six Varieties of Cosmopolitanism in Late Eighteenth- Century Germany. *Journal of the History of Ideas* 60(3), 505 — 524.
McDonald, Kevin (2006). *Global Movements*. Oxford: Blackwell.
Medearis, John (2005). Social Movements and Deliberative Democratic Theory. *British Journal of Political Science* 35(1), 53 — 75.
Meltzer, Bernard N. and Gil Richard Musolf (2002) Resentment and Ressentiment. *Sociological Inquiry* 72(2), 240 — 55.
Mouffe, Chantal (2003). Politik och passioner - demokratins hörnstenar, *Ord och Bild* (3), 85 — 93.
Nowicka, Magdalena and Maria Rovisco (2009). Making Sense of Cosmopolitanism. In: M. Nowicka and M. Rovisco (eds.), *Cosmopolitanism in Practice*. Farnham: Ashgate.
Nussbaum, Martha (1994). Patriotism and Cosmopolitanism. *The Boston Review* XIX(5).
Reddy, William (2001). *The Navigation of Feeling - A Framework for the History of Emotions*. Cambridge: Cambridge University Press.
Scheff, Thomas J. (1990). *Microsociology. Discourse, Emotion, and Social Structure*. Chicago: The University of Chicago Press.
Simmel, Georg (1971). *On individuality and social forms: selected writings*. Chicago: University of Chicago Press.
Smith, Dennis (2001). Organizations and Humiliation: Looking beyond Elias. *Organization* 8(3), 537 — 560.
Stearns, Peter N. (1994). *American Cool - Constructing a Twentieth-Century Emotional Style, Vol. 3*. New York: New York University Press.

Desiring Politics

Wanting More in the Age of Obama

Deborah Gould

This essay[1] considers political hope – its variegated sources, contours, and effects; its different temporal horizons; the sorts of practices, affects, capacities, and socialities it can spur; and what the presence, or absence, of different types of political hope illuminates about people's relation to 'the political', broadly defined. I focus primarily on hope in the 'age of Obama', in a moment, 18 months after Barack Obama's election to the presidency of the United States, when some argue that "Hope Is Fading Fast."[2]

Hope understandably gets a bad rap these days. Indeed, for those seeking progressive or radical social change, it is hard not to be cynical about hope and Obama. U.S. war-making in Afghanistan and Iraq not only continues, it has spread to Pakistan; the "war on terror" seems endless. At home, Obama continues the Bush/Cheney attacks on civil liberties. He also frequently sides with corporate America, including the financial services and oil industries. And meanwhile inhabitants of the U.S. witness growing economic inequality and increasing numbers of people who are below the federal poverty line, homeless, and going hungry; a jobless economic 'recovery' – figures from early 2010 show a 17.2% unemployment and underemployment rate while the Dow regains much of its losses since September 2008 and bailed-out banks report record profits and bonuses (Rich 2010a; Schwartz 2010); health care reform that leaves the for-profit system intact; further erosion of the already-eviscerated welfare state in the form of an Obama administration proposal for a multi-year freeze on "non-security" spending to begin in 2011. The list goes on, providing reason enough for political cynicism and depression among those seeking greater jus-

---

1   Ongoing thanks to my Feel Tank Chicago comrades, in this case especially for discussions during the campaign and after Obama's election. Big appreciations as well to Mayanthi Fernando, Lisa Rofel, and Danilyn Rutherford for comments on an early draft. And to Laurie Palmer, gratitude for comments and for engaging me in discussions about political desire.

2   As a critique of Obama's failure to pursue a progressive agenda, Freshjive's Rick Klotz created a t-shirt in the fall of 2009 with the words "Hope Is Fading Fast" underneath a streaked version of the Obama campaign's iconic "HOPE" poster (by Shepard Fairey), the poster colors running, seemingly a result of the wearer's tears.

tice and equality. It is tempting to give up on hope in the realm of intellectual inquiry as well: the hope surrounding Obama now seems fleeting, transitory, ephemeral, and perhaps, therefore, inconsequential and unworthy of study.

But the phenomenon of hope in this last presidential election, its very presence, offers an avenue into crucial questions about political participation and the meaning of politics to people in the context of their, our, everyday lives. As well, the widespread circulation of hope during the presidential campaign raises important questions about the sources of people's attitudes about *what is* and *what might be*, and how those senses of political possibility shift over time. This moment of political hope, in its multiple registers, offers much to be plumbed, intellectually and politically. Indeed, if we are intent on grappling with questions about people's relations to 'the political', we must attend to political emotion, that is to the ways that feeling states permeate, are shaped by, play out in, and influence all things political, conceived both narrowly, in terms of the electoral realm, and broadly, in terms of any and all arenas where claims-making and struggles over power occur.

Emotion has not been entirely absent from political theorists' discussions of politics, but as Barbara Koziak (2000: 1) argues, "reason and the image of the reason-ruled person have long dominated political philosophy"; emotion, when discussed, mostly has figured as the dangerous cousin to rationality. Political theorists' central concern regarding emotion has been whether it undermines or aids democracy, and conclusions typically align with a theorist's views about the relationship between emotion and reason: those who construe emotions as undermining reason tend to argue that emotions imperil democracy; those who think emotions aid reason tend to argue the opposite.[3]

While important, this debate about whether emotion undermines or aids democracy imagines only a limited role for emotion in political life. Suppose we were to move beyond that debate and instead take as a given that reason requires emotion (see Damasio 1994; 1999), that both feelings and thought can lead to irrational behavior but need not (see Jasper 1998), and that passion is not necessarily or inevitably a threat to democracy (see Marcus 2002). What other questions about emotion and politics might arise?

For starters, rather than wondering whether human emotionality makes people unfit for democracy, we might better flip the question on its head and ask whether representative democracy speaks to people's political hopes and desires.[4] Does democracy, as practiced in the U.S. context for example, address

---

3   See Marcus (2002), Marcus, Neuman, and MacKuen (2000) and Neuman, Marcus, MacKuen, and Crigler (2007).
4   I bracket here the diversity of human political desires and pose the question in a general sense, as political theorists do with regard to the question of emotionality and democracy.

what people want with regard to, say, ways of structuring society and ways of living? Does it allow the governed to view the political realm as a site where alternative worlds, responsive to people's expressed needs and wants, can be discussed and even enacted? The hope and enthusiasm surrounding Obama's campaign and election were striking because we rarely see that sort of passionate political engagement in relation to a politician. In light of their usual rarity, the very presence of those feelings in this instance raises questions about political desire, about people's expectations regarding political leaders, and, most generally, about people's relations to the realm of the political. These are the questions I pursue in this chapter.

I begin this inquiry into political hope with the 1992 election to the presidency of William J. Clinton who, after all, billed himself as "The Man from Hope."[5] That discussion sets us up to consider different sorts of political hope and its various political effects. Next I explore the markedly different meanings and significance of the political hope surrounding Obama's campaign and election. Here, against the dominant view that that hope was in Obama the man, I posit that the hope instead was in large part hope in 'ourselves' and in the sense of opening political possibilities that Obama helped to generate. I conclude with a consideration of the political potentialities activated on this new imaginative and affective terrain, exploring in particular the difficulties of being prepared for 'something better' and reasons why progressive/left activism has seemingly stalled even as the Tea Party right has taken off.

Hope in 1992

An interest in how leftists have characterized the 'Obama phenomenon' partially motivates this essay. As I discuss below, during and immediately following the campaign, many leftist luminaries expressed anxiety about the hope and enthusiasm surrounding Obama. In an effort to illustrate why political hope might raise concerns among some leftists, but also as a way to suggest that political hope arises, when it does, from different sources, takes different forms, and generates different effects, I begin with a discussion of a moment of hope that helped to *de*mobilize a movement – the hope in President Bill Clinton manifested by some in the direct-action AIDS movement in the United States, ACT

---

5   That was the title of the official campaign video shown at the 1992 Democratic National Convention, a biography of Democratic presidential candidate Bill Clinton who was born in Hope, Arkansas.

UP.[6] Based on my own participation in ACT UP and subsequent research, I propose that ours was an exhausted and defeated hope that both ceded our political agency to a politician and his administration and encouraged withdrawal from political activism.[7]

Over the life of the movement, ACT UP participants experienced wide swings in our feelings of political efficacy and senses of possibility. In ACT UP's early years from 1987-1989, amid numerous victories, participants felt optimistic about our capacity to effect change; our overriding goal was to save lives and we did indeed believe we could do that. Concrete victories that prolonged the lives of people with HIV/AIDS continued into the early 1990s, but with deaths continuing to accumulate and movement on the treatment front stalling, many of us began to feel despondent, and pessimistic about the movement's political prospects.

We experienced the 1992 presidential campaign from that affective landscape. As the Democratic presidential nominee, Bill Clinton made big promises regarding AIDS: a dramatic increase in AIDS funding; implementation of the recommendations of the National Commission on AIDS (including controversial proposals in favor of explicit safe-sex education and needle-exchange programs); further expedition of the Food and Drug Administration's drug-approval process; expansion of clinical drug trials for promising treatments; and admission into the United States for HIV-positive Haitians being held without medical care in camps at Guantánamo Bay Naval Base.[8] In echoing a number of ACT UP's demands, Clinton sounded promising. Given twelve years of what we saw as genocidal inaction on the part of the Reagan and Bush administrations, many people with HIV/AIDS and others in the movement felt a sense of urgency about the election, and when Clinton won, optimism swept through the AIDS movement.

I argue elsewhere that Clinton's election – and the resurgent hope his election generated within the direct-action AIDS movement – contributed to ACT UP's decline (Gould 2009). How and why it did so tells us something about the

---

6   Hope in Clinton was not limited to AIDS activists, of course. Cultural theorist Michael Bérubé argues that such hope initially was widespread among liberals and progressives, many of whom felt they had "found a home after more than a decade in the wilderness." http://www.michaelberube.com/index.php/weblog/party_time/ (last accessed September 12, 2009).
7   This section draws from Gould (2009, Chapter 7).
8   The George H. W. Bush administration's use of the Guantánamo Bay Naval Base to confine Haitians with AIDS seeking medical care in the U.S. raises the question of whether the U.S. government's war against people with AIDS during the 1980s and early 1990s was training ground for George W. Bush's "war on terror."

character of political hope in the Clinton moment, allowing a comparison to hope in the age of Obama.

Most important, hope in the newly elected president Clinton derived from the growing despair among many ACT UP participants. Combined with activists' exhaustion after years of being on the front lines of the AIDS war, despair crushed our belief in our own collective political agency, in our ability to effect change through collective direct action, and created a desire to pass the torch. We were ripe for hearing that someone else would fight the battle, and that is essentially what Clinton offered. ACT UP/Chicago member Tim Miller suggests that ACT UP members *wanted* to trust in Clinton, indeed, given our exhaustion and despondency, *needed* to. As Miller puts it, "Everybody just breathed a sigh of relief [when Clinton won]." Continuing in a mocking and self-mocking tone, Miller offers an incisive analysis of the forceful desire to surrender our political agency to the government:

> 'Oh, our savior is here. We're done with the Reagan/Bush folks. Now we've got this liberal youngster in the White House who's gonna give us everything that we could ever ask for'. (...) I think people were exhausted and were happy to pass on the torch to the White House. And hopefully they were gonna take care of everything. Make everything beautiful again (...) [Clinton's] a smart guy. And we bought it. I bought it, and I think a lot of people bought it. We wanted to buy it. And yeah, we should've returned it. (Miller 1999)

We should have returned it not only because Clinton failed to implement many of his promises but also because transferring to Clinton any remaining hopes we might have had in ourselves and our own activism, and thereby surrendering our power to him, contributed to the demise of the direct-action AIDS movement. In Miller's view, Clinton's election and our hopeful belief that Clinton would be "our savior" was "the worst thing to ever happen to the [AIDS] activist movement. Although, I mean, I voted for him. I was so happy that Bush was not in office. But I think it was the worst thing that ever happened to the activism. It just fell apart (...) That was the final straw" (Miller 1999). ACT UP/Chicago member Darrell Gordon similarly links the decline of ACT UP to the hope that Clinton, as our protector, would allow us to retreat from the political realm. "There was this hope that Clinton (...) was going to save us. I think it had a great effect [on ACT UP] (...) People thought that (...) Clinton was going to take care of us, take care of the people in the queer community" (Gordon 2000). We experienced Clinton's election as offering relief from tending to this crisis largely on our own and in the face of unrelenting government hostility. After twelve years of murderous inaction and punitive policymaking from the government, escalating deaths, caretaking and taking to the streets, all of that amid growing exhaustion and despair, we wanted and needed a break from activism.

There is, of course, no necessary connection between intense activism and activist depletion and exhaustion; indeed, activism is often rejuvenating. But in this context, where exhaustion was joined by a forceful despair, the prospect of someone else taking up our battle, the President of the United States no less, was alluring. The contrast between what Clinton seemed to stand for and what had occurred during the Reagan/Bush years – the criminal negligence, the punitive legislation, the active ignorance, the intense homophobia that rendered acceptable the deaths of tens of thousands of gay and bisexual men – was dramatic. How could we not feel some hope? Many ACT UP members, of course, were cynical about Clinton. Nevertheless, the contrast between the Reagan/Bush years and the possibility of better leadership on AIDS from the top was so clear that the skepticism and criticism were initially rather muted. While in retrospect Billy McMillan from ACT UP/Chicago thinks that he was "very naïve," he recalls being thrilled when Clinton won, and moved to tears.

> I was watching his inauguration at home alone. Maya Angelou was reading her poem, and I was just bawling my eyes out (...) I really had hope that maybe we were going to be moving into a new era, that maybe something positive would happen. The Democrats were back in the White House, and I really believed that Clinton was somehow going to help improve things. (McMillan 2000)

Clinton's victory created a sense among many ACT UP members that there was no longer a need to be in the streets: "I think what happened after Clinton's election was that a lot of people felt that things were going to be different and better. Many of us let our guard down and placed hope and trust in him (...) [T]hat was probably the final nail in the coffin of a lot of ACT UPs" (McMillan 2000). In this moment, political hope prompted more ACT UP members to exit the movement, exhaustedly optimistic that the U.S. government would now do the right thing even absent activist pressure. It was, then, a form of hope that not only transferred political agency from the people to a politician, but also bestowed faith in the state as the bearer of change and thereby inspired activist withdrawal from the political. Facing little activist pressure, Clinton hardly mentioned AIDS in his first six months in office, during which time close to twenty thousand people in the United States died of AIDS-related complications. Even worse, he did not act on many of his AIDS-related campaign promises. This history obliges an acknowledgment that hope can quiet and pacify, with disastrous consequences.

After eight years of George W. Bush's regime, the hope surrounding Barack Obama's campaign and election perhaps similarly has been prompted by exhaustion and even despair, but this hope feels different, in terms of both its texture and potential. As I discuss later, it seems more activating than what some AIDS activists felt upon Clinton's election. It is a hope with affinities to what cultural and queer theorist Lauren Berlant talks about as "desire for the political" (Berlant 2008a; 2008b).

Enthusiasm, Apathy, and the Ineloquence of the Political

I begin my analysis of the structure and contours of hope in the age of Obama with a brief discussion of the positive affective intensities that swirled around Obama from the point when he announced his candidacy through the primary season, his election to the presidency, and the first months of his administration. The enthusiasm and excitement that marked this instance of political engagement are striking, especially against a backdrop of widespread political withdrawal. Hundreds of videos on YouTube capture people across the country, and indeed the world, spontaneously flowing into the streets when hearing news of Obama's presidential victory.[9] They document people hooting and hollering, laughing, crying, screaming, hugging, singing, chanting, twirling, beaming, jumping, weeping, cheering, grinning, spinning, high-fiving, dancing – the sorts of reactions we expect when a sport teams wins, not when a U.S. presidential candidate does. If, as political economist Albert Hirschman argues, "boredom and feeling[s] of powerlessness" often characterize political life in a democracy (1982: 106), we have to acknowledge that something quite different was happening here.

The large number of volunteers who joined the Obama campaign suggests extraordinary excitement and enthusiasm as well. Approximately three thousand organizers recruited thousands of volunteer leadership teams which mobilized one and a half million volunteers to hold house meetings, solicit contributions, work the phones, and knock on doors rallying people for the election (Dreier and Ganz 2009). The Obama campaign declared the scale of their campaign operation to be "unprecedented" (Hughes 2008), calling it "the largest field organization in the history of American politics" (Hass 2008a).[10] Political soci-

---

[9] Putting the words "Obama victory celebrations" into the search field on YouTube pulls up 955 videos: http://www.youtube.com/results?search_query=obama+victory+celebrations& search_type=&aq=f (last accessed September 9, 2009).

[10] Others concur: during the primary season, Tom Hayden, Bill Fletcher, Barbara Ehrenreich, and Danny Glover – launching a new organization, Progressives for Obama – noted the "unprecedented numbers of people mobilized in [Obama's] campaign" (Hayden *et al.* 2008). Co-founder of the techPresident blog and editor of Personal Democracy Forum, Micah Sifry,

ologists Peter Dreier and Marshall Ganz write that "the Obama campaign inspired an unprecedented grass-roots electoral movement" (Dreier and Ganz 2009).[11] While this mobilization certainly was facilitated by social networking technologies, the campaign escaped the asociality and passivity of "internet activism" by engaging in phone-banking, door-to-door campaigning, house strategizing meetings, and other face-to-face events. "Individuals in all 50 states (...) created more than 35,000 local organizing groups, hosted over 200,000 events, and made millions upon millions of calls" (Hughes 2008). Speaking just before the Democratic National Convention, Deputy Campaign Manager Steve Hildebrand estimated that 70 percent of the campaign's volunteers had never before been active in a political campaign (Mooney 2008). Indeed, according to one of the organizers at the campaign's blog headquarters, My.BarackObama.com, many volunteers "had never seen themselves as political" before getting involved (Hass 2008b).

Voting statistics indicate immense enthusiasm for Obama as well.[12] His campaign not only registered millions of new voters (Hendricks 2008), it also "drew in legions of voters who had been disengaged and voiceless," according to the *New York Times* (2008: A30). U.S. Census Bureau data show that the number of voters overall increased by 5 million from 2004, with almost all of that increase coming from African American, Latino, Asian, and young voters (U.S. Census Bureau 2009).[13] Although the Pew Research Center for the People & the Press found that Obama did only modestly better among white voters than John Kerry did in 2004, Obama *did* do better, and even more, he made "large gains" among specific groups of whites: the young, the well-educated, and the affluent (Kohut 2008a).

The enthusiasm only increased after Obama's victory. One week after the election, Andrew Kohut from the Pew Center noted that Obama "has received a landslide greeting from the American public" (Kohut 2008a). Despite the dire economic crisis pummeling the country, indeed, the near-collapse of the global economy, Pew found the public to be "highly optimistic that Obama will succeed" (Kohut 2008a). Indeed, "67% of voters believe Obama will be successful in his first term, and 65% in a Gallup survey said the country will be better off

---

writes that Obama's campaign mobilized "the largest volunteer base any presidential campaign has developed in history" (2009).

11 Marshall Ganz was also "the architect of Barack Obama's grassroots organizing juggernaut" (Sifry 2008a).
12 So does the fact that there were 13.5 million contributors to Obama's campaign (Dreier and Ganz 2009).
13 95% of black voters, 67% of Latino voters, 62% of Asian voters, and 66% of voters aged 18-29 chose Obama over McCain (*New York Times* Exit Polls, http://elections.nytimes.com/2008/results/president/exit-polls.html, last accessed April 18, 2010).

four years from now."[14] In striking contrast, "Only 50% saw improvement for the country ahead after Clinton's election in 1992 and Bush's in 2000." It is perhaps unsurprising that immediately following Obama's victory 96% of Democratic voters felt "hopeful," but it is notable that more than two-thirds of Independents (68%) and more than one-third of Republicans (38%) said they did as well (Pew Research Center 2008).

The mobilization and enthusiasm continued in the months between Obama's election and inauguration. Enacting their desire for continuing political engagement, in December volunteers held over 4000 "Change is Coming" house meetings in 2000 cities in all 50 states to reflect on the election and discuss how to "bring change to both Washington and their own communities."[15] Just prior to Obama's inauguration, Pew found Americans to be "enthusiastic about Obama": "Fully 79% of Americans – including 59% of Republicans – say they have a favorable impression of Obama, almost 20 percentage points higher than Bush's personal favorability shortly before he took office in 2001 (60%)" (Pew Research Center 2009a). Regarding the inauguration itself, according to the *New York Times*, "the vast crowd that thronged the Mall (...) was the largest to attend an inauguration in decades, if not ever" (Baker 2009). A letter-writer to the *New York Times* that same day who described himself as a strong supporter of McCain acknowledged his disappointment at the election results but continued: "I can honestly say I was not depressed (...) Obama is honest, extremely intelligent and very capable. He has inspired a groundswell of enthusiasm and optimism greater than any I can recall in my lifetime" (Zinberg 2009).[16] The Pew Research Center found that high levels of enthusiasm and optimism continued into spring 2009 and were well above any such sentiments surrounding other recent presidents during their first one hundred days in office (Pew Research Center 2009b and 2009c; see also Pew Research Center 2009d).

Obama's approval ratings dropped significantly in the summer of 2009 from the low 60% range in June to the low 50% range in September, remained steady in the low 50% range throughout the fall, and then dropped further, into the mid-40% range, in the spring of 2010 (Pew Research Center 2009e; 2009f; Jones 2009; Gallup 2009; 2010). But while this decline in Obama's approval

---

14 "Nearly all Democrats (90%) are optimistic about Obama's first term, as are 67% of independent voters. Republicans are nearly evenly divided; 41% believe Obama's first term will be successful and 44% say it will be unsuccessful" (Pew Research Center 2008).
15 http://my.barackobama.com/page/content/changeiscoming/ (last accessed December 1, 2008); and Hass 2008c and 2008d.
16 For Gallup Poll data that similarly point to very high rates of optimism at the moment of Obama's inauguration, see Saad (2009).

ratings is marked, it is not unexpected given the rough and tumble of partisan politics.

The surprise is the widespread enthusiasm initially surrounding Obama, especially given frequent descriptions of U.S. Americans as politically apathetic. Indeed, that enthusiasm demands that we reconsider standard explanations of political withdrawal as due to apathy, disinterest, and indifference. As my collaborators in Feel Tank Chicago argue, political detachment might instead signal precisely what it is assumed to lack: political desire.[17] A desire, for example, that the state and its representatives actually speak to people's needs, wants, and imaginations, and disappointment that they infrequently do so. That is, rather than being due to disinterest and indifference, high rates of political nonparticipation in the U.S. might better be understood as a response to the ineloquence of the political when it comes to people's desires. Ineloquence specifically in the sense of non-address. Why, indeed, should people care about mainstream political matters, why get involved or even pay attention, if politicians rarely seek to understand and, more rarely still, attend to, people's desires about society and its functioning?

Politics hasn't always been negatively understood. In ancient Greece and Rome, the word 'political' concerned citizens and public life and connoted judiciousness, prudence, and statesmanlike behavior.[18] Today, U.S. Americans tend to see politics as a corrupt and dirty business, controlled by elite moneyed interests and populated by scheming, deceitful individuals; we have come to understand politics as "out of reach to ordinary people," "made by a few," "something distant, done to others," (Colombo and Mascarenhas 2003: 461). We are politically cynical, knowing better than to believe in politicians or expect anything good to happen in the realm of mainstream politics.

Obama's campaign broke through what Berlant characterizes as "a frostbite-like defense against wanting something – from the *mainstream* political sphere" (Berlant 2008a, emphasis hers). Obama's strong and effective challenge to a habituated political cynicism is evident, for example, in the comments of *Daily Kos* contributor 'Ligero1' who describes himself as a jaded guy whom the campaign transformed into an active Obama supporter.[19]

---

[17] Feel Tank defines *apathy* in our "Feel Kit," a keywords project, available at https://coral.uchicago.edu:8443/display/utopianfutures/FeelKit (last accessed December 6, 2009). See also Hirschman who argues critically that the vote "acts as a safeguard against an excessively *expressive* citizenry" (1982, especially ch. 7).
[18] "Politic," Oxford English Dictionary Online, (last accessed September 4, 2009).
[19] Ligero1's post, written in December 2009, asserts that the Democratic Party squandered this moment of movement-building.

This Movement was all the more remarkable (...) in that so many of it's [*sic.*] members were people like myself, guys who had gotten jaded in recent years. Guys like me were disgusted; we pretty much realized that there were really very few differences between the two political parties (...) [T]hings never changed because the real people in power, no matter if there was a Democratic or Republican administration officially 'in power', those *real leaders* called all the shots behind the scenes. We all knew these things going into the 2008 election; they were hard lessons learned over the years. Our dreams of a political revolution were long dead. Then along came Obama, and a Movement took hold.

"Armies of the jaded," continues Ligero1, "got caught up in the excitement." Indicating both the difficulties and possibilities for counteracting entrenched political cynicism, Ligero1 concludes: "although we certainly had our share of doubters who said 'you guys are crazy if you think Obama can really change anything,' we joined up anyway" (Ligero1 2009, emphasis his).[20]

What makes the enthusiasm surrounding Obama's campaign and victory especially stunning, then, is that it emerged against a backdrop of pervasive political cynicism, resignation, and withdrawal. Cynicism provides immunity to political desire and the attendant risks both of being exposed as wanting something and of being disappointed.[21] Political enthusiasm lets its guard down. Although now obsolete, a meaning of *enthusiasm* that was dominant in the 17th century – possession by a god, supernatural inspiration, prophetic or poetic frenzy – shares a connotation of mystical transport and being overtaken by passion with the current principal meaning: rapturous intensity of feeling in favor of a person, principle, cause.[22] Enthusiasm, with its bodily euphoria, fervor, and senses of possibility, is the opposite of cynicism.

Obama is a 'phenomenon' precisely because his campaign generated enthusiastic, expectant political participation. The very existence of such feeling states within, and indeed generated by, the electoral realm raises questions about their more typical absence and why they emerged around Obama. As I've suggested, answers to both questions are found in the fact that the mainstream political realm rarely speaks to our desires. Obama, in contrast, did.

Hope, Now

The enthusiasm about Obama was complex and multiple. It certainly stemmed in part from the perception that Obama's candidacy and victory might close the

---

20   See also Moore (2008) who claims that "Obama appealed explicitly to people turned off by traditional politics."
21   On cynicism offering immunity to politics, see Eliasoph (1998, chapter 6).
22   "Enthusiasm," Oxford English Dictionary Online (last accessed October 10, 2009).

door on this country's racist past and interfere with its ongoing racist present. Obama's candidacy offered white Americans a chance to redeem ourselves and the nation, as if by voting a black man into the presidency we might leave white supremacy behind, and the United States could then, finally, become the great nation it was destined to be.[23] Obama invoked this redemptive, post-racial, nationalist fantasy of unity throughout the campaign: "We are one people. We are one nation."[24] In addition, some of the enthusiasm was likely sheer relief that the Democrats had a candidate who might sweep the Republicans and the disastrous eight years of the Bush administration into history.

I propose that the widespread enthusiasm derived as well from Obama's resurrection of the idea of government as a force for good and, more powerfully, from his incitement to a renewed relation to the political. Amid an epic global economic meltdown that has brought tremendous suffering and has challenged both the ideology and practice of neoliberal capitalism, Obama spoke on behalf of political desire, by which I mean he presented the political realm, and government itself, as a site that should and could be responsive to the citizenry's desires *and thus as a site worth engaging*. Consider Obama's inaugural address: the question, he asserted, "is not whether our government is too big or too small, but whether it works – whether it helps families find jobs at a decent wage, care they can afford, a retirement that is dignified."[25] Indeed, throughout his campaign, Obama challenged an anti-government ideology that has prevailed since Ronald Reagan's presidency, proposing in its place a federal government that assists ordinary people struggling to construct lives on an uneven playing field. Obama not only addressed U.S. Americans who want more from government (a desire expressed by 66% of respondents in the University of Michigan's Na-

---

23 Drawing on an analysis by *New Yorker* writer David Remnick, Danilyn Rutherford argues that "Obama's 'message'... throughout the campaign, rested on the slipperiness" in his usage of the pronoun 'we' (Rutherford 2010). In his speeches, which stylistically drew on "the familiar cadences and syntax of the black church" (Remnick 2008), the 'we' of African American struggle became an American 'we'. "Non-African American listeners slide into the position of an American 'we' by way of pronouns etched in the history of the civil rights struggle. Difference is not erased in this moment, but inhabits the 'we' in a spectral fashion. What 'we' feel is an exhilarating passage through otherness to a new sense of self" (Rutherford 2010), a self that ostensibly transcends racist history and takes part in the building of a new, more hopeful and united, America.

24 See, for example, the remarks of Obama on New Hampshire Primary Night, available at http://en.wikisource.org/wiki/Remarks_of_Senator_Barack_Obama_on_New_Hampshire_Primary_Night (last accessed April 22, 2010).

25 Available at http://www.whitehouse.gov/blog/inaugural-address/ (last accessed May 4, 2010). Reagan, in contrast, promoted hatred of "big government," stating in his 1981 inaugural that "government is not the solution to our problem; government *is* the problem." Available at http://www.reagan.utexas.edu/archives/speeches/1981/12081a.htm (last accessed May 4, 2010).

tional Election Survey in October 2008);[26] the enthusiasm surrounding his campaign and election suggests that he also inspired many to believe that 'change' is indeed possible, and that the political itself – even mainstream electoral politics – can be a site of possibility.

In addition to the thrill of a candidate and victor speaking even mildly on behalf of a government that addresses the populace's needs, then, people cathected to Obama's incitement to a more active relation to the political realm. That is not to deny that Obama's statements during the campaign and on the eve of his election were instrumental; he *is* a politician. But regardless of Obama's intentions, consider the effects of repeated injunctions to "believe" not just in *his* ability to bring about real change, but, more importantly, "in yours."[27] How might people's political subjectivities be affected when a candidate repeatedly states that "real change comes from the ground up" and, following that logic, creates "Obama Organizing Fellowships" intent on training a new generation in "the basics of organizing" and grassroots movement building?[28] Berlant conveys her astonishment at candidate Obama's recurring incitements to grassroots political action: "after 30 years of political parties that wanted apathetic voters, that wanted the political to be delegated to them, we have a mainstream politician who wants people to build their political skills for activism. OMG!" (2008a).

In stating on the eve of his election that "this victory alone is not the change we seek – it is only the chance for us to make that change," Obama invited continuing collective political engagement – in the electoral realm, but also in the realm of the political more broadly construed. Indeed, throughout the campaign Obama argued that continuing political involvement would be necessary, "remind[ing] supporters that the real work of making change would only begin on Election Day" (Dreier and Ganz 2009). Linking Obama's victory to the campaign's successful, market research-backed creation of the Obama brand of hope and change, Naomi Klein (2010) argues that his electoral win "proved

---

26 The National Election Survey found that 66% of those surveyed – a 9-percent increase since 2004 – believe "there are more things government should be doing" compared with 32% who believe "the less government the better" (Campaign for America's Future and Media Matters for America 2009). This statistic provides a counter to Tea Party rhetoric which naturalizes and universalizes sentiments against government.
27 Obama made the following statement in speeches, it permeated his campaign literature and videos, and it remains header on his Organizing for America website, BarackObama.com: "I'm asking you to believe. Not just in my ability to bring about real change in Washington... I'm asking you to believe in yours." http://www.barackobama.com/index.php?splash=false (last accessed 13 April 2010).
28 The campaign created these organizing fellowships in June 2008; see http://my.barackobama.com/page/s/fellowsapp (last accessed July 7, 2010).

decisively (...) that there is a tremendous appetite for progressive change [and] that many, many people (...) very much want to be part of a political project larger than themselves". Against a backdrop of pervasive and long-standing political cynicism, bolstered in no small part by conservative ideology that demonizes 'big government' but also by an 'avoidant' political culture that leaves politics to the experts (Eliasoph 1998), Obama's invitation to a renewed and active relation to the political realm felt different and genuinely exciting to many.

Recalling my discussion about the demobilizing effects of AIDS activists' political hope in Clinton, we must consider the possibility that, rather than feeling a renewed, more participatory relation to politics, some Obama enthusiasts hoped that an Obama victory would allow them to retreat from the political sphere which now would be overseen by a savior-like figure who would, of his own accord, bring about desired change. Characterizations of the American public as politically apathetic support that sort of interpretation: we'd rather someone else did it for us. But I would suggest that the intensity of positive affects swirling around Obama during the campaign and upon his election indicate a different, more appetitive and activating, form of hope.

Appetitive: the hope surrounding Obama overflows with political desire.[29] It has expectations and makes demands of the state. It wants and expects elected officials to be responsive to those they represent, not in a hollow Clintonian "I feel your pain" manner, but rather through concrete policies and actions. It risks believing in change – change with regard to the relationship between those who govern and those who are governed as well as broader social change, the possibility of which Obama came to represent.

What I propose – and I substantiate this claim below – is that Obama's invitation to a renewed relationship to the political realm, and its reception by millions of volunteers and supporters, ushered in a new, more expansive horizon of political possibility. But now, 18 months after Obama's election, we have to reckon not only with the apparent return to 'politics as usual', but also with what appears to be widespread political quiescence among liberals and progressives since Obama's victory, giving support to the idea that people have little desire for the sort of political engagement that Obama invited, preferring instead to leave politics to the experts. What has ensued since Obama's victory, in other

---

29 In this paragraph and subsequently, I use the present tense in order to signal the non-pastness of this political hope, even as I acknowledge that many feel disappointment in Obama and "hope is fading fast" in some quarters. Momentarily, I'll say more about my investment in the present, if largely dormant, existence of this hope. For now I will simply note that the verb tense of the emergent, the not entirely present or manifest, the real but not yet actualized – the verb tense, in other words, of potentiality – is not immediately clear to me.

words, calls into question my claim of expanding political horizons and my characterization of the political hopes associated with his campaign and election.

Hope and (Some) Leftists

Which brings me to doubts or concerns about Obama and the hope and enthusiasm swirling around him that some on the left aired from the start of his campaign. In the face of conservative, liberal, and progressive claims that Obama was left of center, a number of leftists – especially some whom we might characterize as part of what political theorist Jodi Dean (2009) calls the "typing left" – countered that Obama is a neoliberal and Democratic Party centrist. But more than engaging in a disagreement over who Obama is, their reservations had an emotional charge to them, tinged with anxiety about what many dubbed Obamania.[30] Their cautionary warnings interest me because they indicate an ambivalent relation to hope, one which I share to some degree. But I also am interested in considering the possibility that these wary leftists have misconstrued the object of the hopeful's hope. The political potential of the Obama moment looks very different depending on how we understand the object of that hope.

The disparaging ways in which some on the left characterized Obama supporters indicate anxious concern about people's political feelings. During the campaign Doug Henwood, publisher of *Left Business Observer*, questioned the rationality of leftists who, in his words, had succumbed to "Obama Disease" and fallen in love with the candidate's empty rhetoric of change (Henwood 2008). Leftist political scientist Adolph Reed derided other leftists for going "weak in the knees" at the invocation of Obama's past community organizing, admonishing that Obama is a neoliberal centrist and that his rhetoric of "hope and change and new directions" is "empty" (Reed 2008a). Reed lambasted leftists for fantasizing that Obama could be a source of political transformation (Reed 2008b).

In another example of leftist anxiety that hope deludes, two weeks before the election linguist and activist Noam Chomsky advised progressive and leftist voters in swing states to vote "against McCain" and thus "for Obama," but he warned voters to do so "without illusions" (Chomsky 2008). His advice suggested wariness that the enthusiasm and hope surrounding Obama's candidacy

---

30 Berlant (2008d), Davidson (2008), Luis in Paris (2008), and Younge (2009) point to this anxiety as well. J.K. Gibson-Graham (2006: 2) suggest the importance of paying attention not only to the intellectual content of political disagreements but also to "the visceral intensities and emotive narratives that accompany their expression".

might lead voters to hold dangerous illusions. He reminded people to be realistic: "all the elevated rhetoric about change and hope and so on will dissolve into standard centrist Democrat policies." Hope here is either merely the rhetoric of a politician or an opiate that compromises voters' realism.

In an essay published on the internet one day after Obama's victory titled "Uncritical Exuberance," queer theorist Judith Butler also worried that leftists' feeling states were dangerously deluding them (Butler 2008). Reminding her readers that "fascism relied in part on (...) seamless identification with the leader," Butler cautioned leftists (and others) against their "exuberant identification" with Obama. Many on the left, wanting to feel unambivalent love, risk "an uncritical exuberance even when we know better." More warnings: in our uncritical embrace of Obama, we are seduced into believing "that we might overcome all dissonance," that "unity is actually possible," that Obama's election is "the end of struggle." On this last point especially, we would, she cautioned, "be very unwise to regard [Obama's election] that way, even provisionally." We need to disabuse ourselves of our illusions "so that we might remember that politics is less about the person and the impossible and beautiful promise he represents than it is about the concrete changes in policy that might begin, over time, and with difficulty, [to] bring about conditions of greater justice" (Butler 2008). Do not let your hopeful political imaginings and renewed sense of possibility get the better of you, Butler instructed, because politics is a messy business and real change has not yet arrived.[31]

Writer and activist Naomi Klein worried about progressives' and leftists' hope too. In an April 2009 essay in *The Nation*, Klein argued that hope in Obama not only had pulled the wool over many people's eyes, blinding them to the reality that Obama is a centrist Democrat, but also had led them to political passivity vis-à-vis the new administration. But now, finally, progressives and leftists were getting their feelings and reason in order:

> A growing number of Obama enthusiasts are starting to entertain the possibility that their man is not, in fact, going to save the world if we all just hope really hard. This is a good thing. If the superfan culture that brought Obama to power is going to transform itself into an independent political movement, one fierce enough to produce programs capable of meeting the current crises, we are all going to have to stop hoping and start demanding. (Klein 2009).

Hope in Obama was an overindulgence that "felt good at the time but wasn't really all that healthy." Obama fans may be nostalgic for "the rush of optimism

---

31 For direct and indirect critiques of Butler's essay, see Davidson (2008), Luis in Paris (2008), and Wang (2008).

from the campaign trail" and forever trying "to recapture that warm, hopey feeling," but a hopeful posture toward Obama in the wake of his victory "is dangerously deferential" (Klein 2009). Enough with that sort of hope.[32]

Guardian columnist Gary Younge summarized these sorts of comments when he wrote that many have "sneered at [the] joy" expressed by Obama supporters: "Anxious to get their disappointment in early and avoid the rush, they have been keen to point out the various ways in which Obama will fail and betray" (Younge 2009).

Cynical, wary, cautious, anxiety-ridden..., prominent leftist intellectuals appealed for prudence in the age of Obama. How to understand their anxiety about political feelings, hope and enthusiasm in particular? Most leftists privilege rational argumentation above other communicative modes and practices.[33] Raised on U.S. American secularism and cynicism, leftist intellectuals don't quite know what to do with anything that emits even a whiff of religious fervor.[34] Historian and American studies scholar Robin D. G. Kelley (2002: 192) suggests that such uneasiness is long-standing, noting that Marxism has never been able to deal effectively with "magic, spirituality, and the ecstatic". And, as anthropologist Michael Taussig notes, Western intellectuals often correlate lack of hope with profundity and being smart (Taussig 2003: 44-45). Who wouldn't rather appear clear-eyed, realistic, unsentimental, rational, and mature than swept up by the emotion of the moment?

But, of course, all modes of knowing have their emotional dimension, and the leftist intellectuals I cited above might be understood as occupying what queer and cultural studies theorist Eve Sedgwick calls a paranoid position where "bad news (...) [is] always already known" (Sedgwick 2003: 130). Paranoia comforts in its all-knowingness: by 'knowing' in advance that a mainstream politician, no matter how progressive s/he sometimes sounds, is nevertheless beholden to the status quo, you get the pleasure of feeling like you have some control, at least in the realm of knowledge. But as Sedgwick (2003: 130) notes, "paranoia knows some things well and others poorly". To be sure, we have good reason to expect our leaders will pursue policies that systematically and dramatically advantage the few over the many. But a paranoid approach to politics has consequences beyond providing a ready-made analysis. Its mode of knowing

---

32 By January 2010, Klein seemed to be reading hope in the Obama moment differently, now pointing out, as I wrote above, that the "embrace of Obama's brand" proved that "there is a tremendous appetite for progressive change" (Klein 2010).
33 For a challenge to this rationalist bias in leftist politics, see Duncombe (2007).
34 For a discussion of secularist intellectuals' anxiety about religious faith and fervor, see Pellegrini (2009).

crowds out space for uncertainty, ambiguity, indeterminacy, and surprise, not to mention hope.[35]

As my discussion of AIDS activists' optimism regarding Clinton indicates, I do not posit hope as an unadulterated good for progressive/left politics. But not only do I think the cautionary warnings about the hope surrounding Obama are misplaced – a point I return to below – I also worry that leftists' counsel toward political 'realism' fundamentally misunderstands a crucial role that emotion plays in political life. The affective landscapes in which we find ourselves, *and which we help to create*, shape our political imaginaries and thus influence what sorts of politics are possible (Gould 2009).[36] We therefore need to consider the political effects generated when we align cynicism with realism and hope with naïveté. We need to ask what sorts of politics are possible when people feel resigned to the corruption, hollowness, and curtailed possibilities of the political sphere, and what becomes possible when people feel more hopeful.

Leftists' expressed anxieties about hope vis-à-vis Obama are multiple: in addition to risking disappointment, this hope deludes, makes stupid, misdirects, pacifies, deactivates. Those certainly are possible outcomes, but what if wary leftists have misconstrued both the hopeful and the object of their hope? Queer and cultural studies scholar Lisa Duggan posits that "Obama the politician will surely disappoint every part of the left," but, recognizing that this surge in political hope might have legs beyond the Obama moment, she asks "what might the impact of mobilized hopefulness nonetheless be?" Bracketing for a moment her suspicions and anxieties, Duggan suggests that hope "can arrive in collective, political and insurgent forms," that it can be without delusion, and when that is so, she asks, might hope generate "future possibilities beyond any present expectation?" (Muñoz and Duggan 2009: 276).

Hope and Its Doings

The object of political hope matters when the question is about what futures might flow from it. Hope in President Clinton – that he would take the torch

---

35 Sedgwick (2003: 129) does not argue that we should dispense with paranoid forms of knowing entirely; indeed, paranoiacally structured inquiry is often necessary for nonparanoid forms of knowing.
36 Žižek (2008) puts it slightly differently, focusing on the power of fantasy and illusions in politics: "The position of the cynic is that he alone holds some piece of terrible, unvarnished wisdom. The paradigmatic cynic tells you privately, in a confidential low-key voice: 'But don't you get it that it is all really about (money/power/sex), that all high principles and values are just empty phrases which count for nothing?' What the cynics don't see is their own naivety, the naivety of their cynical wisdom that ignores the power of illusions".

from ACT UP and implement important policy changes – helped to derail the direct action AIDS movement. Who or what is the object of hope in the Obama moment?

More than hope in a savior, I contend that the object of this hope is 'ourselves'. The 'we' here is vague, an amorphous imagined collectivity of people who desire progressive or even radical social change that would challenge inequality and injustice.[37] Obama's campaign made millions aware that they themselves and their friends, intimates, acquaintances, co-workers, colleagues, classmates, neighbors, compatriots have desires and expectations for a different and better world as well as the capacity to collectivize their efforts and work toward bringing such a world, or worlds, into being. What electrified, and continues to, is *politics*, the experience, in philosopher Simon Critchley's words (2008), "of a people suddenly present to itself and aware of its awesome power". The experience of sensing political efficacy astonishes in its challenge to long-standing, widespread feelings of political powerlessness. Drawing on the work of philosopher Brian Massumi (2002),[38] I would use the word *potentiality* to describe what swirled around Obama's campaign and election, and what continues to exert force in the present. Potential: what might emerge, what steps I/you/we might take, the unpredetermined, open, unpredictable, surprising qualities of any moment. People felt, and feel, the potentiality of political desire and collective political action. That is what hope in the age of Obama derives from and revolves around: a changed affective relation to the political and the potentialities that emerge on that altered terrain.

In saying that Obama himself is not the object of hope I am not saying that he plays no role in its generation and amplification in this moment. Indeed, the specific content of his rhetoric and his style of oratory matter a great deal: drawing from his history as a community organizer, Obama continually acknowledges people's dissatisfactions with the status quo, reminds that nothing about *what is* is inevitable or immutable, expresses faith in the collective agency of ordinary people, invokes a different future generated by those very people, and asserts (and thereby invites) belief in that potentiality.[39] His speeches repeatedly

---

37 "Red Pepper Obama" blogger Rob Augman also challenges the notion that the hope resides only with Obama himself: "the radical left's hope has not to do with Obama, but with the grassroots mobilization that put him in office and the new political climate" (Augman 2008). See also Younge (2010): "Some of us drew hope from the energy, activism and diverse nature of Obama's base, which we believed might emerge as a movement. That hasn't happened. But it was rooted in an understanding not that he would lead us leftward but that there might now be enough of us to push him leftward and that he might be responsive to that pressure."
38 Massumi draws from Spinoza and Deleuze.
39 Describing Obama as someone "who takes pleasure in the language of organization and struggle, who sees movement politics not as a sentimental exception to ordinary life but as

offered that sort of 'bottom-up' theory of social change. Consider excerpts from just two: the speech he gave about race in March 2008 in Philadelphia, "A More Perfect Union," and his victory speech after winning the Iowa caucus in January 2008:

> [W]ords on a parchment would not be enough to deliver slaves from bondage, or provide men and women of every color and creed their full rights and obligations as citizens of the United States. What would be needed were Americans in successive generations who were willing to do their part – through protests and struggle, on the streets and in the courts, through a civil war and civil disobedience and always at great risk – to narrow that gap between the promise of our ideals and the reality of their time.[40]

> Hope is the bedrock of this nation. The belief that our destiny will not be written for us but by us, by all those men and women who are not content to settle for the world as it is, who have the courage to remake the world as it should be. That is what we started here in Iowa (...) Together, ordinary people can do extraordinary things (...) We are ready to believe again.[41]

To believe..., not in Obama as our messiah, but in the collective action of an imagined 'we' that desires, and has the capability to fight for and bring, change. It was Obama's call to politics specifically that aroused many. Describing his students' "inspired and dazzled" responses to Obama's acceptance speech, English professor Joon Oluchi Lee wrote, "They are uplifted by the call for struggle, to do something to make things happen in this country, and so am I" (Lee 2008). Obama spurred hope, helped to shape its content, authorized and amplified it, but the hope is in that imagined politicized collectivity rather than Obama alone.

This hope, then, does not delude people about a leader or locate the directionality of change from the top down. Nor does it promote a passive relation to politics, or even a limited relation à la representative government. In other words, this hope does not entail a ceding of agency, as happened in the case of AIDS activism. Incited and intensified by Obama's invitation to an engaged, participatory relation to the political, this hope in ourselves thrills, excites, charges people up, and potentially activates.

---

what ordinary life requires for entrenched structures of inequality, insecurity, and injustice to be forced to change," Berlant (2008c) also links the hope surrounding Obama to a revitalized relation to the political. Ganz similarly argues that "the excitement is about empowerment, working with others to organize, advocate, and practice politics" (in Sifry 2008b).

40 "A More Perfect Union," March 18, 2008, available at http://my.barackobama.com/page/content/hisownwords (last accessed December 7, 2009).

41 Available on YouTube: http://www.youtube.com/watch?v=yqoFwZUp5vc (last accessed December 7, 2009). Obama made similar statements throughout his campaign, from the announcement of his candidacy in Springfield, Illinois on February 10, 2007.

The very structure of the Obama campaign's field operation – with its mantra of "Respect. Empower. Include." – affirmed and radiated belief in people's capacities to collectivize and themselves bring change. To be sure, the campaign was not run by the "grassroots" nor was it as bottom-up as the Obama brand proclaims. Like all political campaigns, Obama's listened to the big money donors and the financial, energy, health, military sectors (Sifry 2009); their influence is reflected in many of Obama's positions and policies. As well, the campaign's message and overall strategy were determined from the top down.[42] But even so, those who got involved in Obama's campaign found a considerably decentralized structure that, in contrast to more typical campaigns, devolved responsibility and authority, allowing volunteers to develop leadership skills and in many cases to exercise creative initiative.[43] Staff "field organizers" enlisted volunteers to become "neighborhood team leaders" each of whom oversaw a team working a specific "turf;" team leaders recruited volunteers to coordinate different tasks (Exley 2008). By all accounts, the campaign gave volunteers, even those who were young and inexperienced, "responsibility galore" (Berry 2009). As journalist Elizabeth Méndez Berry notes, "Volunteers on most large-scale campaigns can expect to phone-bank or door-knock and not much else. But on the Obama campaign, they could be promoted to several key roles: team leader, campus captain, data coordinator, phone-bank captain or house party captain" (Berry 2009). According to the training director of Organizing for America, Nicole Derse, "Our success as a campaign depended on young people's leadership. At Penn State, we told our volunteers, 'If *you* don't organize your dorms, they're not going to get organized. If *you* don't get them registered to vote, they probably won't vote'" (quoted in Berry 2009, emphases in original). By encouraging volunteers "to run their own activities" rather than follow campaign staff directives (Mirza 2008), these "technologies of decentralization and self-organization" (Exley 2008) cultivated political skills along with independence. As one campaign worker said,[44] "We're organizing ourselves. The

---

42 For a critique of the Obama campaign that usefully distinguishes between distribution of work and decentralization of power, see Teachout (2007).
43 Former MoveOn.org staff member and the Kerry campaign's online communications director, Jack Exley, quotes volunteers contrasting their experiences in the Obama campaign with work on previous political campaigns. He also notes the power that decentralization gave to the Obama campaign, writing: "After visiting my fourth or fifth [Obama neighborhood] team, it was painfully clear that an enormous amount of power is unlocked by this incredibly simple act of distributing different roles to people who actually feel comfortable taking them on. And I say 'painfully' because I couldn't stop thinking about all the union and electoral campaigns I've worked on where we did not do this" (Exley 2008).
44 From the campaign's "Signs of Hope & Change" video, available on YouTube: http://www.youtube.com/watch?v=EcRA2AZsR2Q (last accessed December 7, 2009). On the campaign's

campaign helps us, they're there to help us, but we're organizing ourselves" (BarackObama.com 2008).

That campaign structure not only empowered volunteers; it also afforded them opportunities to experience collectivity and immersion in something larger than themselves as well as a growing sense of political efficacy and political possibility. The words of volunteers indicate how vitalizing, pleasurable, and activating those bodily experiences were. Writing for the *Daily Kos* blog about volunteer precinct work for the campaign, "kid oakland" (Paul Delehanty) conveys his feelings of empowerment.

> We were last minute volunteers getting trained at Obama Headquarters in downtown Oakland; we were to be plugged into precincts that had yet to find a captain. Each of us was to become responsible, with a partner, for 70-100 voters. Door-knocking, precinct walking, calling, leaving door hangers in the AM and following through with each of our voters on election day till the polls close. The woman training us (...) told us to act on our own convictions. To learn the script and then make it our own. Those voters were ours (...) It's hard work (...) My knuckles hurt from rapping on doorjambs. I've been on my knees all day shoving lit under doors, I've been stuck outside security trellises squinting into homes at faces I can't see. But there's 77 people in Oakland who are counting on me; I've walked and called and persuaded today. I'm their guy. (kid oakland 2008).

More than buttressing volunteers' belief in their own and other people's capacity to engage politically and collectively bring change, the structure of the campaign allowed them, and the wider public, to feel, viscerally, the potency of "people power," the power of collective political action. As historian Tithi Bhattacharya wrote after attending Obama's victory celebration in Grant Park, "Every single woman, man and child came out (...) because they powerfully felt that a major change had been achieved. I say achieved, as opposed to a change that just happened (...) [A]s in the case of countless other political victories[45] (...) the participants experienced a confident surge of empowerment for the gain achieved was in part because of them" (Bhattacharya 2008; see also Berry 2009), specifically because of their active engagement in politics. In an era of "communicative capitalism" where "[political] doing is reduced to talking, to contributing to the media environment" (Dean 2009: 32) through, for example, blogging, the very physicality of the campaign provided a different experience of politics. It widened people's senses of political possibilities, flooding them with faith in their collective political efforts and hope about the potentialities thereby unleashed. Writing about her experiences volunteering for the Obama

---

willingness to allow self-motivated volunteers to organize themselves, see also Vermonter (2007).

45 Bhattacharya mentions, for example, the ousting of the British from India.

campaign in Philadelphia, sociologist Magali Sarfatti Larson described what felt so different compared to the campaign work she had done in 2004: "The interest and enthusiasm of those we visited, those we dragged out of their homes to go vote, those who finally voted, (...) and our own sense that something, this time, had to change because we were doing this together" (Larson 2009). Something *felt* different, even for those not directly involved in the campaign. The pleasures and potentialities of collectivity. Swirling energy, feelings, creativity. New senses of possibility. Political desire.

Is Hope Fading Fast?

What happens when the political realm comes to be seen by many as a site of engagement and a place of possibility? What potentialities pepper this new terrain?

It is tempting to answer pessimistically given what has and hasn't happened since Obama's inauguration. From a progressive or leftist perspective, the Obama administration hasn't so much brought change to Washington as engaged in business as usual, politics in the register of the same old, same old. In addition, liberals, progressives, leftists seemingly have engaged in little political mobilization and activism since Obama took office. We might, then, come to regard the hope around Obama's campaign and election as a misplaced feeling, more passive than I argued, and fleeting besides.

That would be to misunderstand this hope and the seeming political quiescence since Obama's victory as well. Let me suggest a different way to make sense of political mobilization since Obama's election. First, we should consider our sources of information. The corporate media infrequently cover progressive/left activism. As just one example, the only mention in the *New York Times* of the U.S. Social Forum in Detroit in June 2010 where 10-20,000 progressive and leftist activists gathered to discuss their work and strategize was in 3 readers' comments; in contrast, putting the phrase "tea party convention" into the *New York Times'* search engine turns up 2530 results.[46] For those of us who get our information from the corporate media, our perspective about how much and what sorts of activism are happening is strongly skewed.

How we define activism matters as well. In interviews with thirty young Obama campaign workers conducted about a year after the election, Elizabeth

---

46 I did both searches at http://www.nytimes.com/ on July 15, 2010. Also important as a point of comparison, the *New York Times* never mentioned the first U.S. Social Forum which took place in Atlanta in 2007.

Méndez Berry found that "almost all (...) continued their activism well after the endorphins of winning wore off" (Berry 2009). A few worked in Obama's administration, some formed and joined non-profit organizations, and many got involved in community organizing. "Of the nineteen campaign coordinators AFSCME [American Federation of State, County and Municipal Employees] hired last spring to work on healthcare reform, fifteen are Obama campaign veterans" (Berry 2009). Some might not consider all of that work to be activism – definitions vary – but the evidence indicates that many Obama enthusiasts have remained politically engaged.[47]

Even so, if I am correct that the hope manifested around Obama's campaign and victory was hope not in Obama the man but rather in people's capacities to fight for and bring change, an activating feeling connected to an expansion in political horizons, then we might expect more, and more massive, political mobilization in general in this period. The dominant model in the study of social movements, the political process model with its political opportunity thesis, certainly would predict increased progressive/left mobilization in the wake of Obama's victory, especially in this moment of economic crisis.[48] So, what gives?

Most important, in my view, are an organizational vacuum and, even more, an organizational culture that is ill-suited to meet people's recently unleashed political desires. I've argued that the hope, enthusiasm, and excitement swirling around Obama's campaign and victory in large part revolved around Obama's invitation to a more participatory relation to the political. People tasted the joys and sensed the possibilities unleashed by collective political engagement, and many wanted more. Revved up and ready to go, an obvious place to turn would be Obama's campaign organization itself. But post-victory, Obama for America shifted away from participatory politics. Under the new name "Organizing for America," Obama for America was folded into the Democratic National Committee (DNC) and thereby became part of the Democratic Party apparatus with its top-down leadership style. According to Micah Sifry, "the local base of the Obama campaign had no meaningful say in the creation and structure of Organizing for America, and there is no evidence that OFA is actually driven by anything but what its DNC-paid staff and White House advisers want" (Sifry 2009).[49] That is not especially surprising: Obama's rhetoric aside, no mainstream politician or party is committed to genuine people power.

---

47 For more evidence, see Sifry (2010).
48 Exemplars of the political process model include McAdam (1999), Tarrow (1994; 1998), and McAdam, McCarthy, and Zald (1996).
49 Both Sifry (2010) and Evry (2010) indicate frustration about Organizing for America among people who volunteered for Obama's campaign and were energized by the experience.

Another place to turn would be toward the groups that helped to get Obama elected and that generally support his agenda – unions, community organizations, internet groups like MoveOn.org. But those groups, according to Peter Dreier and Marshall Ganz, "pushed the pause button" once Obama won, replacing the "'outsider' mobilizing strategy" that got Obama elected with "insider tactics" like closed-door meetings, lobbying, and advertising that left campaign volunteers who were "all fired up" essentially "twiddling [their] thumbs" (Dreier and Ganz 2009). Dreier and Ganz quote a volunteer from Delaware County, PA following the election saying, "Here, *all* the leader volunteers are getting bombarded by calls from volunteers essentially asking 'Nowwhatnowwhatnowwhat?'"(Dreier and Ganz 2009). Similarly, Sifry (2009) mentions hearing many stories "of Obama supporters who desperately wanted to keep the grassroots campaign going after November 4th, of youthful staffers in the Chicago office blindly trying to field their calls for guidance, and of leaders offering no direction".

Desire for continuing active political engagement evidently persisted, but existing organizations within and closely aligned with the Democratic Party did not and have not become vehicles for that desire. And with their more hierarchical structures, insider tactics, and strong Democratic Party loyalty, most of them are unlikely to become such vehicles. Existing progressive and left organizations have not become that vehicle either, and the shift many of them have taken away from a participatory structure suggests that neither are they poised to become such vehicles. Marshall Ganz argues that many progressive organizations have become "top down," professionalized, "mailing list operations" that maintain paid staffs that develop strategy themselves and then fight the battles in the courts, legislatures, and the media, leaving their 'members' with little to do but give money and sign petitions (Dicum 2005; cited in Duncombe 2007). From an organization's perspective, allowing for more participation entails greater risks: of contestation, conflict, losing control; a top-down structure is less threatening. With the important exception of many anarchist and autonomous Marxist organizations, even progressive/left organizations oriented toward protest politics have tended toward a hierarchical and minimally participatory structure. Duncombe argues that, aside from ACT UP and its spin-offs,

> the dominant progressive protest model throughout the 1980s and 1990s was dull and deadly. It went something like this: Leaders organize a 'mass' demonstration. We march. We chant. Speakers are paraded onto the dais to tell us (in screeching voices through bad sound systems) what we already know (...) While these demonstrations were often held in the name of 'people's power,' they were profoundly disempowering. Structured within this model of protest was a philosophy of passive political spectatorship: they organize, we come; they talk, we listen. (Duncombe 2007: 69).

With the current anti-war movement as an exemplar, the model that Duncombe describes continues to characterize much progressive protest politics.[50] People energized by Obama's invitation to active political participation are unlikely to find that more top-down organizational culture especially enticing.

In the face of relatively low levels of political activism since Obama's victory, we might conclude, as Sifry (2009) does, that those people who were energized by Obama's campaign "thought that Obama would be more of a change-agent, and never really embraced their own role" as protagonists. There is something to this explanation that I will say more about momentarily, but a more accurate account, in my view, is that many people did indeed embrace their role as agents of change but have been stymied in their efforts to actively engage the political by the dearth of organizational venues that practice participatory politics in a manner that genuinely recognizes and respects people's intelligence, agency, and capacities. What inspired people during the Obama campaign? Not on-line activism where you click a button to sign yet another vital petition, and then sit back and watch what happens. Not representational politics where (some) people vote and decisions are delegated to the alleged experts. Not being lectured about the correct political analysis or talked at from the stage at another rally. Not the endless stream of commentary on blogs and alternative media outlets. What inspired and gave hope was the sense that people can want and even expect something from the political and can collectivize their efforts and actively fight for, and potentially realize, their needs and wants. Most existing liberal, progressive, and leftist organizations are not sites for the sort of active and participatory collective political engagement that many desire.[51] In the face of that organizational vacuum, spectator democracy (Chomsky 1991) where passive watching replaces live engagement again becomes the default mode of politics.

Capacities, Potentialities, Openings

There is, then, something important to consider in the claim that people have not yet embraced their role as political protagonists. But rather than being due to

---

50 Although the first decade of the 21st century saw the emergence in the U.S. of more participatory alter-globalization organizations, many of them are relatively small and not always visible to a wide public. Historian Barbara Epstein suggests another barrier to participation is that many of these organizations require a level of involvement that is difficult for those with ordinary jobs that do not overlap with their political activity (Epstein 2009).

51 Again, there are exceptions among anarchist, autonomist, and smaller community-based organizations.

lack of desire, I posit that a key reason for this slow embrace is that the dominant political culture in the U.S. provides little practice in political protagonism, making it difficult to develop a more active relation to the political. As sociologist Nina Eliasoph (1998) argues, in our everyday lives and interactions we have learned and we reproduce political passivity, keeping politics at arm's length and leaving policy matters and decision making to our leaders and experts; we tend to avoid even talking about politics. Few sites exist in U.S. society where people can unlearn that political passivity, which is precisely why the Obama campaign, in its provision of just such an organizational vehicle, was so remarkable.

The Obama campaign and victory is a story of potentiality, of what has not yet occurred, but might. Those events ushered in a new affective and imaginative terrain that, characterized by people's hope and belief in their own collective political capacities, bursts with potentiality. The potentiality of people's changing relation to the political, of expanding political horizons among millions who have come to see themselves as protagonists, has an indeterminacy and open-endedness to it, generating energies and intensities that could go in multiple and surprising directions. As I suggested earlier, the Democratic Party has captured and contained some of that potential, lassoing much of the campaign's vitality into the politically centrist and structurally hierarchical Organizing for America and Democratic National Committee; they offer the more typical message of a representative democracy: "you voted, we'll take it from here." Leaders on the right, meanwhile, recognizing changes in the emotional and imaginative landscape that the economic crisis and election unleashed, have tapped into and (re)generated reactive emotional states that have helped to mobilize conservatives who feel threatened by the potentialities unleashed by the current political-economic conjuncture; the Tea Party movement both manifests and regenerates the often racist resentments, hatreds, and fears circulating in this moment of demographic, political, cultural, and economic change and anxiety.[52]

What about the left? The changed affective and imaginative terrain presents tremendous opportunities for leftists, but they/we have been unprepared to meet this moment of political opening. One reason is that many leftists, with our efforts oriented toward fundamental social transformation, are disinclined to get involved in anything having to do with mainstream electoral politics, even if that is the realm where a tremendous sense of political possibility has emerged in this moment.

Another, related reason is the tendency on the left to inhabit a cynical and paranoid relation to politics that I discussed earlier. Certain that mainstream

---

52 On demographic anxiety among tea partiers, see Rich (2010b).

politicians will always disappoint, many have sat this one out. As Gary Younge notes, "being on the left you are always prepared for disillusionment. That is the psychological nature of the left" ("Holding" 2008). The real challenge, he continues, and one that leftists have not been able to muster to any large extent, is "to be prepared for hope, and to be prepared for something that is actually better" ("Holding" 2008). Leftists certainly have utopian visions, but they are usually futural, deferred to some distant moment after the revolution has swept away all that is bad. The hope swirling around Obama, in contrast, is a hope in the potentialities of our capacities *now*. The standard leftist genre of doom and gloom makes us unsure how to deal with that surge in present-tense hope, our own and other's, except with suspicion that those feeling it are deluded and naïve.

Suspicion of the hope swirling around Obama's campaign and victory, and of those feeling it, leads to a third reason why leftists have been unprepared to address the potentialities of this moment. The excitement, enthusiasm, and hope of the Obama moment revolve(d) around Obama's invitation to a different, more active relation to the political. That should appeal to those on the left, but as much as we talk about the importance of popular political participation, the top-down, representational structure and practices of many progressive/left organizations suggest little confidence in people's capacities to self-organize. An older style of politics instead prevails in many sectors of the left: distinguishing between leaders and led, it grants leaders a monopoly on answers to the questions of what is to be done and how to do it, even in the face of the left's post-1989 loss of its eschatology and in a moment when no one is quite sure how to proceed. Seeking assurance and surety in an uncertain world, we disavow the notion that, in Rebecca Solnit's words, "activism (...) is a plunge into the unknown" (2004: 58). The unscripted quality of genuine popular political participation, and thus its unpredictability and possible ungovernability by 'leaders', makes many on the left anxious. That anxiety helps to explain why we don't yet have a leftist organizational vehicle or vehicles that might cultivate and facilitate the sort of active political participation that during the campaign many indicated they want.

The challenge for leftists is to address this newly enlivened desire for more active political participation, to respond to this altered affective landscape and cultivate its political potential. More horizontally-organized groups that embrace bottom up, DIY/do-it-together, prefigurative politics, many of which are anarchist or anarchist-leaning and participate in the alternative globalization movement and in venues like the U.S. Social Forum, are moving the left in that direction.

I will end here with one more point about the question of political hope and its effects. I want to argue for a longer time horizon. Something was set in motion by Obama's campaign and victory, and it won't be easily turned off. We don't know yet what sort of legs it has, how long they will be, where they will go. But consider what sorts of intensities, affections, creativities, capacities are set in motion when people cast off their resignation about the inevitability and immutability of the status quo and come to believe that their collective political action can bring change. New constellations of feelings have the capacity to unravel the prevailing taken for granteds and shake people out of our deeply grooved patterns of thinking and feeling and doing. Collectivity, reciprocity, political agency and efficacy, new senses of possibility...one is changed after getting a taste of those experiences and affects. We can view this period through a paranoid and cynical lens that grants us the aura of realism and clear-eyed unsentimentalism: Obama's election meant nothing, nothing ever changes, nothing ever will. But what might ensue if we instead acted as if something indeed happened with Obama's campaign and election, and tried to inhabit this new affective and imaginative terrain? The new horizon of political possibility that opened during the Obama campaign continues to emit a charge even if its intensity diminished in the first year of Obama's presidency. In this open moment with no determinate conclusion, the task is to recognize "the openness of [the] situation" and to experiment with "liv[ing] that openness" (Massumi 2003: 214) and cultivating its political potential.

References

Augman, Rob (2008). Left Hope after Bush? *Red Pepper blog*. 6 December. Available at http://redpepperobamablog.blogspot.com/2008/12/left-hope-after-bush.html (last accessed July 24, 2010).

Baker, Peter (2009). A Milestone in History. In Sober Address, He Pledges to Begin Remaking Nation—A Million Celebrate. *New York Times*. 21 January, p.A1.

Berlant, Lauren (2008a). Other People's Optimism. *Supervalent Thought blog*. 6 May. Available at http://supervalentthought.com/2008/05/06/other-peoples-optimism/ (last accessed April 1, 2010).

Berlant, Lauren (2008b). Looking for Mr. (W)Right. *Supervalent Thought blog*. 7 May. Available at http://supervalentthought.com/2008/05/07/looking-for-mr-wright/ (last accessed April 1, 2010).

Berlant, Lauren (2008c). Sarah Palin, Female Complainer. *Supervalent Thought blog*. 17 September. Available at http://supervalentthought.com/2008/09/17/sarah-palin-female-complainer/ (last accessed April 1, 2010).

Berlant, Lauren (2008d). Political Happiness–or Cruel Optimism? *Supervalent Thought blog*. 9. November. http://supervalentthought.com/2008/11/09/political-happiness-or-cruel-optimism/ (last accessed April 1, 2010).

Berry, Elizabeth Méndez (2009). The Obama Generation, Revisited. *The Nation.* 23 November. Available at http://www.thenation.com/article/obama-generation-revisited?page=full (last accessed March 30, 2010).

Bhattacharya, Tithi (2008). Why I Went To Grant Park on November 4th. *Lenin's Tomb blog.* 9 November. Available at http://leninology.blogspot.com/2008/11/why-i-went-to-grant-park-on-november.html (last accessed July 24, 2010).

Butler, Judith (2008). Uncritical Exuberance? *San Francisco Bay Area Independent Media Center.* 5 November. Available at http://www.indybay.org/newsitems/2008/11/05/18549195.php (last accessed July 24, 2010).

Campaign for America's Future and Media Matters for America (2009). *America: A Center-Left Nation.* 27 May. Available at: http://cloudfront.mediamatters.org/static/pdf/caf_mm-20090526-4.pdf (last accessed September 12, 2009).

Chomsky, Noam (1991). Media Control: The Spectacular Achievements Of Propaganda. *Open Media.*

Chomsky, Noam (2008). In Swing States Vote Obama, Without Illusions. *The Real News Network.* 20 October. Available at http://therealnews.com/t/index.php?option=com_content&task=view&id=31&Itemid=74&jumival=2593 (last accessed September 12, 2009).

Cillizza, Chris (2009). Obama Announces 'Organizing for America.' *Washington Post.* 17 January. Available at http://voices.washingtonpost.com/thefix/white-house/obama-announces-organizing-for.html (last accessed July 14, 2010).

Colombo, Pamela and Tomas Bril Mascarenhas (2003). We're Nothing; We Want To Be Everything. In Notes from Nowhere (ed.), *We Are Everywhere: The Irresistible Rise of Global Anti-Capitalism.* London/New York: Verso.

Critchley, Simon (2008). What's Left After Obama? All this Talk of Change May Amount to Little More than a Fantasy. *Adbusters.* 12 November. Available at https://www.adbusters.org/features/after_obama.html (last accessed April 13, 2010).

Damasio, Antonio (1994). *Descartes' Error. Emotion, Reason, and the Human Brain.* New York: Putman's.

Damasio, Antonio (1999). *The Feeling of What Happens.* London: Random House.

Davidson, Cathy (2008). Historicizing Critique. *HASTAC.org blog,* November 11, http://www.hastac.org/blogs/cathy-davidson/historicizing-critique (last accessed October 22, 2010).

Dean, Jodi (2009). *Democracy and Other Neoliberal Fantasies: Communicative Capitalism and Left Politics.* Durham & London: Duke University Press.

Dicum, Gregory (2005). Green: The Sierra Club at a Crossroads. *SF Gate.* 31 August. Available at http://www.sfgate.com/cgi-bin/article.cgi?f=/g/a/2005/08/31/gree.DTL (last accessed July 14, 2010).

Duggan, Lisa and José Esteban Muñoz (2009). Hope and hopelessness: A dialogue. *Women & Performance: a journal of feminist theory* 19(2), 275 – 283.

Dreier, Peter and Marshall Ganz (2009). We Have the Hope. Now Where's the Audacity? Kennedy passed the liberal torch to Obama. Let's run with it. *Washington Post.* 30 August.

Duncombe, Stephen (2007). *Dream: Re-imagining Progressive Politics in an Age of Fantasy.* New York: The New Press.

Eliasoph, Nina (1998). *Avoiding Politics. How Americans Produce Apathy in Everyday Life.* Cambridge: Cambridge University Press.

Epstein, Barbara (2009). Why the US Left is Weak, and What to Do About It. *ZNet.* 14 July. Available at http://www.zcommunications.org/why-the-us-left-is-weak-and-what-to-do-about-it-by-barbara-epstein (last accessed July 16, 2010).

Evry, Marta (2010). Jeremy Bird—OFA Deputy Director—Respect, Empower, Include, 'Unfriend' UPDATED! *Venice for Change blog.* 6 January. Available at http://veniceforchange.blogspot.com/2010/01/jeremy-bird-ofa-deputy-director-respect.html (last accessed July 17, 2010).

Exley, Zack (2008). The New Organizers: What's Really Behind Obama's Ground Game. *Huffington Post.* 8 October. Available at http://www.huffingtonpost.com/zack-exley/the-new-organizers-part-1_b_132782.html (last accessed December 8, 2009).
Gallup (2009). *Gallup Daily: Obama Job Approval.* Available at http://www.gallup.com/poll/113980/Gallup-Daily-Obama-Job-Approval.aspx (last accessed December 6, 2009).
Gallup (2010). *Gallup Daily: Obama Job Approval.* Available at http://www.gallup.com/poll/113980/Gallup-Daily-Obama-Job-Approval.aspx (last accessed April 19, 2010).
Gibson-Graham, J.K. (2006). *A Postcapitalist Politics.* Minneapolis: University of Minnesota Press.
Gould, Deborah B. (2009). *Moving Politics: Emotion and Act Up's Fight Against Aids.* Chicago and London: The University of Chicago Press.
Hass, Christopher (2008a). What Happened on Tuesday. *Organizing for America.* 10 November. Available at http://my.barackobama.com/page/content/hqblog (last accessed July 24, 2010).
Hass, Christopher (2008b). I learned that change is possible. *Organizing for America.* 14 November. Available at http://my.barackobama.com/page/community/post/stateupdates/gGxqsk (last accessed July 24, 2010).
Hass, Christopher (2008c). This Weekend: Still Fired Up? *Organizing for America.* 11 December. Available at http://my.barackobama.com/page/community/post/stateupdates/gGxzCj (last accessed July 24, 2010).
Hass, Christopher (2008d). Message from David Plouffe: What you're saying. *Organizing for America.* 19 December. Available at http://my.barackobama.com/page/community/post/stateupdates/gGx8gc (last accessed July 24, 2010).
Hayden, Tom, Bill Fletcher, Barbara Ehrenreich and Glover, Danny (2008). Progressives For Obama. *Progressives for Obama blog.* 24 March. Available at http://progressivesforobama.blogspot.com/2008/03/progressives-for-obama_25.html (last accessed, April 19, 2010).
Hendricks, Tyche (2008). Millions of new voters register in swing states. *San Francisco Chronicle.* 10 October.
Henwood, Doug (2008). Would You Like Change With That? An Analysis of Obamamania. *Left Business Observer* 117 (March). Available at http://www.leftbusinessobserver.com/Obama.html (last accessed April 14, 2010).
Hirschman, Albert O. (1982). *Shifting Involvements: Private Interest and Public Action (20th Anniversary Edition).* Princeton, NJ: Princeton University Press. 2002
Holding Obama's feet to the fire. 2008. *Red Pepper.* 24 August. Available at http://www.redpepper.org.uk/Holding-Obama-s-feet-to-the-fire (last accessed July 22, 2010).
Hughes, Chris (2008). Moving Forward on My.BarackObama. *Organizing for America.* 7 November. Available at http://my.barackobama.com/page/community/post/chrishughesatthecampaign/gGxZvh (last accessed December 7, 2009).
Jasper, James (1998). The Emotions of Protest: Affective and Reactive Emotions in and around Social Movements. *Sociological Forum* 13(3), 397 – 424.
Jones, Jeffrey M. (2009). Obama Approval Holding Steady in Low 50s; Averaging 52% approval in September. *Gallup.* 24 September. Available at http://www.gallup.com/poll/123182/Obama-Approval-Holding-Steady-Low-50s.aspx (last accessed December 6, 2009).
kid oakland (Paul Delehanty) (2008). Respect. Empower. Include. *Daily Kos.* 4 February. Available at http://www.dailykos.com/story/2008/2/4/20835/87521/677/449856 (last accessed December 8, 2009).
Klein, Naomi (2009). A Lexicon of Disappointment. *The Nation.* 15 April. Available at http://www.naomiklein.org/articles/2009/04/lexicon-disappointment (last accessed September 12, 2009).
Klein, Naomi (2010). How Corporate Branding Took Over the White House. *AlterNet.* 18 January. Available at http://www.alternet.org/media/145218?page=entire (last accessed April 17, 2010).

Kohut, Andrew (2008a). Post-Election Perspectives. *Pew Research Center for the People & the Press.* 13 November. Available at http://pewresearch.org/pubs/1039/post-election-perspectives (last accessed September 4, 2009).

Kohut, Andrew (2008b). High Hopes. *New York Times.* 14 November. Available at http://pewresearch.org/pubs/1035/high-hopes (last accessed September 4, 2009).

Koziak, Barbara (2000). *Retrieving Political Emotion: Thumos, Aristotle, and Gender.* University Park: The Pennsylvania State University.

Larson, Magali Sarfatti (2009). Si se puede! Working for Obama at K and A. *Sociological Forum* 24(2), 429 – 436.

Lee, Joon Oluchi (2008). Love Hangover. *Lipstick Eater blog.* 9 November. Available at http://lipstickeater.blogspot.com/2008/11/love-hangover.html (last accessed April 14, 2010).

Ligero1 (2009). How the Democrats Actually Succeeded In Squandering a Movement. *Daily Kos.* 26 December. Available at http://www.dailykos.com/story/2009/12/26/819319/-How-the-Democrats-Actually-Succeeded-In-Squandering-a-MOVEMENT (last accessed April 17, 2010).

Lucchetti, Aaron and Stephen Grocer (2009). Wall Street On Track To Award Record Pay. *Wall Street Journal* 14 (October). Available at http://online.wsj.com/article/SB125547830510183749.html (last accessed July 24, 2010).

Luis in Paris (2008). In response to Judith Butler's "Uncritical Exuberance." *Luis in Paris blog.* 9 November. Available at http://luisinparis.blogspot.com/2008/11/in-response-to-judith-butlers-excessive.html (last accessed July 24, 2010).

Marcus, George E. (2002). *The Sentimental Citizen: Emotion in Democratic Politics.* University Park, PA: Penn State University Press.

Marcus, George E., W. Russell Neuman, and Michael MacKuen (2000). *Affective Intelligence and Political Judgment.* Chicago: The University of Chicago Press.

Massumi, Brian (2003). Navigating Movements: An Interview with Brian Massumi. In Mary Zournazi (ed.), *Hope: New Philosophies for Change.* New York: Routledge.

McAdam, Doug (1999). *Political Process and the Development of Black Insurgency, 1930-1970, 2ed.* Chicago: The University of Chicago Press.

McAdam, Doug, John D. McCarthy and Mayer N. Zald (eds., 1996). *Comparative Perspectives on Social Movements: Political Opportunities, Mobilizing Structures, and Cultural Framings.* Cambridge: Cambridge University Press.

Mirza, Rayyan (2008). The Obama Campaign: A Progressive Sourcebook. *Red Pepper Obama blog.* 2 September. Available at http://redpepperobamablog.blogspot.com/2008/09/obama-campaign-progressive-sourcebook.html (last accessed December 7, 2009).

Mooney, Brian C. (2008). Obama's Paid Staff Dwarfing McCain's; Democrat Targets 50 States as Rival Focuses on Tossups. *Boston Globe.* 20 July. Available at http://www.boston.com/news/nation/articles/2008/07/20/obamas_paid_staff_dwarfing_mccains/?page=full (last accessed July 24, 2010).

Moore, Martha T. (2008). Obama Volunteers Plan to Keep in Touch. *Usa Today.* 21 November. Available at http://www.usatoday.com/news/politics/2008-11-20-volunteers_N.htm (last accessed July 24, 2010).

Neuman, W. Russell, George E. Marcus, Michael MacKuen, and Ann N. Crigler (2007). *The Affect Effect: Dynamics of Emotion in Political Thinking and Behavior.* Chicago: The University of Chicago Press.

New York Times (2008). The Next President. Editorial. 5 November: A30.

Pew Research Center for the People & the Press (2008). High Marks for the Campaign, a High Bar for Obama. *The Pew Research Center for the People & the Press.* 13 November. Available at http://people-press.org/report/471/high-bar-for-obama (last accessed September 4, 2009).

Pew Research Center for the People & the Press (2009a). Strong Confidence in Obama—Country Seen as Less Politically Divided; America's Pre-Inauguration Mood. *The Pew Research Cen-*

ter for the People & the Press. 15 January. Available at http://pewresearch.org/pubs/1080/pre-inauguration-mood (last accessed September 4, 2009).
Pew Research Center for the People & the Press (2009b). Unusually Wide Gap in 'Satisfaction,' 'Right Direction' Measures. *The Pew Research Center for the People & the Press* 26 March. Available at http://pewresearch.org/pubs/1169/right-track-versus-satisfaction-polling (last accessed September 4, 2009).
Pew Research Center for the People & the Press (2009c). Obama at 100 Days: Strong Job Approval, Even Higher Personal Ratings; Better Ratings for Foreign Policy than Domestic Issues. *The Pew Research Center for the People & the Press.* 23 April. Available at http://people-press.org/report/509/obama-at-100-days (last accessed September 4, 2009).
Pew Research Center for the People & the Press (2009d). Obama's High Ratings Hold Despite Some Policy Concerns. *The Pew Research Center for the People & the Press.* 18 June. Available at http://pewresearch.org/pubs/1257/obama-economic-effect-foreign-policy-tough-health-care (last accessed September 4, 2009).
Pew Research Center for the People & the Press (2009e). Obama's Ratings Slide Across the Board; Public Supports Health Care Goals, But Not Current Proposals. *The Pew Research Center for the People & the Press.* 30 July. Available at http://people-press.org/report/532/obamas-ratings-slide (last accessed September 4, 2009).
Pew Research Center for the People & the Press (2009f). Obama's Approval Ratings Slide: By the Numbers. *The Pew Research Center for the People & the Press.* 4 September. Available at http://pewresearch.org/pubs/1333/obama-approval-falls-across-most-major-demographics (last accessed September 4, 2009).
Reed, Adolph (2008a). Obama No. *The Progressive.* May. Available at http://www.progressive.org/mag_reed0508 (last accessed September 4, 2009).
Reed, Adolph (2008b). Where Obamaism Seems to be Going. *The Progressive.* 29 July. Available at http://www.progressive.org/mag/reed_072908.html (last accessed September 4, 2009).
Remnick, David (2008). The Joshua Generation; Race and the campaign of Barack Obama. *New Yorker.* 17 November. Available at http://www.newyorker.com/reporting/2008/11/17/081117fa_fact_remnick?currentPage=all (last accessed July 24, 2010).
Rich, Frank (2010a). The Other Plot to Wreck America. *New York Times.* 10 January: WK10. Available at http://www.nytimes.com/2010/01/10/opinion/10rich.html (last accessed July 24, 2010).
Rich, Frank (2010b). The Rage Is Not About Health Care. *New York Times.* 28 March: WK10. Available at http://www.nytimes.com/2010/03/28/opinion/28rich.html?_r=1&scp=1&sq=%22rage%20is%20not%20about%20health%20care%22&st=cse (last accessed July 20, 2010).
Rutherford, Danilyn (Under Review). Chapter 8: The Appeal of Slippery Pronouns. In *Laughing at Leviathan: Essays on Sovereignty and Audience in West Papua.* Chicago: University of Chicago Press.
Saad, Lydia (2009). Optimism Abounds as Power Changes Hands in Washington; Public predicts brighter future for the country and success for Obama. *Gallup.* 20 January. Available at http://www.gallup.com/poll/113890/Optimism-Abounds-Power-Changes-Hands-Washington.aspx (last accessed December 6, 2009).
Sedgwick, Eve Kosofsky (2003). *Touching Feeling: Affect, Pedagogy, Performativity.* Durham & London: Duke University Press.
Schwartz, Nelson D. (2010). Wall St. Hiring in Anticipation of an Economic Recovery. *New York Times.* 10 July: A1. Available at http://www.nytimes.com/2010/07/11/business/11rebound.html?ref=nelson_d_schwartz (last accessed July 24, 2010).
Sifry, Micah L. (2008a). Marshall Ganz on the Future of the Obama Movement. *techPresident.* 20 November. Available at http://techpresident.com/node/6545 (last accessed July 14, 2010).
Sifry, Micah L. (2008b). The Other Transition: Whither Obama's Movement. *techPresident.* 6 December. Available at http://techpresident.com/node/6586 (last accessed July 14, 2010).

Sifry, Micah L. (2009). The Obama Disconnect: What Happens When Myth Meets Reality. *techPresident*. 31 December. Available at http://techpresident.com/blog-entry/the-obama-disconnect (last accessed July 14, 2010).

Sifry, Micah L. (2010). Respect, Empower, Include, Unfriend? The Story of One Disillusioned Obama Organizer [Updated]. *techPresident*. 6 January. Available at http://techpresident.com/blog-entry/respect-empower-include-unfriend-story-one-disillusioned-obama-organizer (last accessed July 14, 2010).

Solnit, Rebecca (2004). *Hope in the Dark: Untold Histories, Wild Possibilities*. New York: Nation Books.

Tarrow, Sidney (1994). *Power in Movement: Social Movements, Collective Action and Politics*. Cambridge: Cambridge University Press.

Tarrow, Sidney (1998). *Power in Movement: Social Movements and Contentious Politics*, 2nd edition. New York: Cambridge University Press.

Taussig, Michael (2003). Carnival of the Senses: A Conversation with Michael Taussig. In Mary Zournazi (ed.), *Hope: New Philosophies for Change*. New York: Routledge.

Wang, Dan S. (2008). A Response to Judith Butler: Working the Optimism. *eipcp: european institute for progressive cultural policies*. November. Available at http://eipcp.net/n/1226801857 (last accessed July 23, 2010).

Teachout, Zephyr (2007). You Don't Have the Power. *techPresident*. 10 October. Available at http://techpresident.com/blog-entry/you-don%E2%80%99t-have-power (last accessed July 23, 2010).

U.S. Census Bureau (2009). Voter Turnout Increases by 5 Million in 2008 Presidential Election, U.S. Census Bureau Reports Data Show Significant Increases Among Hispanic, Black and Young Voters. *U.S. Census Bureau News*. 20 July.

Vermonter (2007). It's Your Campaign! *techPresident*. 11 October. Available at http://techpresident.com/blog-entry/you-don%E2%80%99t-have-power#comment-3209 (last accessed July 14, 2010).

Younge, Gary (2009). Celebrate the Moment. From Then, It's Not Who Obama Is, but What He Does. *The Guardian*. 19 January.

Younge, Gary (2010). Believers in Great Men Think Alike. *The Nation*. 13 January. Available at http://www.thenation.com/article/believers-great-men-think-alike (last accessed July 24, 2010).

Žižek, Slavoj (2008). Why Cynics Are Wrong: The Sublime Shock of Obama's Victory. *In These Times*. 13 November. Available at http://www.inthesetimes.com/article/4039/why_cynics_are_wrong/ (last accessed July 24, 2010).

About the Authors

Andrew J.W. Civettini is Assistant Professor of Political Science and International Relations at Knox College in Galesburg, IL. His work focuses on the psychology of political decision making, particularly voting behavior, and has appeared in *Political Psychology* as well as *The Affect Effect* (2007, University of Chicago Press). Civettini's dissertation work focused on the role of affective reactions in directing information search and memory for information in a political campaign environment. Civettini earned his Ph.D. and M.A from the University of Iowa and a B.A. from Grinnell College.

Marcos Engelken-Jorge received his doctoral degree in political science from the University of the Basque Country, where he works as a Post Doctoral Fellow. His primary research interests are in political theory, in particular democratic legitimacy and deliberative theory, democratic innovations and discourse analysis. His work has appeared in *Journal of Political Ideologies*, *Foro Interno: Anuario de Teoría Política* and *Política y Sociedad*.

Oliver Escobar (Galicia, 1979) is a political scientist (MA Hons, MM, MPhil, University of Santiago de Compostela) currently working as a doctoral researcher at the School of Social and Political Science of the University of Edinburgh, where he is also the Project Officer of the Public Policy Network. Oliver's areas of research are: political communication, deliberative democracy, participatory policymaking, public engagement, social policy, and science & society. He has held positions as a Public Engagement Fellow of Edinburgh Beltane (UK Beacons for Public Engagement), and as member of the Dialogue Research Project (Queen Margaret University). Besides academia, he has done work in management, scriptwriting, and radio broadcasting, as well as published three poetry books.

Deborah Gould is an assistant professor of sociology at the University of California, Santa Cruz. Her interests are in contentious politics and political emotion. She has published essays in the collections *Passionate Politics*, *Rethinking Social Movements*, and *Gay Shame*. Her first book—*Moving Politics: Emotion and ACT UP's Fight Against AIDS*—was published by the University of Chicago Press (2009). Her next project explores the conditions of possibility for political optimism and pessimism. She was involved in ACT UP for many years as well as the Chicago group, Queer to the Left, and is a founding member of the art/activist/research collaborative group, Feel Tank Chicago.

Pedro Ibarra Güell is a former Professor of Political Science (retired) at the University of the Basque Country. His research interests are in contemporary political theory, political sociology and participatory democracy. He is the former Group Co-ordinator of the research team *Parte Hartuz* on participatory democracy and the former director of the Department of Political Science at the University of the Basque Country. Among his latest publications are: *Relational Democracy* (2008, Center for Basque Studies, University of Nevada), *Nacionalismo: Razón y Pasión* (2005, Ariel) and *Manual de Sociedad Civil y Movimientos Sociales* (2005, Síntesis).

Mary-Kate Lizotte is an Assistant Professor at Birmingham Southern College in Birmingham, Alabama. She recently received a doctoral degree in political science from Stony Brook University. Her main area of research is on gender differences in public opinion and most of this research investigates to what extent gender differences in values accounts for public opinion differences. As a secondary focus, she is also interested in the study of emotions and politics.

Ramón Maiz Suárez is Professor of Political Science at the University of Santiago de Compostela (Galicia, Spain). His research interests are in contemporary political theory, history of political thought and the comparative analysis of nationalisms and federalist systems. He is the current Group Co-coordinator of the research team on political analysis at the University of Santiago de Compostela and Vice-chair of the Research Committee on Politics and Ethnicity, International Political Science Association.

Carmelo Moreno del Río is Professor of Political Science at the University of the Basque Country. His main research interests are political theory, political identities and nationalism, critical discourse analysis and, more recently, political humour. His work has appeared in *Revista Española de Ciencia Política*, *Teorías Políticas Contemporáneas* (Tirant lo Blanch, 2001 and 2009) and *Ideologías y Movimientos Políticos Contemporáneos* (Tecnos, 2006).

Alan Sandry lectures in Political Theory at the University of Wales Institute Cardiff. He is the co-author of *Devolution in the United Kingdom* (Edinburgh University Press, 2007) and has just completed a monograph entitled *Plaid*

Cymru: An Ideological Analysis (Welsh Academic Press, 2010). Dr Sandry was one of the founders of, and is the current Group Co-ordinator of, the Welsh Nationalism Study Group. He is also on the Scientific Board of the Centre Maurits Coppetiers, Brussels and is a Research Associate at the Institute of Contemporary European Studies, Regents College, London. Dr Sandry is currently undertaking a series of political interviews for publication in *Planet Magazine*.

Brad Verhulst received his doctoral degree in political science from Stony Brook University and is currently a Post Doctoral Fellow at the Virginia Institute for Psychiatric and Behavioral Genetics at Virginia Commonwealth University. His primary area of interest is in political psychology and most of his research deals with the forming, maintaining and changing attitudes. More specifically, he is interested in exploring the underlying mechanisms that result in stable or malleable attitudinal preferences at both the biological and cultural levels.

Åsa Wettergren, PhD, is an Assistant Professor at the Department of Sociology, University of Gothenburg, Sweden. Her main research interests are emotions and collective identities (social movements, organizations, national identities); and emotions in and of migration and social exclusion/inclusion. She was the coordinator of the European Sociological Association's Research Network of the Sociology of Emotions 2005-2007.

VS Forschung | VS Research
Neu im Programm Politik

Cornelia Altenburg
Kernenergie und Politikberatung
Die Vermessung einer Kontroverse
2010. 315 S. Br. EUR 39,95
ISBN 978-3-531-17020-6

Markus Gloe / Volker Reinhardt (Hrsg.)
**Politikwissenschaft
und Politische Bildung**
Nationale und internationale Perspektiven
2010. 269 S. Br. EUR 39,95
ISBN 978-3-531-17361-0

Farid Hafez
Islamophober Populismus
Moschee- und Minarettbauverbote
österreichischer Parlamentsparteien
2010. Mit einem Geleitwort von Prof.
Dr. Anton Pelinka. 212 S. Br. EUR 34,95
ISBN 978-3-531-17152-4

Annabelle Houdret
**Wasserkonflikte
sind Machtkonflikte**
Ursachen und Lösungsansätze
in Marokko
2010. 301 S. Br. EUR 34,95
ISBN 978-3-531-16982-8

Jens Maßlo
Jugendliche in der Politik
Chancen und Probleme einer
institutionalisierten Jugendbeteiligung
2010. 477 S. Br. EUR 49,95
ISBN 978-3-531-17398-6

Torsten Noe
Dezentrale Arbeitsmarktpolitik
Die Implementierung der Zusammen-
legung von Arbeitslosen- und Sozialhilfe
2010. 274 S. Br. EUR 39,95
ISBN 978-3-531-17588-1

Stefan Parhofer
**Die funktional-orientierte
Demokratie**
Ein politisches Gedankenmodell
zur Zukunft der Demokratie
2010. 271 S. Br. EUR 29,95
ISBN 978-3-531-17521-8

Alexander Wolf
**Die U.S.-amerikanische
Somaliaintervention 1992-1994**
2010. 133 S. Br. EUR 29,95
ISBN 978-3-531-17298-9

Erhältlich im Buchhandel oder beim Verlag.
Änderungen vorbehalten. Stand: Juli 2010.

www.vs-verlag.de

Abraham-Lincoln-Straße 46
65189 Wiesbaden
Tel. 0611.7878-722
Fax 0611.7878-400

PGMO 08/08/2018